Manuel Lisa

and the Opening of
the Missouri Fur Trade

MANUEL LISA

and the Opening of
the Missouri Fur Trade

By Richard Edward Oglesby

UNIVERSITY OF OKLAHOMA PRESS
NORMAN

The publication of this volume
has been aided by a grant from the FORD FOUNDATION.

LIBRARY OF CONGRESS CATALOG CARD NUMBER: 63-9956

For Genie

Preface

IN the unfolding epic of the fur trade of the American West, Manuel Lisa appears a shadowy figure hovering in spectral attendance on the opening of the Missouri trade—there because he had undeniable significance, obscure because his story has not yet been told. The same is pretty much true of the period in which he lived, long neglected by writers in favor of the much more exciting, and much more fully documented, story of furs commencing in 1822, two years after Lisa's death. This is passing strange, for not only does the earlier era contain its share of larger-than-life figures, John Colter, Edward Rose, and others, and comprehend episodes fully as dramatic as any in which Jim Bridger or Jed Smith participated, but Manuel Lisa himself had most of the features usually associated with the frontier hero: strength of limb, courage and perseverance in the face of overwhelming adversity, involvement in events of great moment. In fact, Lisa lacked only one of the important attributes, the crucial one as far as posterity is concerned with a man of business: outstanding success. Without any massive accumulation of cash, without any stunning single catch of furs to draw notoriety, Lisa has been disregarded by those who have seen the beginning of the fur trade in the highly publicized and relatively successful voyages of William Ashley.

And in sort of a limbo Lisa has remained. Mentioned as the first private trader to ascend the Missouri with an organized party to trade and trap after the government-sponsored Lewis and Clark expedition, founder of the Missouri Fur Company, opponent of Wilson Price Hunt and his Astorians in a fantastic keelboat race up the Missouri, and occasionally as an Indian agent during the War of 1812, Lisa's sketchy story usually acts as prologue to the main show after 1822. But Manuel Lisa not only wrote that prologue, he set the stage and laid out the plot for future actors.

Rising from an obscure background, this self-made man—one of the few who did not botch the job—cut a wide swath in early Missouri. Not only was he the first trader to ascend the river with an organized force, but the second, the third, the fourth; indeed, the history of the Missouri River from 1807 to 1820 is the narrative of Lisa's several voyages, his trading and trapping adventures, and his dealings with the natives. He was the founder of not one but several Missouri Fur Companies, in addition to lesser partnerships, all designed to acquire a share of the vast riches of the northern Rocky Mountains. Fiercely opposing anyone who attempted to compete with him, Astorians included, Manuel Lisa and his various associations managed to maintain a practical monopoly of commerce on the great river. As subagent for the Indians of the Missouri during the War of 1812, he not only successfully retained their friendship in the face of determined British efforts to wean them away but actually put the Sioux, Omahas, and Poncas in the field against their brethren who had declared themselves antagonistic to the United States.

In addition, he made several attempts to open the Santa Fe trade, both from St. Louis and the upper Missouri. His early policy of sending out trapping parties from mountain posts spread Americans all over the northern Rockies. These men made contact with the frontiers of British and Spanish influence in the West, indicating to those powers that the United States was determined to make its claim to greater Louisiana valid, and demonstrating that "Manifest Destiny" was something more than a catch slogan. In the area of Indian relations, Lisa stood out. Having great sympathy for the natives, and seeing the inevitable destruction of their way of life, Lisa sought to help them make the transition from their primitive, nomadic existence to a more sedentary subsistence, providing them with the seed, tools, and technical knowledge to commence farming. He fought to help them preserve their lands as owners, and to keep white poachers from their hunting grounds. For all of these things and more, Manuel Lisa deserves better remembrance than has been his.

To thank appropriately all those whose contributions helped produce this work would require another volume of equal size. However, there are some who deserve special mention. My particular gratitude is owed to Mr. and Mrs. Harold G. Basquin, Altadena, California, and to Mrs. Jane E. Dawson, Glenview, Illinois, whose interest, confidence, and material succor enabled the research to be completed; to Mr. Odo B. Stade, Glendora, California, a genius with languages who provided translations of letters that otherwise would have remained incomprehensible; to Mr. and Mrs. Lyman Fay Barber, Tujunga, California, who donated their "Casa Quonsetta" in the wilds of the Mojave Desert for a period of uninterrupted writing; and to Mr. and Mrs. Alfred D. Day, who provided their castle in Altadena, California, for the same purpose.

While pursuing research at several depositories, I was overwhelmed by the generous help provided by the staffs of the Henry E. Huntington Library, San Marino, California, the Illinois State Historical Society, Springfield, Illinois, and the Kansas State Historical Society, Topeka, Kansas. Mrs. Dorothy Thomas Cullen of the Filson Club, Louisville, Kentucky, and Miss Caroline Dunn of the Indiana Historical Society, Indianapolis, Indiana, kindly took time to comb their files for materials, as did Mr. Archibald Hanna of the Yale University Library, New Haven, Connecticut, and Mr. Frederick Hall of the Newberry Library, Chicago, Illinois. A special thank-you is due the Missouri Historical Society, St. Louis, Missouri, and its entire staff for their considerable help, but particularly to Mrs. Frances H. Stadler, Society archivist. Her intimate knowledge, not only of the Society archives but of the history of her city, saved many an hour, and turned up much material that might otherwise have been missed. Miss Mildred Goosman, associate curator of the Joslyn Art Museum in Omaha, Nebraska, graciously provided reproductions of paintings in the Bodmer Collection for use as illustrations in this book.

My interest in Manuel Lisa began at Northwestern University under Professor Ray Allen Billington, whose uncanny ability to transfer to his students his own unbounded enthusiasm for the subject of Western history has bred a generation of frontier historians. He nursed this project through its initial stages with helpful criticism, read the entire manuscript, and provided valuable suggestions for change. To him belongs the credit for whatever merit this book has. Finally, as is tradition, although I have always felt it should be placed first as most important, my deepest obligation is owed my wife, Eugenia Basquin Oglesby, who not only put up with an oftentimes irascible author but gave up many an evening to the typewriter which might have been better spent. To these, and others unnamed, goes the credit for such value as this work has. The shortcomings I managed to accomplish despite their best efforts.

RICHARD EDWARD OGLESBY

Charleston, Illinois
April 30, 1963

Contents

Preface   *page* vii
I   Manuel Lisa: Apprenticeship   3
II   The Fur Trade: Theater of Operations   35
III   The Missouri Fur Company: Great Expectations   65
IV   The Missouri Fur Company: Retrench-
          ment and Reorganization   99
V   The Missouri Fur Company: Demise   126
VI   War and Trade: One Last Attempt   150
VII   Manuel Lisa: Accomplishments and Legacy   179
       Appendix I: A Typical Fur Hunter's Contract   197
       Appendix II: A Standard Indian Treaty   200
       Appendix III: Articles of Agreement—
          St. Louis Missouri Fur Company, 1809   202
       Appendix IV: Articles of Agreement—
          Missouri Fur Company, 1812   209
       Bibliography   217
       Index   235

Illustrations

Manuel Lisa   *facing page* 66
Auguste Chouteau   67
William Clark   82
Sylvestre Labbadie and Pierre Chouteau   83
Blackfeet Indians   114
A Mandan Chief's Hut   115
Fur Traders Attacked by Indians   130
Mackinaw or Cordelle Boat   131
Beaver Building a Hut   146
Buffalo and Elk on the Upper Missouri   147
The Stone Walls on the Upper Missouri   162
The Great Falls of the Missouri   163

MAP

Manuel Lisa's Theater of Operations
    in the American Northwest   *pages* 42–43

Manuel Lisa

and the Opening of
the Missouri Fur Trade

I

Manuel Lisa
Apprenticeship

THE main topic of discussion in St. Louis the first week of
August, 1808, whether over rum at Yosti's or Landreville's, or over after-dinner wine at the stately mansion of Auguste Chouteau, was the impending trial of George Drouillard
for the murder of Antoine Bissonette. As a conversation piece
it was not new, for Bissonette's death had taken place nearly
fifteen months earlier, and the town had been well apprised of
the circumstances at that time. But the principals, George Drouillard and his employer Manuel Lisa, had just arrived from the
headwaters of the Missouri River and were being held in de-
tention by the town constable. Edward Hempstead, one of the
attorneys for the defense, was even then appealing for the release
of the prisoners on a writ of habeas corpus.[1]

No one thought the government had much of a case against
the half-blood hunter-trapper-interpreter who had served with
such distinction on the Lewis and Clark expedition. Drouillard
was an honest, loyal individual who harbored ill will toward
no man. Besides, Bissonette had broken his legal engagement
and had deserted from the expedition he had contracted to join.

[1] Letter, Edward Hempstead to Hon. J. C. B. Lucas, Aug. 8, 1808, Lucas Papers,
Missouri Historical Society, St. Louis, Missouri (hereinafter cited as MHS).

3

He deserved, opinion among the traders had it, no better treatment than he had received. For while the hunters and boatmen fulminated against such summary action toward one of their own, the traders were concerned lest, by a conviction of Drouillard, the courts destroy the inviolability of contracts and make it almost impossible to maintain any discipline in an organized company of men.

Manuel Lisa, the leader of the expedition on which Bissonette and Drouillard had been employed, posted $5,000 to bind himself and Drouillard to the trial,[2] which took place before the Honorable J. C. B. Lucas, presiding, and the Honorable Auguste Chouteau, associate, on September 23, 1808. The deliberations proceeded much as the knowing had predicted they would, but with the details more closely spelled out. Manuel Lisa, in partnership with Pierre Menard and William Morrison, two merchants of Kaskaskia, in the Illinois country, had organized a trading and trapping expedition over the winter of 1806–1807 to exploit the untapped riches of the upper Missouri.[3] Menard and Morrison, preferring to remain at home, had designated George Drouillard as their representative on the voyage.

Among the *engagés*[4] of the company, which left St. Louis on April 19, 1807,[5] was Antoine Bissonette, who had signed a typi-

[2] Receipt, Aug. 9, 1808, Manuel Lisa Papers, MHS.

[3] The partnership may have been formed in October, 1806, for that was when Lisa cleared up his account with Morrison. Bryan and Morrison Store, Kaskaskia Ledger D, 267; and Daybook 16, 19, microfilm in Illinois Historical Survey, Lincoln Hall, University of Illinois, Urbana, Illinois. Morrison's connection with the fur trade is conveniently summarized in John L. Tevebaugh, "Merchant on the Western Frontier: William Morrison of Kaskaskia, 1790–1837," Ph.D. thesis, University of Illinois, 1962.

[4] An *engagé* was any individual who had signed a contract of employment for wages as a boatman or hunter. These contracts generally had a number of conditions to be met by either of the signatories, with the length of service usually specified as one of the conditions.

[5] Walter B. Douglas, "Manuel Lisa," *Missouri Historical Society Collections,* Vol. III (1911), 249.

cal contract to hunt, trap, mount guard, and the like, binding himself to the service of his employers for a period of three years. On May 14, 1807, 120 miles upstream, at the mouth of the Osage River, it was discovered that Bissonette was missing. Lisa, hoping to prevent any future desertions, ordered Drouillard to go after the deserter and bring him back "dead or alive."[6] Drouillard complied with his instructions, bringing in his prisoner hovering somewhere between the two states stipulated by Lisa, having, in the course of his capture, shot and seriously wounded the fugitive. "That's well done, that's a rascal who got what he deserved," Lisa had remarked at the time.[7] In front of the witnesses in camp, Lisa had questioned Bissonette about the reasons for his actions, but he would give none. The wounded man was then placed in a canoe and dispatched to St. Charles for medical attention while the rest of the company continued upstream. The next day, before reaching St. Charles, Bissonette died of his wound.

It was proved that that unfortunate individual had deliberately planned his desertion, having planted two caches of blankets and other articles along his projected escape route. With this evidence in hand, the lawyers for the defense, Hempstead, William Carr, and Rufus Easton, ably and forcibly demonstrated the legality of Drouillard's action, with Carr pointing out that if anyone was to blame for the death of the deserter it was Manuel Lisa, who had given the order to bring him in "dead or alive."[8] Drouillard, who was quite shaken by the proceedings, evidently felt much the same as Carr, for he later wrote to his half-sister: "Thoughtlessness on my part and a lack of reflec-

[6] Deposition of Augustin Dubrouil, Aug. 5, 1808, Lisa Papers, MHS.
[7] *Ibid.*
[8] The account of the trial is taken from the *Missouri Gazette* (Oct. 12, 1808). This newspaper went through a number of name changes, including *Louisiana Gazette*, *Missouri Gazette and Public Advertiser*, and *Missouri Gazette and Illinois Advertiser*, all under the ownership of Joseph Charless. For the sake of uniformity, I have called it *Missouri Gazette* throughout.

tion in this unhappy moment is the only cause of it, and more-over encouraged and urged by my partner, Manuel Lisa, who we ought to consider in this affair as guilty as myself for with-out him the whole thing would never have taken place."[9] At length the attorneys ceased extolling the character of the de-fendant, and completed outlining the meritorious services he had rendered the captains Lewis and Clark. The jury retired and, after a fifteen-minute debate, returned a verdict of not guilty.

The judgment was a victory for all traders who engaged men in their employ. Theretofore, men, once out of touch with civili-zation and the agencies of law enforcement, all too easily found it convenient to disregard their legal contracts. Upriver, habit and convention helped keep the order and discipline so neces-sary for protection against Indian attack, but in the main the bourgeois had to rely on force. Not even necessity could always be depended upon to bind together the dissident elements of such an expedition. This case abundantly demonstrated that the exercise of force, even to the extent of taking a life to maintain discipline, was compatible with the law. Now the traders could look forward to some semblance of order on future voyages.

While the excitement of the trial died away, an even more important source of concern manifested itself to the merchants of the city. Manuel Lisa was back in town after an absence of eighteen months—back from the headwaters of the Missouri; back from the Rocky Mountains. Moreover, he had returned "idemnified . . . by considerable benefits."[10] Here was a point to be pondered by the closed group of French merchants, led by Auguste Chouteau and his half-brother Pierre, who had, up until this time, held the economic destiny of St. Louis in their cautious, conservative hands. For the first time their status was

[9] Olin D. Wheeler, *The Trail of Lewis and Clark, 1804–1904*, I, 110–11.

[10] Henry M. Brackenridge, *Views of Louisiana, Together with a Journal of a Voyage up the Missouri River, in 1811*, 92.

challenged by a man who, if he continued his profitable course, bid fair to surpass them all. They could not afford to let Manuel Lisa's newly won monopoly of the trade of the Northwest go unchallenged.

Auguste Chouteau had been one of the founders of the town of St. Louis, coming to the site in 1764 as the teen-aged clerk of Pierre Laclède Liguest, the man who actually picked the spot for the French trading post. He had prospered, aided by the generous treatment accorded by the governments under which he had lived, and in time became, and was to remain, the wealthiest man in St. Louis. Much of his wealth was in the form of land, some acquired through government grants, but to which he had added considerably by accepting property in lieu of cash in payment for his goods and services. Chouteau became the unofficial banker to the community,[11] and men drew on him for credit to make their purchases from the other merchants of the place. Together with his half-brother Pierre, Auguste Chouteau had long enjoyed the exclusive trade of the near-by Osage Indians,[12] a trade from which he still derived some profit. These men were cautious in their investment, partially by choice, but mainly because they had to be. Their need was the need of the frontier everywhere: fluid capital, long-term credit, and cash money. So scarce was cash in St. Louis that for years the most abundant and acceptable money was in the form of the skins of deer and beaver, with beaver being the most stable and valuable.

The Chouteau brothers were content to trade the usual cheap goods with the neighboring tribes for deerskins and beaver, and to act as outfitters for the few individuals who made tentative excursions on the lower Missouri as independent traders and trappers. They were also merchandisers to the town, supplying everything from handkerchiefs to hardware, from raw lead to

[11]There are many such accounts in the papers of the merchants of St. Louis contained in the files of the MHS. See especially the Chouteau Collection.

[12] See a discussion of it later in this chapter.

7

fine imported French wines.[13] With contacts in Montreal, New Orleans, and London, the Chouteaus had built up a thriving business. But it was an unstable one. They paid their distant creditors in skins, and were totally dependent on the market value of the pelts, which fluctuated greatly from season to season. They had, no doubt, thought of extending their trade to the upper Missouri, and listened eagerly to the tales of teeming beaver streams in the northern Rockies brought back by Lewis and Clark, but they were not ready to launch any plans for the exploitation of the area when the brave captains returned from their epic voyage to the Pacific Ocean. Only one man in St. Louis, restrained by no such caution, was prepared to act. That man was Manuel Lisa.

If Manuel Lisa is an enigma in our time, he was an anomaly in his own. A fighter for freedom in a despotic age, he was constantly, in his youth, at odds with the government of his Spanish countrymen, particularly as it was practiced by the paternalistic representatives in the town of St. Louis. Finding himself stifled under the mercantilistic blanket of the benevolently protective state, which doled out monopolies of trade to the highest bidder, Lisa, shortly after his arrival in the Spanish province in 1798, cried out for liberty in the field of economic competition. Although he probably never heard of Adam Smith, his utterances made him sound as if he was one of that great economist's most ardent disciples. Even when granted the choicest plum of all, the exclusive trade with the Osage Indians, which he received in 1802 as much to silence his revolutionary tongue as for any other reason, Manuel Lisa protested against the defects and restraints of the system. Even the charms of American freedom did not beguile him at first, for he found himself in conflict with the representative of that government shortly after the United

[13] For examples of the great variety of merchandise carried by Auguste and Pierre Chouteau, see the several Chouteau ledger books and the Chouteau Collection, MHS. The variety defies belief.

States came into possession of Louisiana. But the freedom he sought was there, and it was not too many years before Lisa could finally say, "I have suffered enough in person and property, under a different government, to know how to appreciate the one under which I now live."[14]

According to the memorial stone erected by his wife to mark the great pioneer's grave, Manuel Lisa was born in New Orleans on September 8, 1772.[15] This date is in doubt, however, because Lisa on one occasion spoke of his "older brother" Joaquin,[16] whose date of birth was recorded in New Orleans as December 21, 1774.[17] His place of birth is equally in question. It may have been, as one novelist would have it,[18] at the bottom of an Indian burial pit somewhere along the Gulf Coast east of New Orleans, with a dying crone as midwife and a howling hurricane above, matching screams with the newborn infant, or, more likely, a conventional birthplace, the Lisa home in Cuba, New Orleans, or elsewhere. Christobal de Lisa of Murcia, Spain, and Maria Ignacia Rodriquez of St. Augustine, Florida, were the infant Lisa's parents,[19] but little else is known about them. Manuel's father came to Louisiana in the service of the government of Spain at the time that nation took possession of the country, and continued in that service until his death. What his position was is unknown, although since his son Joaquin later entered the employ of the United States as a customs official, Christobal may have held a similar office.

Although nothing is known of Manuel's early years, it is fair

[14] Letter, Manuel Lisa to William Clark, July 1, 1817, printed in the *Missouri Gazette*, (July 5, 1817).

[15] Lisa's grave was originally in the Hempstead burial plot, which is now part of Bellefontaine Cemetery, St. Louis, Missouri.

[16] Petition for Land for Joaquin Lisa, July 16, 1799, Lisa Papers, MHS.

[17] Birth Certificate of Joaquin Lisa, Lisa Papers, MHS.

[18] Shirley Seifert, *Those Who Go against the Current.*

[19] Testimony of Eugenio Alvarez, *American State Papers*, Vol. XVII, Public Lands II, 545.

to assume that the hustling life of the New Orleans water front, with its ocean-going vessels whose crews spouted sentences in languages unknown, and its river keelboats populated with the reckless and wild Americans from such exotic-sounding places as Kentucky, Ohio, and Pennsylvania, appealed to his adventurous spirit. He early saw the field of trade as the one in which to make his fortune, for in 1796 he was already a "merchant of New Orleans," and had captained his own boat as far up the Mississippi as New Madrid,[20] in what is now the state of Missouri. Later in that same year, although it would seem he had been there before, Lisa had gone to Vincennes, on the Wabash, Northwest Territory. There, on August 12, he was the signer of the baptismal certificate of Rachel Chew,[21] the gravely ill daughter of Polly Charles Chew. The fact that the child's godmother was Lisa's own mother indicates that Manuel was already the husband or about to become the husband, of the tragic widow of Samuel Chew. Less than three years prior to the child's baptism, the Chew family, residing out on the Indiana frontier, had been attacked by Indians. Samuel was killed, and Polly and her infant child held captive until ransomed. Manuel saw them shortly after their release and so pitied their miserable condition that he married Polly, though "the charms of her beauty had all fled," in order to take care of her and her child, which he did until their deaths.[22]

[20] New Madrid Archives, Vol. III, No. 528, MHS.

[21] Copy of Church Register, Vincennes, Indiana, Lisa Papers, MHS. This is a photostat of the original in the Lassalle Collection, Indiana State Historical Society, Indianapolis, Indiana.

[22] Richard Edwards and M. Hopewell, *Edwards's Great West*, 302–303. This story has a decidedly apocryphal flavor, particularly since the ransomer was "General Harrison." William Henry Harrison was in the Northwest Territory during this period on the staff of General Anthony Wayne, and was put in charge of Fort Washington (Cincinnati) when only an ensign in 1796. He was promoted to captain the following year. Nonetheless, Manuel was married to Polly Chew, and the story probably helped to make him one of the more romantic characters in early St. Louis even during his own lifetime.

It may have been Lisa's original intention to settle in Vincennes, for he had a store there as early as 1796, and had accounts with such prominent citizens as Francisco Vigo[23] and Touissant Dubois. From Vigo he no doubt learned that the successful trader of that era would always be beset by jealous enemies who constantly would attempt to put him out of business, either by unfair competition, spreading false rumors among the Indians, or, failing these, trying to have him killed. All these things happened to Vigo, and Lisa was to have them happen to him in turn. From Dubois, Manuel bought over two thousand acres of rich Indiana bottom land for $1,700,[24] showing that he was a man of substance at that early date. The land, however, he would never settle, for the press of his business kept him constantly on the move, both to the east and west. He caused some consternation in official American circles when, in 1797, he appeared in Cincinnati as a traveler going west. William Henry Harrison, then in charge of Fort Washington, wrote the Secretary of War that he was worried lest this unknown and foreign-looking individual prove a spy. He managed to find out that Lisa was a New Orleans merchant on his way to Vincennes, where he had a store.[25] Manuel remained connected with Vincennes as late as 1799, in which year he was subject to a levy there,[26] but had earlier transferred his base of operations west of the Mississippi, making voyages between Vincennes and Ste. Geneviève.

The first notice of Manuel Lisa in the town of St. Louis, which was to remain his home for the rest of his life, was a public one: a dispute between himself and Joseph Robidoux, a merchant of long standing, which came before Lieutenant Governor Zenon

---

23 There are one letter and an account notation between Lisa and Vigo in the Vigo Collection, Indiana Historical Society, Indianapolis, Indiana.

24 Deed, Apr. 7, 1797, Lisa Papers, MHS.

25 Bernard C. Steiner, *The Life and Correspondence of James McHenry, Secretary of War under Washington and Adams*, 263.

26 Levy, Jan. 1, 1799, Lisa Papers, MHS.

Trudeau for judgment on September 5, 1798.[27] It seems that Robidoux was the cosigner of a note owed Lisa by one Tynan Chatigny, and Lisa was trying to collect from Robidoux. The sum involved was over two thousand dollars, and Lisa complained that up until that time all he had received in the way of payment were two banquets, at which the principal bill of fare was rum. A not very serious matter, but it marked the first of a long series of incidents in which Lisa and the men who occupied the lieutenant governor's chair, particularly the last of the Spanish officials, Charles Dehault Delassus, faced each other across the official desk. By the time of the American occupation six years later, Delassus was happy to let the new administration deal with the litigious Lisa.

Not until the next summer did Lisa decide to make the Missouri country his permanent home. Why he did so is difficult to imagine. Perhaps the challenge of breaking into an area already overstocked with merchants and traders appealed to him. He may already have sensed the value of the theretofore untapped fur trade, and the vast possibilities of the country to the north and west. It may have been that, as a Spaniard, he expected to get preferential treatment from the Spanish government, especially since there were so few of his countrymen in and around St. Louis. Whatever his reasons for settling, he meant to be well established. After first purchasing a sixty-arpent[28] tract from Joseph Taillon, Lisa, on July 16, 1799, petitioned the Lieutenant Governor:

> . . . that it being his intention to establish himself in this country with his family, which is now ascending the river in a boat of his own, therefore, the petitioner wishes to obtain a concession for six thousand arpens of land in superficie, upon one of the banks of the river Missouri, in a place where there may be found some

[27] Official Statement, Lisa Papers, MHS.

[28] An arpent is a French unit of measure equivalent to between an acre and an acre and a half.

small creek emptying into the said river, in order to facilitate the raising of cattle, and, with time, to be able to make shipments of salted as well as dried meat to the capital.[29]

On the same day he petitioned for a similar grant for his brother Joaquin, who was coming up from New Orleans with his family, also preparing to become a permanent resident.[30]

Manuel, always a merchant and trader, had no intention of settling down and raising cattle, but he knew that such an indication would best serve to obtain so large a grant from the Governor. Trudeau was extremely lenient in the granting of land as an inducement for immigration to Missouri, but he, and the Spanish government generally, was interested in bringing in farmers, peaceful men to till the soil and cause no one, particularly the government, any difficulty. Another merchant in St. Louis might be the spark to set off trouble. Still, the following day, the Governor granted both petitions,[31] and Manuel Lisa was established as a considerable landholder. He continued his commercial operations, probably opening a typical frontier store similar to the one he had in Vincennes, carrying everything imaginable, and what he did not have in stock he could get from his friends in New Orleans. Lisa did not neglect his old contacts in New Madrid, Ste Geneviève, and Vincennes, and they were to help him in several later ventures. As the year progressed Manuel bought a house and lot in the town proper, and prepared to win his share of the trade of St. Louis.

The town he had chosen for his home was not much of a place, even by frontier standards.[32] It consisted of three streets

29 United States Congress, House of Representatives, *H. R. Doc. No. 59*, 24 Cong. 1 sess., Serial 288, Vol. III, 129–30.

30 Petition for Land for Joaquin Lisa, July 16, 1799, Lisa Papers, MHS.

31 Certificate of Lands Claimed by Manuel Lisa, Book B, 91, Concession from Zeno Trudo to Joaquin de Lisa, 6000 arpens, July 17, 1799; Concession from Zeno Trudo to Manuel Lisa, 6000 arpens, July 17, 1799, Bates Papers, MHS.

32 This description is a composite drawn from articles, advertisements, and notices

laid parallel to the river and several cross streets laid at right angles to the others, all situated below the natural rock levee which rose several hundred yards back from the water's edge. The houses were of mud, stone, and rough-hewn log construction, with the logs standing vertically instead of being laid horizontally in the conventional American method. As one early traveler described it, "St. Louis as you approach it, shows, like all the other French towns in this region, to much the greatest advantage at a distance. The French mode of building, and the white coat of lime applied to the mud or rough stone walls, gives them a beauty at a distance, which gives place to their native meanness when you inspect them from a nearer point of view."[33] It was a dirty town, whose unpaved streets became quagmires in the rain and were dust choked in their normal condition. The common method of waste disposal was to pitch it into the street, and woe to the passer-by. Dead cattle were left to rot where they fell, their incense becoming a calling card for the hordes of mosquitoes and flies which made summer life almost unbearable for the nearly one thousand residents. On the hill above the town stood the imposing fort and wall, constructed at an earlier day to protect against Indian attack, the fort now being used as a jail.

By contrast, the environs struck all visitors with their beauty. Over one hundred different species of trees were counted in the surrounding countryside. Hardwoods, walnut, maple, oak, cherry, and the rest were plentiful, and cabinet-makers produced some worthy furniture for local consumption. So abundant was walnut that it was sawed up into shingles, available to the purchaser for three dollars per thousand. The forest abounded in game and no man with a gun was more than a few minutes' walk from his choice of turkey, bear, elk, deer, raccoon, and hundreds

in the early issues of the *Missouri Gazette*, and from the accounts of early visitors such as Thomas Ashe, *Travels in America, 1806.*

[33] Timothy Flint, *Recollections of the Last Ten Years*, 110.

of other species of game, including an occasional buffalo. This was the reason for the excess of loiterers in town. With food so plentiful, there was no need to work for it.

Society was, however, genteel, at least so it seemed to later chroniclers who compared it to the St. Louis of the American occupation. French hospitality was extended to all travelers as the homes of the wealthy were opened to them. Those of affluence demonstrated their position with fine silver, glassware, and substantial libraries. Parties and dances were regularly scheduled, and excellent food and expensive entertainment made each one a delight. It was a French society, dominated by the figures of Auguste Chouteau, founder of the town, and of the Lieutenant Governor, himself born a Frenchman, but long devoted to the service of Spain. The major portion of the population was also French, having migrated across the Mississippi from the Illinois country when the British began taking over in that area after 1763. Their French heritage was that of the monarchy, and when the later revolutionary agents of Citizen Genêt appeared in St. Louis hoping for support, they were sadly disappointed.

The main occupation of the citizenry, outside the common one of farming, was trade—trade on the Mississippi and Ohio rivers, trade with the near-by Indians for pelts and deerskins, and local trade in merchandise and groceries. Heading the list of merchants were the familiar Auguste and Pierre Chouteau. They were the oldest and wealthiest residents of St. Louis, and, in addition, held the best of the monopolies granted by the Spanish government, the trade with the Osage Indians.

The Osages had been known for many years as the most warlike and dangerous of the tribes west of the Mississippi, and their trade was equally renowned as the most profitable. French *coureurs de bois* had exploited the tribe long before the founding of St. Louis, and so valuable was their business that as early as 1768, one Antoine Hubert was able to pay one Alex Langlois

15

eight hundred livres to trade with the Osages for him for the period of one year.[34] The warlike tendencies of this tribe had given the Spanish government much cause for alarm, but the wheels of administration and policy ground slowly, if at all, in the Spanish system, and nothing had been done about the situation. To send an expedition against the Osages to protect the tiny and unprofitable village of St. Louis was simply too expensive, so the outlying settlers lived in constant fear for their scalps.

The Chouteaus, in 1794, had proposed a solution to the problem. They would, at their own expense, build, arm, and supply a fort at the Osage village, sign a treaty of friendship with the tribe, and extend that friendship to all of the settlers. The fort was to be manned by twenty men, and the government was to pay the Chouteaus one hundred dollars per man per year for their maintenance. In return, the proprietors of the post asked for an exclusive grant of trade with the Osages from that date, May 18, 1794, "to the year 1800 inclusive." At the end of that period the government was to get the whole establishment at no cost.[35]

This was a bargain that the penurious Spaniards could not refuse, and the license was issued accordingly. The Chouteaus kept their part of the bargain in excellent fashion, and the Osages gradually became the tribe most friendly to the whites, although this did not come about without great struggle. In 1797 the Osages were causing trouble on the frontier, and Chouteau's rivals were quick to point it out to the Governor, which prompted Auguste Chouteau to write in explanation.[36] When, he wrote, a band of Osages had gone on a rampage along the Arkansas

[34] Agreement between Alex Langlois and Antoine Hubert, Aug. 14, 1768, Fur Trade Papers, MHS.

[35] Chouteau Petition, George Rogers Clark, MSS, Vol. XLI, Spanish Document C, 1793–95, Draper Collection, Wisconsin State Historical Society, Madison, Wisconsin; copy in Illinois Historical Survey.

[36] Letter, Auguste Choteau to Baron Carondelet, Apr. 18, 1797, Chouteau Collection, MHS.

River, Pierre Chouteau had brought the responsible chiefs to St. Louis to be held until the Governor should decide their fates, an indication that they were doing all in their power to control their Indian charges. Chouteau complained of the "brutishness" of those savages, and despaired of ever making "good men" of them.[37] Indian troubles continued to plague the monopolists until, by 1799, wars on the frontier had become so general that the Osages were afraid to go out and hunt, and Chouteau was unable to meet expenses. He asked the Governor for help in the form of three thousand weight of powder.[38] When the original concession was up at the close of 1800, the Chouteaus were again granted the privilege, this time for four years.[39] By the time Lisa arrived on the scene, the Osage trade was the established perquisite of the Chouteaus.

Among the other prominent merchants of St. Louis was Jacques Clamorgan,[40] a Portuguese of dubious ancestry and background, who held title to the largest of the monopolistic grants, the one comprising all of the tribes of the Missouri and the Rocky Mountains. Recognizing the potential value of the upper Missouri, and their own inability to finance the organization necessary to open the area to trade, a number of St. Louis merchants formed the Company of the Discoverers and Explorers of the Missouri, organized to explore the Spanish lands of Louisiana, and on to the Pacific if possible, as well as to open the trade of the upper Missouri. As the director of the company, Clamorgan had the opportunity to make a fortune if he could persuade the government to back him with enough funds to get the unwieldly

[37] Letter, Auguste Chouteau to Manuel Gayoso de Lemos, June 24, 1799, *ibid.*

[38] Letter, Auguste Chouteau to Manuel Gayoso de Lemos, Apr. 14, 1799, *ibid.*

[39] A. P. Nasatir, ed., *Before Lewis and Clark; Documents Illustrating the History of Missouri, 1785–1804*, II, 591.

[40] Very little is published illuminating this romantic adventurer. An all too brief summary of his life is in A. P. Nasatir, "Jacques Clamorgan: Colonial Promoter of the Northern Border of New Spain," *New Mexico Historical Review*, Vol. XVII (Apr., 1942), 101–12.

firm into operation. By the time of Lisa's arrival in St. Louis the company had sent three expeditions up the Missouri, but because of inadequate equipment and inept leadership none got farther than the Mandan villages, in modern North Dakota, and only one that far. None was successful as a trading venture.

By 1800 the merchants of the company, and those outside it as well, were becoming restless. They had always cordially disliked Clamorgan the adventurer, who had been, among other things, a slave trader in the West Indies, merchant, land speculator, explorer, keeper of a Negro harem, church warden, and bachelor father of four children. His partners hated him for his harem but respected him for his inordinate influence over the Governor's councils. His lack of success, however, brought them to the point of overthrowing his control. Even though the Missouri company was a failure, Clamorgan knew how to deal with the Indians, and understood well the advantages of giving them presents. He could never convince the authorities that money spent for good will would bring dividends in later trade. Lisa learned this lesson well, and never failed to court good will with adequate presents wherever he went.

With all the Indian trade in the hands of the Chouteaus and Clamorgan's group, Lisa had a considerable amount of vested interest to overcome if he was ever to achieve a share. Fortunately for him, others were dissatisfied under the strict governmental controls, and were tired of trying to work within and around the Missouri company. While Lisa was establishing himself in a number of enterprises in 1800 and 1801, including buying and selling land, slaves,[41] and the hiring of Juan Gatzeze to work for him as a baker,[42] others were making the first moves against Clamorgan's monopoly.

On April 26, 1800, Gregory Sarpy and J. P. Cabanné peti-

[41] The St. Louis Archives, MHS, contain over twenty entries in the years 1801, 1802, and 1803, in which Lisa is involved in either buying or selling land or slaves.

[42] Contract, May 29, 1800, Lisa Papers, MHS.

tioned for the exclusive trade of the Kansa Indians,[43] in consideration whereof they would make a treaty of peace with that nation. Lieutenant Governor Delassus at St. Louis, fully aware of the benefits received from the similar bargain struck with the Chouteaus regarding the Osages, recommended the plan and sent it on to New Orleans for official approval. Governor Casa Calvo agreed, and the necessary license was issued. On March 14, 1801,[44] Charles Sanguinet petitioned for the exclusive trade of the Omahas and Poncas. This was granted for two years on July 11. The same day licenses were given to Clamorgan (Republican Sioux), Chauvin (Pawnees), Pratte (Des Moines river country), Benito Vasquez (Missouri Loups), and Sarpy and Cabanné (Kansas and Otos).[45] This was not exactly free trade, but it was at least a step in that direction.

But Manuel Lisa, who did not share in this broadening of the franchise, did not want to content himself with a fraction of the trade, even if it be exclusively his. Confident of his ability to capture a fair share if unrestrained competition prevailed, he chose to strike at the whole principle of the monopolistic system. In a memorial to the Governor, signed by a number of merchants and citizens, including three who already had exclusive grants, Sarpy, Sanguinet, and Chauvin, and his old antagonist Joseph Robidoux,[46] Lisa, in a reasoned argument, pleaded the case for free trade. He cited the benefits to be obtained:

> The trader, stimulated by eagerness for gain, and restrained by fear of losing the confidence of the merchant, [would make a

[43] Indians Papers, MHS.

[44] Indian Trade and Fur Companies Papers, MHS.

[45] Delassus' List of Licenses, July 11, 1801, Indians Papers, MHS.

[46] This antagonism is best demonstrated in a humorous story related in Rudolph F. Kurz, *Journal*, trans. by Myrtis Jarrell and ed. by J. N. B. Hewitt, 66–67:

> Both were traders to the Pawnee. Each of them tried to acquire by trade as many pelts as possible for himself without being at all squeamish as to the means employed, and, for that reason, they often quarreled. In order to pre-

fortune for his family, and he] would give all his attention to curbing the savages, and to securing the most important parts of the exploration entrusted to him. The *engagé*, sure of receiving his salary in current money, would become more careful and economical, in the hope of acquiring some landed property.

The tiller of the soil, assured of selling his products and receiving a price at their current value, would increase his means [of production], and would give all his attention to agriculture. We would see industry revive; speculations would quickly follow one another; and various enterprises would be formed which would tend to regenerate the country and make it flourish.[47]

Nor did he forget practical matters, pointing out that the only currency of value was peltry, and to make that the exclusive possession of the few could not but be detrimental to the economy of the entire province. In addition to this statement, Lisa attempted to arm himself with a power of attorney from a large citizen group in St. Louis, including the signers of the memorial,

vent such wrangles and under the conviction that neither had the power to ruin the other, they pledged reciprocally to be "loyal," i.e., if a band of Indians arrived at their trading posts for the purpose of exchange and barter, neither would attempt to take advantage of the other. Manuel Lisa, however, had no intention of trading on honorable terms for any length of time; accordingly, upon occasion when both of them expected a band of Pawnee he tried to circumvent Robidoux. While he ordered his post supplied in secret with commodities to barter with the Pawnee, he went over to see Robidoux by way of putting him off his guard, by his own presence there to hinder operations, and to see what was really going on in the other storehouse. Robidoux played the part of unsuspecting host just as well as his opponent played his role; acted just as though he had allowed himself to be really duped. He invited Lisa to drink a glass of champagne to the success of the prospective trade; but regretted that on account of his gout he was not able to stoop down, and therefore would have to ask Lisa to fetch the flask from the cellar himself. The latter obligingly raised the trapdoor in the room and went down the steps. Joe let fall the door, rolled a cask upon it, and with mocking words left his opponent imprisoned, in order that he might trade alone with the Pawnees.

[47] Nasatir, ed., *Before Lewis and Clark*, II, 647–48.

to act in their behalf in New Orleans to help persuade the Governor General of the proper course of action. Delassus, disapproving of the entire petition as a criticism of his administration, refused to sanction such a power, but Lisa went to New Orleans anyway, carrying a signed document authorizing him to act for the group of citizens.[48] In New Orleans, Manuel wrote directly to the Intendant General, pointing out the justice of his petition, and asked that august personage to intercede with the King for the memorialists and have free trade instituted. In all, his was a well-organized crash campaign to abolish the monopolistic system.

Unfortunately, the move was ill timed. The Spanish government was in no mood to be dictated to by a handful of minor citizens from one of its least profitable outposts, and it certainly was not going to lose the many benefits deriving from the policy of granting exclusive licenses of trade to individuals. Although the petitioners obtained some unsolicited support from former governor Miró, who wrote that he understood the point they were trying to make and sympathized with their position, even he had qualms about free trade and feared the problems it would bring. But if Miró was tolerant, the rest of Spanish officialdom was appalled. Delassus, in forwarding the memorial to New Orleans, manifested his disapproval in no uncertain terms, and expressed his astonishment at finding the signatures of those men who already had received exclusive grants.[49] He took great pains to send along an annotated list of the signatories, giving a bit of their background, and, where he could, some reason for their signing. The meticulous Governor further pointed out that the province had had free trade prior to 1792, and the results of that experiment had been something close to disastrous.

Delassus' alarm proved unnecessary, for the memorial elicited

[48] *Ibid.*, 667.
[49] *Ibid.*, 641.

a scathing reply,[50] not even graced by a signature, which completely and, it was hoped, permanently demolished the arguments of the memorialists, and severely chastised them for even making such a suggestion as free trade. The answer was a classical defense of the paternalistic system, waxing philosophical in calling for a return to the "good" pastoral life, where man's communion with the land produced the fruit of his toil and put him at peace with the world. Asking a practical question, the reply hit at a weak point in the petitioner's stand: if an organized group of merchants could not put up enough money to make a trading venture successful, how could an individual expect to do so? The Spanish government wanted no part of the chaotic system proposed by the memorialists. It was interested in law and order, peace and quiet, and that it would have under a closely controlled system. The memorial was dismissed.

If Lisa had stopped to analyze the causes for his setback at the hands of the Governor, he might have realized that the addition of one more name to the memorial might have turned the balance in his favor, for no one was more respected, or wielded more power, than Auguste Chouteau. But Chouteau, already happy in the arms of privilege, would never be a party to a free-trade movement. There was, of course, no point in taking needless risks. So Manuel decided to teach that venerable gentleman an object lesson on the evils inherent in the monopolistic system by attempting to wrest the trade of the Osages from him. If he could not have free trade, Manuel would at least have the most profitable of the monopolies.

Well aware that Chouteau had been given the Osage trade for four years, terminating at the end of 1804, Lisa also knew that the Frenchman recently had not added anything of value to the Spanish coffers. Not only that, he had had to ask for help in maintaining his grant. Manuel reasoned that the government's

[50] *Ibid.*, 651.

investment in the fort and its equipment was steadily depreciating, and that the government would no doubt be interested in obtaining more value in return for the right of exclusive trade than they were presently receiving. If Chouteau had procured the grant with what amounted to a bribe, why could not Lisa take the trade away from him with a larger one? His was a cynical evaluation of the Spanish government, but not the less valid. For this purpose, Manuel formed a partnership with Charles Sanguinet, Gregory Sarpy, and Francis Marie Benoît, and was back in New Orleans petitioning the Governor on June 4, 1802.[51]

Knowing that one of the problems faced by the authorities in St. Louis was the clandestine trade across the Mississippi with the Americans, and cognizant of the fact that the Americans had, among other things, better-ground flour, the petitioners shrewdly promised to build in St. Louis "a water mill to make flour as fine as that of the Anglo-Americans," thus partly cloaking their purely profit motive by contributing to the general welfare of all of the citizens of upper Louisiana. The supplication continued in the same vein, with the partners expressing their patriotism and zeal for the Spanish crown, and, in order to demonstrate concretely that zeal, they offered a one-thousand-dollar "gift" to the royal treasury. Their repeated protestations of love for country and interest in the general welfare of the populace ultimately convinced the Governor, and on June 12, 1802, "bearing in mind that it is just that all the honorable and powerful residents profit from the trade with the Indians," the Governor had "come to yield to the reiterated solicitations, which under date of the fourth instant, the inhabitants of the town of St. Louis, Illinois, Don Manuel de Lisa, Don Carlos Sanguinet for himself and his son-in-law Don Francisco Maria Benoît, and Juan Bautista Sarpy in the name of his brother Don Gregorio made

---

[51] *Ibid.*, 677.

to me, conceding to them for the precise term of five years, to all four in common, the trade with the Osage Indians."[52] The Governor also let it be known that he, too, was acting in the public interest, since the recipients of the grant were to construct and operate the proposed mill.

Manuel Lisa, Benoît and Company, as the group was known, now possessed the exclusive trade of the Osages, and Lisa lost no time in personally presenting his grant to Delassus, in order that they might begin the trade at once. Delassus was shocked and unhappy that Lisa, who had gone over his head directly to New Orleans, should succeed in depriving his good friend Auguste Chouteau of a trade which was rightfully Chouteau's possession for another two and one-half years. Twice Lisa had disrupted the normal order of things, first with the memorial for free trade, and now by snatching the Osage trade from its legal owner. He was a man to be watched closely, and cut down to size if possible. To keep the record straight, Delassus called Chouteau into his office and, in the presence of Lisa and Benoît, had the new license read so that there would be no misunderstanding of its contents. The document specifically gave the monopoly of the trade of the "Osage of the Missouri" to the Lisa group.

Chouteau, although he bowed to the superior authority, was not a man to take such a rebuke without fighting back, and he did so in the most effective ways possible. First, he made sure that the loss of trade did not deprive him of the contract to provision the garrison at the Osage fort.[53] This not only allowed him to snatch a bit of profit from under the noses of the new monopolists but gave him a valuable inroad into the Osage country. That he would exploit this opportunity was shown early in

[52] *Ibid.*, 698. There is a handwritten contemporary copy with slightly different wording under the date of June 15, 1802, Indians Papers, MHS.

[53] Letter, Morales to Delassus, June 18, 1802, Chouteau Collection, MHS. This letter confirms Delassus' action in giving the contract to Chouteau.

1803 when Lisa discovered and captured a boat, loaded with brandy, within the bounds of his Osage grant. The vessel, piloted by one José Ortiz, had for its object the sale of liquor to the Osages and Lisa's traders at the post. Lisa suspected, probably correctly, that Chouteau was behind the incident, and complained to the Lieutenant Governor. The complaint fell upon deaf ears. This slight by the Governor, the latest in a long series of injuries, real and fancied, suffered by Lisa and company at the hands of Delassus, was the more serious because Manuel had bought out Sarpy and Sanguinet, so that only Lisa and Benoît shared the Osage trade.

It was enough to provoke Manuel to write a scathing memorial[54] to the Lieutenant Governor, condemning his action, or, rather, the lack thereof, in the Ortiz incident, and mentioning all the other injustices he had received from official hands. The event showed, said Lisa, "without the least doubt the little or no justice we are to receive in the future from you, which statement we make without fear, more so knowing that your intention at all times has been to ignore us and give us sufficient and equivocal proofs of the antagonism which you have towards us in matters pertaining to the trade of the Missouri." This was too much, even for the mild-mannered Delassus, and Lisa immediately found himself looking out at the world through the bars of the St. Louis prison.

The memorial had been written on March 14, 1803, and by March 17, Lisa had had enough. He wrote to Delassus in humble supplication, "I am very sorry and I retract all my statements in said writing which you might have taken as personal offense, and also retract any thing that I might have said in this writing against you personally, and if your heart is really pious, you will have mercy on me, and you will feel sorry to see my property lost, my work delayed and my family in deep affliction."

[54] Memorial, Lisa to Delassus, Mar. 14, 1803, Lisa Papers, MHS.

Not only that, but "My health is injured on account of the dampness of this place."[55] Delassus certainly had a pious heart, but only to the extent that he moved Lisa from the dank calaboose and confined him to his (Lisa's) home. On the nineteenth Lisa was moved to repeat his plea, stating, "It is not right that a subject like I should criticize or conceive any wrong idea of the actions of a superior person, who at all times has shown his good heart."[56] He promised to conduct himself properly in the future, and on that condition was released. The whole matter was reported to New Orleans, and Governor Salcedo wrote to Delassus on May 3, commending his action, and saying that "Lisa must be informed that hereafter he will have to behave himself, and if he does not comply with the requirements, he shall be taught a lesson and punished."[57] Thus the errant sheep was brought back into the fold.

Fortunately the mail took a long time getting between St. Louis and New Orleans, for at the time Salcedo was writing, Lisa was again embroiled with Delassus. The original partners in Manuel Lisa, Benoît and Company, in order to finance their "gift" to the royal coffers, begin construction of the mill, and outfit themselves for the Osage trade, had given out a note for fifteen hundred dollars. Auguste Chouteau had promptly bought it up, and, when payment was due, on April 30, 1803, he presented it to Lisa for collection. Manuel, who not only was short of cash but was having difficulty in making the Osage trade show a profit, refused to meet the demand. The major problem with the trade was that Pierre Chouteau had persuaded Clermont's band of Osages to separate from the rest of the tribe and settle on the Arkansas, out of the jurisdiction of Lisa's grant. This had cut seriously into the hoped-for profits of the partners.

Chouteau, the same day, appealed to Delassus for action and

---

[55] Lisa Papers, MHS.
[56] In *ibid.*
[57] Chouteau Collection, MHS.

instituted suit to recover the debt in the Supreme Tribunal in New Orleans. Sarpy, Benoît, and Sanguinet immediately stated that they were willing to pay their shares of the note, and added that there was no formal organization of Manuel Lisa, Benoît and Company, and each man acted independently. Lisa, defying logic, wrote that as long as Chouteau had appealed to the court, he was willing to wait for its decision, and, further, that he thought it would be in his favor. Delassus then ordered the three willing partners to pay equal shares and to withhold from the partnership the amount of Lisa's share until it should be paid.[58] Delassus took this summary action no doubt prompted by the fact that Sarpy had recently complained that he had had to stand the entire cost of constructing the flour mill himself, and desired Delassus either to make the others contribute their shares or give the trade of the Osages exclusively to him.[59] This request was sent on to New Orleans, where Salcedo, on August 26, ordered Delassus to make the partners pay their shares or give the trade to Sarpy or any others who would contribute to the construction of the mill.[60] But while these machinations went on, matters of world-wide significance were beginning to sift into the isolated town on the west bank of the Mississippi—matters which would work permanent change and relegate these petty disputes into the limbo of the past.

News of the secret Treaty of Ildefonso, signed between France and Spain in 1800, ceding the Louisiana Territory back to France, caused a great stir in St. Louis. Almost simultaneously came word that Napoleon was negotiating with the United States for the sale of that vast area. The very day Chouteau was pressing Lisa for payment of his note, Louisiana was sold to the United

[58] All the correspondence back and forth is contained in the Lisa Papers, MHS, and printed in Frederic L. Billon, *Annals of St. Louis in Its Early Days under the French and Spanish Dominations*, 334–37.

[59] Petition, Sarpy to Delassus, May 4, 1803, Indians Papers, MHS.

[60] In *ibid.*

States. The impending arrival of Americans in St. Louis brought mixed reactions. For Delassus it must have been a blessing. No more walking the tightrope of trying to please his superiors in New Orleans and his subjects in St. Louis; no longer would he have to listen to the interminable disputes of the traders. The coming of Americans meant retirement and a little peace and quiet. To some, particularly the older French inhabitants, it meant the loss of an old way of life. They knew that the American flag would be followed, if not actually preceded, by the drunken, brawling boatmen and hunters from Kentucky. They had heard of them on the Ohio and Mississippi, and of horse races in the streets, no-holds-barred fights in which the loser, if not dead, was maimed for life, and taverns with billiards and gambling, all of which things would give their town an "under the hill" similar to that of Natchez.

To others, the coming of American rule meant the loss of privilege and position, for the Americans, they knew, did not stand on formality, and granted no special favors to specific individuals. A man was free to make of himself what he would. This was good news to Lisa, for though it would occasion the loss of the exclusive trade with the Osages, that trade would still be open to him along with other, perhaps richer, areas. Now he could begin to think seriously of the vast reaches of the upper Missouri, where, it was said, beaver abounded. There was also the possibility of opening a new trade with his now former countrymen in Santa Fe, far across the prairies and deserts of the West. For the moment, however, there was business to be done.

The winter of 1803–1804 found a gathering of Americans across the Mississippi at the mouth of the Wood River, nearly opposite that of the Missouri. Under the leadership of Meriwether Lewis, former secretary to the President of the United States, and William Clark, fiery-haired former soldier and son of a prominent Virginia family, they were preparing to embark on an incredible voyage across the North American continent at the behest of Thomas Jefferson, third President of the United States. They were to ascend the Missouri River to its sources, cross the Rocky Mountains to the Pacific Ocean, and return, exploring that vast country, acquainting themselves with the inhabitants, noting the resources, animal, mineral, and vegetable, ascertaining the extent of British influence and activity in the area, and determining to some extent the size and boundaries of the Louisiana Territory so recently purchased. These men would need recruits, supplies, and all of the information they could get concerning the upper country. Manuel Lisa would be among their suppliers.

It was natural that the American captains should turn to Lisa as well as to the Chouteaus and others for supplies. Throughout his early years in St. Louis, Manuel had steadily developed his retail business, as the account books of the Chouteaus and others indicate. Selling everything from fine glassware to chamber pots, from coffee to guns, he continued to deal in land and slaves as well, building himself into a place of prominence. In 1804, particularly, perhaps taking advantage of the departing Spanish officials, Lisa added much acreage to that which he already had. On July 18 of that year, Joaquin Lisa deeded to his brother the six thousand arpents he had been granted in 1799.[61] Joaquin was returning to New Orleans to make that place his permanent home. Possessing two lots and houses in St. Louis,[62] Manuel Lisa, despite all opposition, was a power to be reckoned with.

Lisa no doubt paid at least one visit to the encampment at Wood River to see the massive preparations in progress, and there met men with whom he later would become associated: George Drouillard, the half-Indian in whom Lewis had enough confidence to send on a recruiting expedition to Tennessee;[63]

[61] Deed, Joaquin Lisa to Manuel Lisa, Lisa Papers, MHS.

[62] Notes on Owners of Lots and Description of Houses, Mar. 10, 1804, Frederic Billon Collection, MHS.

[63] Letter, Meriwether Lewis to William Clark, Dec. 17, 1803; "Drewyer ar-

John Colter, chafing under soldierly restraints, fully confident that he was prepared to meet any eventuality and eager to be on the way; Edward Robinson; John Potts; Peter Wiser; and others of their wild kind, submitting themselves to military discipline only for the opportunity to make the voyage. This was a labor of love for these men. It had to be, for the material rewards were minimal, and the incredible record of not losing a man on the voyage attests not only to their hardy constitutions and excellent training but to their desire to make the expedition a success. Here were men who, when they returned, would be valuable assets to a trader thinking of opening new vistas in trade to the northwest.

Preparations proceeded at a rapid rate, with the two captains constantly on the move, picking up volunteers, purchasing equipment. On February 18, 1804, Lewis wrote to Clark:

> If Mr. Manuel will let us have the men you mentioned, pray engage them immediately, if you think from their appearance and characters they will answer the purpose. . . .
>
> My compliments to Govr. Lassuse and Mons. Dabuche, & Msrs. Gratiott and A. Chouteau—not forgetting my most profound respects to *Mdam. Manuel.*[64]

Perhaps "the charms of her beauty" had not altogether fled. By May 6, however, as the party was making final preparations prior to setting out, relations were not so cordial, for Lewis wrote:

> Damn Manuel and triply damn Mr. B. They give me more vexation than their lives are worth—I have dealt very plainly with these gentlemen, in short I have come to an open rupture with them; I think them both great scoundrels, and they have given me abundant proofs of their unfriendly dispositions toward our government and it's measures—these [the word "gentlemen"

rived here last evening from Tennisee with eight men." William Clark Collection, MHS.

[64] In *ibid.*

was scratched out in the original] (no I will scratch it out) these puppies are not unacquainted with my opinions; and I am well informed that they have engaged some hireling writer to draught a petition and remonstrance to Govr Claibourne against me; strange indeed, that men to appearance in their senses, will manifest such strong sumtions of insanity, as to be *wheting knives to cut their own throats.*[65]

Whatever the cause of this outburst, it could not have been as serious as Lewis made it sound. At least neither he nor Clark ever held it against Lisa, because Lewis later became the patron of Lisa's Missouri Fur Company, and Clark was associated in partnership with Manuel for many years.

While preparations were under way for embarkation, Major Amos Stoddard arrived on the scene to preside over the formal exchange of the Louisiana Territory. Delassus wrote him, detailing all the information Stoddard had requested in a letter of his own, and included a last shot at Lisa, recommending that Chouteau be given back the Osage trade. On March 9 the Spanish flag was taken down and replaced by the French. Since France had never taken formal possession of the land, the Spanish had to transfer it to the French before the Americans could have it. Upon the plea of the French inhabitants, their national banner was permitted to fly overnight, and the exchange was completed the next day. The Stars and Stripes floated above one of the finest land purchases in history, worth all of the pangs it cost Mr. Jefferson's conscience. "The Spanish troops after the evacuation of the Fort were marched down the hill to a large old French house of logs at the southwest corner of Third and Elm streets, the property of Manuel Lisa, from whom it had been rented by Governor Delassus, for quarters for the Spanish troops, until they could depart for New Orleans."[66] Although this allowed Lisa to squeeze a last few doubloons from the departing Span-

---

[65] In *ibid.*
[66] Billon, *Annals*, 361–62.

iards, it may have been a mixed blessing, for Delassus did not get the troops out of there until October.

With the final settlement of the political situation and the resumption of a stable market for furs and skins, Lisa set out to consolidate his finances before entering wholeheartedly into the business of opening new avenues of commerce. A considerable portion of the years 1805 and 1806 were spent in the courtroom, where Manuel instituted suit after suit in an attempt to collect money owed him by people who had either borrowed cash or made purchases on credit, and were unable, or unwilling, to make payment. He prosecuted more than twenty individuals in suits totaling several thousand dollars.[67]

The largest of these suits was against Robert McClellan. McClellan, one of the early romantic characters of the Western fur trade, had served with honor under General "Mad Anthony" Wayne in the latter's campaigns against the Indians, and had taken to the rough, outdoor life. He drifted westward after leaving the service and in 1805 turned up in St. Louis, outfitting himself for a trading trip to the Omaha nation. The hardy frontiersman purchased from Lisa and Benoît, and from Lisa alone, a considerable outfit, buying, as was the prevailing practice, on short-term credit. The trading venture proved not too successful, for McClellan was faced with competition from the British traders on the Missouri who had penetrated that far south.[68]

McClellan apparently did not pay on time, and Lisa sued him for $2,000.00 in damages.[69] Manuel won the case, although the

[67] Almost one entire envelope of the three comprising the Lisa Papers, MHS, is taken up by notices and receipts of court cases, but unfortunately there is rarely any disposition of the cases given.

[68] Hiram M. Chittenden, *The American Fur Trade of the Far West*, I, 159. This is the Academic Reprint edition, Chittenden's original work having been published in three volumes (New York, 1902). I have used the 1954 edition throughout.

[69] Notice of Suit, 1806, Lisa Papers, MHS. Judgment appears under Manuel Lisa vs. Robert McClelland, May 28, 1806, Missouri Minute Book of the Supreme Court, 1805–1808, MHS.

jury awarded him only $810.50, which was probably the sum owed him plus court costs. McClellan countersued for $5,000.00, claiming that he had contracted to buy "Merchantable Indian goods such as the Michilimackinack Merchants usually furnish to those employed in the Indian Trade."[70] This, he claimed, he had not received, and, as a consequence, his trade was ruined. His goods possibly were somewhat inferior to those used by the British, although the St. Louis merchants used a preponderance of English goods brought in through Montreal, but it was British competition, not inferior goods, which cut into the trader's profits. The British were always able to sell their trade goods for nearly what Americans paid for theirs, and wherever British and Americans competed for Indian favors, the British invariably were victors. The firm of Lisa and Benoît then sued for their bill, and on November 10, 1806, the jury awarded the plaintiffs $1,185.33½ plus court costs.[71] Thus Lisa helped his financial situation but incurred the enmity of a man who would return to plague him in later years.

The year 1806 was the turning point in the career of Manuel Lisa. The news of the returning Lewis and Clark party filtering into St. Louis fired his imagination and stiffened his determination to become a part of events of great moment. The small business ventures of trading on the Mississippi, Ohio, and Wabash rivers, his mercantile establishments in Vincennes and St. Louis, and the trade with the Osage Indians had been an important apprenticeship for the new ventures he planned and was about to execute. The talented Spaniard had dealt with all the prominent merchants in the area, and had learned from them. His intensive, firsthand study of the Indian character had allowed him to gain an understanding of its mysteries. Manuel had gath-

---

[70] Notice of Suit, 1806, Lisa Papers, MHS.

[71] Notice of Suit, 1806, *ibid.* Judgment under M. Lisa & F. M. Benoît vs. Robert McClelland, Nov. 10, 1806, Missouri Minute Book of the Supreme Court, 1805–1808, MHS.

ered a fund of information from the Chouteaus, from Clamorgan, from the Osages, and from his late friend Regis Loisel.[72]

Loisel had been a partner of Jacques Clamorgan in Clamorgan, Loisel and Company, which had been formed to utilize the many grants and considerations given by the government to Clamorgan's Missouri company. When the progress of the larger company bogged down, Loisel struck out on his own, although still financed in part by Clamorgan. He made several trips up the Missouri for relatively short distances and, in 1802, built a post on Cedar Island to trade with the Sioux. From these wanderers of the Plains, Loisel learned of the wealthy tribes of the West, the Arapahoes of the sources of the Platte, the Crows of the *Roche Jaune* (Yellowstone), and the mighty Blackfeet of the watershed of the Missouri. The trader also learned of a river rising near the source of the Missouri which flowed to the south, through Spanish territory, and ultimately into the Gulf of California, a fact which Lisa later tried to utilize to connect the Northwest with Santa Fe. With this information feeding his fertile imagination, Lisa prepared to strike out into uncharted territory.

[72] The best description of Loisel and his activities is contained in Pierre-Antoine Tabeau, *Tabeau's Narrative of Loisel's Expedition to the Upper Missouri*, 3–52.

II

The Fur Trade
Theater of Operations

BY July 1, 1806, Lisa felt that he was equipped to make his first move. Entering into an agreement with Jacques Clamorgan, the two indebted themselves to the firm of Francis W. Geisse, Tayesse, and Snyder for the sum of $12,000,[1] of which $6,459 were due and payable in April, 1808.[2] The merchandise purchased from the Philadelphia firm was to outfit a trading expedition to "the frontier of New Mexico near the town of Sta. Fe."[3] To implement this venture, Lisa obtained a license to trade with the Republican Osages, whose territory lay across the route westward to the Spanish settlement. The expedition, headed by Louison Beaudoin, an old St. Louis trader possessed of the necessary lack of scruples the job called for,[4] and accompanied by Clamorgan himself, left St. Louis in the summer of 1807. At that time Clamorgan wrote to Mrs. Lisa and to Manuel's agent in St. Louis, Hyacinte Egliz, notifying them of his departure.

---

[1] Copy of the agreement sent to Lisa by Clamorgan, Feb. 19, 1810, Lisa Papers, MHS. Clamorgan was trying to get Lisa to pay off a portion of the debt due in 1810.

[2] Letter, Jacques Clamorgan to Mrs. Lisa and Hyacinte Egliz, July 21, 1807, in *ibid.*

[3] *Ibid.*

[4] Beaudoin had had furs confiscated for illegal trapping as early as 1799. Early Litigations Envelope, MHS.

They replied that they knew nothing of such an expedition, and that Manuel, then absent on a voyage up the Missouri, had verbally broken his partnership with the Portuguese, and had told him that he wanted nothing to do with the Santa Fe venture.[5]

The reason for this wish to disassociate himself from so noteworthy an enterprise can be found in the fact that somehow this expedition fell athwart the plans of that master schemer, General James Wilkinson, then acting governor of the Louisiana Territory. Lisa had been in trouble with governments before and realized that this was not the time to assert his independence and be jailed while others acquired riches in the trade. The summer of 1806 found Wilkinson sending Lieutenant Zebulon M. Pike on an exploring trip to the sources of the Arkansas River, which rose somewhere near the Spanish claims in the Southwest. Pike had recently returned from a similar assignment to find the source of the Mississippi, which object he had failed to accomplish. What Wilkinson's plans were are unknown, for that worthy kept his own counsel, and historians and others have speculated on them ever since Pike's return. Their almost universal feeling has been that whatever Wilkinson had in mind, Pike was only a tool, and knew of no object for his travels other than those given in his instructions.

The Pike expedition got off to a bad start when Lisa, seeing an opportunity to collect another of his outstanding debts, caused the sheriff to arrest Baroney Vasquez, Pike's interpreter, for a debt of between three and four hundred dollars.[6] Vasquez, unable to pay, was required to return to St. Louis with the law. At Cantonment Missouri the prisoner and his escort met Governor Wilkinson, where the latter became Vasquez' security, allow-

[5] Letter, Mary Lisa and H. Egliz to Jacques Clamorgan, July 22, 1807, Lisa Papers, MHS.

[6] Major Zebulon M. Pike, *An Account of Expeditions to the Sources of the Mississippi*, 112.

ing the interpreter to rejoin Pike. Writing to the explorer on July 18, 1806, Wilkinson stated:

> I have recd. your letter of yesterday and concerning yr interpreter without date. I had taken arrangements to secure Bennette [Baroney Vasquez] when he appeared here and I have now become his security. Manual is a Black Spaniard. He dined here yesterday and left here this morning before the arrival of your letter—this was well for him . . . I shall dress Manual and Cadet assui. I will teach them how to interrupt national movements with their despicable intrigues.[7]

Apparently they did not need special instruction. On August 14, Pike met three *engagés* of Pierre Chouteau, who informed him that the Little Osages had taken to the warpath against the Kansas, an event which Pike attributed to Lisa's chicanery. Five days later Pike arrived at Lisa's post at the Osage village, where he found three of Manuel's men who also had just arrived. From Baptiste Duchoquette dit Larme, the leader of the three, Pike learned only that Lisa had sent them out to tell the Osages that Sylvestre Labbadie was coming up in the fall to trade with them,[8] which was, apparently, true, as Lisa obtained a license from Joseph Browne on August 29 for one barge and eight men to engage in trade with the Osages.[9] This is not the stuff from which great intrigues are made. Since the three men did not have passports to be in that country, Pike sent them back to St. Louis and reported the incident to Wilkinson.

In a letter dated Cantonment Missouri, August 6, 1806, Wilkinson described to Pike what he thought Lisa was up to in the West:

[7] Major Zebulon M. Pike, "Papers of Zebulon M. Pike, 1806–1807," ed. by Herbert E. Bolton, *American Historical Review*, Vol. XIII (July, 1908), 814–15.

[8] Pike, *Account*, Appendix, 41. Duchoquette's deposition appears in Pike, "Papers," *loc. cit.* 823–24.

[9] License, Aug. 29, 1806, Lisa Papers, MHS.

It is reduced to a certainty that [Lisa] and a society of which he is the ostensible leader, have determined on a project to open some commercial intercourse with Santa Fe, and as this may lead to a connection injurious to the United States, and will, I understand, be attempted without the sanction of the law or the permission of the executive: you must do what, consistently, you can to defeat the plan. No good can be derived to the United States from such a project, because the prosecution of it will depend entirely upon the Spaniards, and they will not permit it, unless to serve their political, as well as their personal interests. I am informed that the ensuing autumn and winter will be employed in reconnoitering and opening a connection with the Tetaus, Panis, &c, that in the fall, or the next winter, a grand magazine is to be established at the Osage towns, where these operations will commence; that [Lisa] is to be the active agent, having formed a connection with the Tetaus. This will carry forward their merchandise within three or four days travel of the Spanish settlements, where they will deposit it, under a guard of 300 Tetaus. [Lisa] will then go forward with four or five attendants, taking with him some jewelry and fine goods. With those he will visit the governor, to whom he will make some presents, and implore his pity with a fine tale of sufferings which will have been endured by the change of government: that they are left here, with goods to be sure, but not a dollars worth of bullion, and therefore they have adventured to see him, for the purpose of praying his leave for the introduction of their property into the province. If he assents, then the whole of the goods will be carried forward; if he refuses, then [Lisa] will invite some of his countrymen to accompany him to his deposit, and having there exposed them to his merchandise, he will endeavor to open a forced or clandestine trade; for he observes, the Spaniards will not dare to attack his camp. Here you have the plan, and you must take all prudent and lawful means to blow it up.[10]

It was a magnificent conspiracy, one worthy of a dreamer of

[10] Pike, *Account*, Appendix, 38. Pike, in his published work, leaves blanks instead of using names. Elliott Coues, editor of Pike's *The Expedition of Zebulon*

grandiose schemes such as Manuel Lisa or Jacques Clamorgan, or James Wilkinson. Whether this was the actual plan or not, Clamorgan visited the Governor in Chihuahua and asked for trade privileges in Santa Fe.[11]

Why Lisa dropped his active participation in the Santa Fe venture at this time remains a mystery, for he continued to maintain his financial interest in Clamorgan's journey, and never lost sight of the New Mexican capital as a trade possibility. Perhaps the "Black Spaniard" did fear reprisals from Wilkinson if he persisted, although that would not be in character. Or perhaps the dream of the Missouri seemed within his grasp, and he wished to attain it before Wilkinson sent the wandering Pike to seek out the sources of that river.

At any rate, Manuel, already in serious debt with the New Mexican adventure, formed a partnership—there was no other way to obtain even the minimum of capital necessary to initiate an enterprise—with Pierre Menard and William Morrison of Kaskaskia, in the Illinois country, for the purpose of sending a trading and trapping expedition to the headwaters of the Missouri River. The St. Louis group of merchants apparently wanted no part of the spirited Spaniard and his schemes, for Lisa, having first formed a partnership with the outcast Clamorgan, now had to go entirely outside the city for financial backing. His new partners, however, were not strangers.

Lisa may have met Pierre Menard as early as his days in Vincennes, since the Illinois merchant had lived there for a time and was well known in the area, having done business with Vigo, Dubois, and perhaps Lisa himself. William Morrison had long been established in Kaskaskia, and early had been interested in

Montgomery Pike, II, 574–75, inserts Lisa's name in all the blanks. This seems more logical than the theory of R. I. Holcomb, *History of Vernon County, Missouri*, 122, who uses both the names Lisa and Chouteau, and indicates the fact that Lisa was working for Chouteau at the time.

11 J. J. Hill, "An Unknown Expedition to Santa Fe in 1807," *Mississippi Valley Historical Review*, Vol. VI (March, 1920), 560–62.

the Santa Fe trade. He had, in 1804, sent out Baptiste La Lande with a small outfit to the Spanish outpost to scout trade possibilities.[12] Morrison heard nothing from his agent and assumed him dead, or at best held prisoner by the Spanish. Not until Pike's return did he learn that La Lande had liked Santa Fe and its señoritas so well he had simply decided to stay. Morrison had also come into possession of the note owed by Lisa and Clamorgan to Geisse and company.[13] This could well have prompted him to remain close to Manuel, and to aid him in this venture. The failure of Lisa to pay promptly became the cause of bitter feeling between the two men at a later date.

The return of Lewis and Clark, with their extremely favorable report of the potentialities of the upper country, galvanized the partnership into action. Menard and Morrison, who preferred the privilege of placating their creditors at home, left the command of the actual expedition to Lisa and designated George Drouillard, lately discharged from government service, as their representative on the planned voyage. Lisa and Drouillard managed to recruit from fifty to sixty men,[14] many of them recently released from the Lewis and Clark contingent, to man two keelboats.[15] Since it was a combined trading and trapping promotion, the boats carried an outfit valued at about $16,000, $12,-649 of which had been purchased from G. Gillespie and Company of Michilimackinac through the St. Louis trader Myers Michaels.[16] Well aware of the odds they faced, considered by many to be insuperable, this hardy band set out for the moun-

[12] Chittenden, *American Fur Trade*, II, 491.

[13] William Morrison Account, Mar. 22, 1807, Kaskaskia Papers, MHS.

[14] United States Congress, Senate, *Sen. Doc. No. 90*, 22 Cong., 1 sess., Serial 213, Vol. II, Joshua Pilcher's Report dated St. Louis, Dec. 1, 1831, 11.

[15] Brackenridge, *Views of Louisiana*, 89.

[16] Frederic L. Billon, *Annals of St. Louis in Its Territorial Days from 1804 to 1821*, 32, gives the value of the outfit as $16,000. The Gillespie purchase is in the St. Louis Records, Book D, 375, Office of the Recorder of Deeds, City Hall, St. Louis, Missouri, and, Deposition of Security by Auguste Chouteau for a bill of Manuel Lisa with Myer Michaels & Company, Aug. 10, 1806, June 14, 1808,

tains in the spring of 1807, the first organized trading and trapping expedition to ascend the Missouri to the Rocky Mountains.

This first commercial voyage to the mountains started inauspiciously enough, although setting a pattern for all later departures of a similar nature. After embarkation, Lisa had to return to St. Charles to bring along forcibly one of his *engagés*, Jean Baptiste Bouché,[17] who had imbibed a bit too freely and was unwilling to leave the bottled comforts of civilization. It was common practice when signing an *engagé* to contract, to advance him a small portion of his wages, ideally so that he could clear up his obligations and purchase whatever personal articles he wanted to take along, but practically so that he could have one last spree before setting out for the wilderness, where hardship was severe and alcohol dear. Tavern owners were free with credit to such men, knowing that their employers would pay up all bills rather than have the creditor lawfully detain the *engagé* for debt and hold up the entire party. This was a scene played with monotonous regularity every time a group left for the mountains. In this case, Lisa would have saved himself much grief and money had he left Bouché to the tender mercies of the barkeep, but since Bouché had been paid for his services, Manuel was determined to extract his money's worth of labor from the fellow.

The first and most persistent difficulty encountered by the party was met the day the boats nosed into the turbulent waters of the Missouri from the relatively placid Mississippi. The mighty Missouri, aptly described as too thin to plow but too thick to drink, had a personality all its own, and was seemingly bent on destroying every boat that attempted to conquer its murky brown waters. The current of this giant was about four miles per hour,[18] much too strong for the clumsy, hand-powered

Henry Chouteau Dyer Collection, MHS. The purchase was made on August 8, 1806, and paid in the early part of 1809.

[17] Douglas, "Manuel Lisa," *loc. cit.*, 251.

[18] Lewis C. Beck, *A Gazetteer of the States of Illinois and Missouri*, 173.

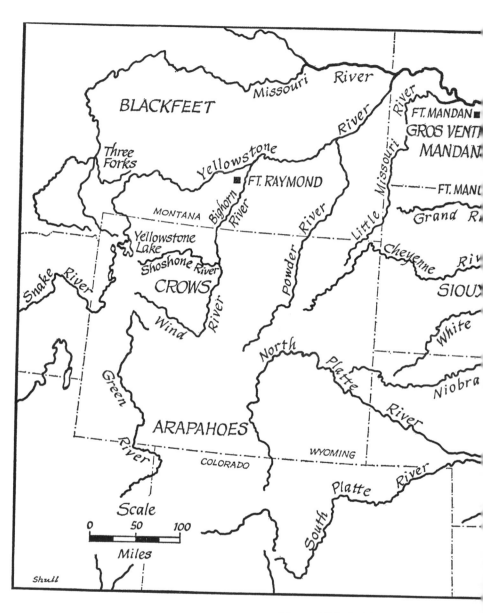

Manuel Lisa's Theater of Operation

n the American Northwest

keelboats, and so the vessels were forced to navigate close to the bank, usually the farthest one from the main channel. The means of propulsion were several, and all save one required sheer muscle power. The main reliance was on poling along in the shallow, fairly calm water close to shore. Each boat was equipped with walkways along either gunwale; on these the men would position themselves, with the rounded knobs of their long poles fitted against their shoulders. On a given signal the men, facing the stern, would lean into their poles and literally walk the boat forward under their feet. As each man reached the stern he hurried quickly back to his original position, and the process was repeated. Where this was not possible because of deep water or a soft bottom, the cordelle, a long length of rope attached to the mast and pulled by men scrambling along the bank, was used to inch the craft upstream. When neither of these methods sufficed, or to supplant the cordelle in operation, each boat was fitted with several pairs of oars. The center mast was also equipped with a square rigged sail for use when the wind and the boat happened to be going in the same direction. Unfortunately for the boatmen, this all too rarely happened.

Not content with leaving the men to their tedious and back-breaking means of propulsion, the cantankerous river did everything in its power to stop them completely, and, failing that, to sink the boats. When the crew would bed down for the night along a relatively quiet stretch of water, they might be awakened in the blackness of midnight to find a raging torrent lapping not too gently at their blankets. Overhanging trees would sweep men from the decks; banks would cave in without warning; the channel would shift from one side to the other in a matter of minutes. In addition, the river set snares to catch the unwary steersman. Sawyers, whole trees swept into the stream at some point above, and anchored to the river bed by their roots, bobbed menacingly in the current, now above water, now hidden under the surging waves. Should one of them come up under a boat, it could slash the bottom open from end to end, or flip it over in less time than it takes to tell. Another potential danger was the embarras, a floating aggregation of tangled trees, dead buffalo, and flotsam of all kinds. A crushing force while being swept downstream, the embarras was an even greater menace when hung up in midstream on a sawyer or rock. There it formed a veritable island, constantly increasing in size, breaking the current around itself to either bank, making keelboat passage almost impossible. The river also had a nasty habit of piling up an embarras between the upper end of an island and the lee shore, causing the crew, who preferred these quiet channels, either to cut a path through the tangle or to retrace their steps and pass along the current side of the island, both of which methods caused delays of from hours to several days. The Missouri was a river to make strong men weep and rich men poor.

Aside from the normal difficulties furnished by the river, the Lisa party experienced no trouble up to the mouth of the Osage, where Bissonette deserted. After the delay caused by that affair, the expedition continued in good time to the mouth of the Kansas, where, on June 3, François LeCompt, a half-blood trader of renown who had spent much time with the Kansa Indians, hailed the passing boats. He was promptly signed to a contract for three years at a salary of five hundred dollars.[19] Thus Lisa added another to his array of men who were well acquainted with the north country, and had firsthand knowledge of the Indians as well. These men, John Potts, Peter Wiser, Edward Robinson,[20] and the others who had been with Lewis and Clark, provided seasoned leadership for the greenhorns, and were able to impart to

[19] Douglas, "Manuel Lisa," *loc. cit.*, 251.

[20] List of Notes of the "Men" on the Missouri Belonging in Part to Pierre Menard, Menard Family Papers, Illinois State Historical Society, Springfield, Illinois. This definitely identifies Robinson as one of Lisa's original men, and his presence indicates that his boon companions, John Hoback and Jacob Reznor, were also along.

them the knowledge necessary to keep alive in the wilderness, to catch a beaver or lift a scalp.

While struggling through the vicious eddies and many sand bars that marked the mouth of the river Platte, thereafter considered the far boundary of civilization and the gateway to the prairies, the company received a stroke of good fortune in the person of John Colter,[21] canoeing his solitary way down-river toward civilization. This intrepid Virginian had already traversed the continent with Lewis and Clark, and was no doubt delighted to see some of his old comrades among the men of the Lisa expedition. Colter had received an early discharge from the government group at Fort Mandan[22] to join Forrest Handcock and Joseph Dixon, two independent trappers, in a partnership to hunt and trap in the vicinity of the Rocky Mountains through which he had so recently come. There he had trapped out the winter in company with Handcock and Dixon, but in the spring of 1807 the association was dissolved, and Colter headed for the settlements from which he had so long been absent. So valuable an asset was not allowed to slip through Lisa's fingers, and his entreaties, the presence of Colter's friends, and a good offer, probably including the status of free trapper,[23] served to turn the wanderer's eyes once more toward the mountains.

It is not difficult to understand John Colter's choice. He had already become familiar with nights on the prairie, with the only sound the whisper of the river gliding eternally seaward, and with the bright and mysterious stars, set in a blanket of blackest blue, pressing so close that they seemed within reach. He knew

[21] Brackenridge, *Views of Louisiana*, 89.

[22] Meriwether Lewis, *Original Journals of the Lewis and Clark Expedition, 1804–1806*, ed. by R. G. Thwaites, VII, 360.

[23] The "free trapper" was that individual who had not bound himself to serve any man or company while in the mountains. He usually worked for his passage upstream by hunting and taking an occasional turn at helping the boatmen over rough spots, but once in trapping country was free to trap wherever and trade with whomever he chose. Often these individuals had *engagés* bound to them.

the exhilaration of standing on a lofty eminence and gazing out upon a panorama of untrammeled nature, drinking in the beauty of her infinite variety: the crystal blue of a high mountain lake, the diamond sparkle of a tiny streamlet splashing over stone into a deep and quiet pool, the somber green of the stately pines all cast against the azure profundity of a cloudless sky. He had heard her sounds, from the tinkling music of a mountain rill to the deep-throated growl of a grizzly bear; from the roar of her thunder to the hushed silence attending the coming of a summer shower. John Colter had walked in the cathedral quiet of a virgin forest and understood that he was one with nature. Here all a man needed was a sack of "possibles,"[24] a little skill, and nature would provide. Mountain life was immensely preferable to the rush and crush of civilization, even civilization as represented by the St. Louis of 1807.

Difficulties began to mount shortly after Colter joined the party. The company apparently carried only enough food to reach the vicinity of the Platte, that being the practice of later expeditions, and had the misfortune to find a scarcity of game. The land of the Sioux, where they were after passing the Platte, was poor country for hunting, though not usually because of any lack of wildlife. Those wandering bands of Indians liked nothing better than to fall upon a lone forager and take home his scalp as a trophy. But even with such expert hunters as Drouillard and Colter scouring the countryside, the party, by July 12, was reduced to one quarter pound of meat per day per man.[25] Here it was that Bouché, having already caused the delay in

[24] "Possibles" were a collection of the many things an individual needed in the wilderness. The "possible sack," hung by a thong around the neck, usually contained a few tools for the repair of a rifle, bullet mold, awl, flint and steel, perhaps a needle and thread, and similar articles.

[25] Deposition of Manuel Lisa, Mar. 18, 1811, Lisa Papers, MHS. This remarkable document was first brought to light by Burton Harris, *John Colter: His Years in the Rockies.*

embarkation, and more trouble by refusing to obey orders after the crew got under way, was accused of stealing meat from the larder with the intention of causing the expedition to fail.[26] The charge may well have been true judging from that *engagé*'s later activities, for he continued to be a troublemaker during the rest of his stay in the mountains. There was little that could be done with the man, short of shooting him, and no one wanted that responsibility.

Sioux country was traversed without meeting any of that tribe, although Bouché did his best to make the encounter possible by absenting himself on an unauthorized hunting trip. Lisa held up the voyage for four days waiting for him, preferring to keep trouble under surveillance and in camp rather than worrying about what real mischief Bouché might do wandering alone in the wilderness.[27] This peaceful passage was another bit of luck that few later expeditions would share. However, by the time real trouble occurred, what in April had been a green and unseasoned group of men had become a hardened and veteran crew of boatmen and hunters, capable of meeting any eventuality.

Their first encounter with hostile Indians came at the Arikara village. This tribe, an offshoot of Caddoan stock, had originally migrated northward with the Pawnees from the Red River of the South. They had split from their companions and settled in villages, living a semisedentary life, being visited by, and trading with, a number of the tribes of the West. Of volatile and unpredictable temper, the Rees, as they were known to the traders, became the most dangerous and treacherous Indians on the Missouri. The Lisa party, on its arrival, found two to three hundred warriors drawn up along the bank. The Indians fired upon the boats when they came into range, and ordered them to land. Lisa complied with the demand, but, upon touching shore, summarily commanded the natives not to set foot on his boats, which order

26 *Ibid.*
27 *Ibid.*

the Indians respected. As the Indian women began to appear carrying sacks of grain with which to trade, a brave dashed among them, slashing the bags with his knife, and spilling the contents on the ground. Taking this as a hostile sign, Lisa ordered the men to arms and had the boat-mounted swivels leveled at the crowd. The Rees, startled by the sudden action, fell back in confusion, but soon came forward with pipes of peace and bade Lisa council with them. He agreed to meet the chiefs, smoked and talked with them, and distributed the usual presents before the party left the village.[28] He was then, and continued to be, a believer in giving substantial gifts to the many tribes with which he came in contact. This was part of the great success he enjoyed as a trader, and helped give him considerable influence over those tribes. The Arikaras seemingly were undecided themselves about what their course of action would be against the white men, and Lisa's quick action convinced them that a battle was not in their best interest. Lisa always seemed to know when a show of force would be most effective.

The Mandans, next tribe encountered, and thereafter, in contrast to their neighbors to the south, the most consistently friendly of the Missouri tribes, provided the company with several anxious moments before being safely passed. After the experience with the Rees, Manuel wisely decided to proceed alone and on foot through the three villages while the boats remained offshore, ready either to fight or to run on a moment's notice. All went well until Manuel arrived at the uppermost of the villages. There the chief refused the presents Lisa brought to council, and demanded a quantity of powder. The situation was tense, but Lisa was its equal. He "knew that his life was in no danger while his death could not procure them his goods, and resisted their repeated solicitations in a bold and firm manner."[29] Again resolution accomplished his purpose as the chief capitulated, accepted

---

[28] Brackenridge, *Views of Louisiana*, 90.
[29] *Ibid.*, 91.

the presents as offered, and allowed the party to pass in peace. The men were gaining an invaluable lesson in Indian diplomacy, and the wiser saw that the Indian always respected the strong and the brave, and the man who kept his word. Possibly Lisa left a small outfit with this sedentary branch of the Sioux, but if he did his limited resources were taxed to the utmost.[30]

A few days later the expedition was confronted by a huge war party of Assiniboines massed on the bank of the river. There were so many Indians that, as Lisa himself put it, "the whole prairie was red with them."[31] Manuel, again following the policy of taking the initiative, directed the boats straight toward the waiting horde. He then ordered all the small arms and swivels discharged into the air. "This was intended to strike them with terror; the effect was ludicrous, they fell back, tumbled over each other, and fled to the hills with precipitation."[32] Only a few chiefs approached to smoke the pipes and to receive the presents which Lisa offered them. By a thorough knowledge of the Indian character, and the ability to play a bold hand in the face of great odds, Manuel Lisa had carried his men unharmed through three potentially dangerous situations. Down-river another group, struggling against the same sort of difficulties, did not fare as well, and the repercussions of that failure were to touch Lisa upon his return.

On May 18, 1807, the official party for the return of the Mandan chief, Shahaka, and his entourage, to his village departed from St. Louis."[33] Shahaka and his followers had come down to visit the United States with the returning Lewis and Clark contingent in 1806, with a view to meeting President Jefferson. One

[30] Chittenden, *American Fur Trade*, I, 118, suggests that "He probably left a small outfit of goods at this point."

[31] Brackenridge, *Views of Louisiana*, 91.

[32] *Ibid.*, 91.

[33] Letter, William Clark to Secretary of War Henry Dearborn, May 18, 1807, William Clark Collection, MHS, photostat of original in National Archives.

of the conditions of his journey was that the government give him safe conduct home. Unable to spare more men, or completely oblivious to the danger facing a small party traveling up the Missouri, the government trusted more to good luck than common sense to get Shahaka home safely. In command of the organization was Ensign Nathaniel Pryor, who had been a sergeant under Lewis and Clark, and had been promoted to take charge of this detail. He had under his command fourteen soldiers.[34] With the military was a trading party of twenty-three men directed by Pierre Chouteau, Jr., going upriver to establish a post at the Mandan villages.[35]

The joint expedition moved slowly upriver but found no difficulty until its arrival at the Arikara village, where the same reception Lisa's party had faced was waiting.[36] On this occasion the Rees, after some preliminary sparring, attacked and defeated the water-borne group, killing three outright, and seriously wounding several others, one of whom later died. The expedition returned to St. Louis without having accomplished its mission, indeed barely managing to get the chief back unharmed. The reasons for the attack were not clear. Perhaps it came out of spite for having been cowed by Lisa's show of force; perhaps the Indians were encouraged by the conciliatory approach used by Pryor, which made it seem that they would meet little resistance; or perhaps it happened because, as René Jessaume, Shahaka's interpreter, later wrote to the President, the Arikaras were jealous of the attention shown the Mandan chief.[37]

Whatever the cause, Pryor, on his return to St. Louis, wrote a letter to William Clark giving his report of the incident and

[34] *Ibid.*

[35] *Ibid.*

[36] Elliott Coues, "Letters of William Clark and Nathaniel Pryor," *Annals of Iowa*, Vol. I (April, 1893), 616.

[37] Letter, René Jusseaume to President Jefferson, December 3, 1807, Jefferson Collection, MHS.

seriously implicating Manuel Lisa. As he described it, shortly
after the arrival of the expedition at the Arikara village:

> A Mandan woman who had been a captive for several years,
> came on board, from whom I obtained information which could
> probably have been derived from no other quarter.
>
> She informed me that Manuel Lisa, a St. Louis trader had
> passed up some time before: that he had given the Ricaras, through
> *compulsion* I conjecture, a number of guns and a considerable
> quantity of powder and ball. This man you recollect obtained a
> license from Mr. Bates before your arrival and before the plan
> which the government had adopted with respect to the Mandane
> was known at St. Louis. He was however, still at St. Charles and
> it is not forgotten that Mr. Bates having occasion to visit that vil-
> lage informed him of the change of arrangement in the upper
> country, and desire him to remain until my Boats should be
> equipped that he might accompany the expedition.
>
> *This*, we understand he consented to do—and his failure in
> those engagements, has probably obliged him to divert the storm
> which threatened *his own boat*, by diverting the attention of the
> Ricaras to *ours*.
>
> He told them; as we learn from this woman, that two boats
> might very soon be expected; that we had the Mandane Chief on
> board; and that we were to remain, for the purpose of trade at
> their villages.—On this, they pillaged him of about half his
> goods, and suffered him to pass on determining in their councils
> at the same time to kill him on his return, and to lose no time in
> preparing to murder the Mandane and his escort as soon as we
> should arrive.[38]

Pryor went on to say that, in his opinion, a force of at least four
hundred men would be necessary to surmount the Arikaras and
return the Mandan chief unscathed.

The letter caught up with Clark in Louisville on October 24,
from where he sent on a brief report of the incident to Washing-

---

[38] Coues, "Letters," *loc. cit.*, 616–17.

ton,[39] holding Pryor's letter for further study and later transmission. In his report Clark remarked to the Secretary of War that "Young Mr. Chouteau behaved verry well," and went on to deplore the activities of the British traders in the Northwest, seemingly implying that the British were behind the hostilities of the Arikaras. If they were, the British could have selected no better time to demonstrate to the natives the inadequacy of the power of the Great White Father in Washington.

The charge which Pryor had made against Lisa was a grave one, but apparently Clark did not take it seriously for he made no comment about it in his report, nor did he in a later covering letter under which he sent Pryor's report. There was no investigation; in fact, the matter was never again brought up. Had Lisa arranged the destruction of the government expedition, the facts would have certainly come to light. There were too many people who would have liked to see Lisa stopped to have let the matter drop so easily. News of the defeat spread quickly. Frederick Bates, writing to a friend in Michigan, mentioned Pryor's misfortune, but adduced no cause save the temperament of the Indians.[40] Thus Bates, whom Pryor claimed as a witness, had nothing to say about the charge.

Among the other groups on the river that year, hurrying to take advantage of the information brought back by Lewis and Clark, was one headed by Lisa's old antagonist Robert McClellan, now in partnership with Ramsay Crooks. Crooks had recently come to St. Louis from the Michilimackinac country, and undoubtedly was the financial half of the partnership, for McClellan could not have had much left after the court had finished with him. They got a late start, met Pryor returning with his wounded,

---

[39] Letter, William Clark to Secretary of War Henry Dearborn, Oct. 24, 1807, William Clark Collection, MHS, photostat of original in National Archives.

[40] Letter, Frederick Bates to the Honorable August B. Woodward, Oct. 20, 1807, printed in *Michigan Pioneer and Historical Society Collections*, Vol. VIII (1886), 559–60.

and, not wishing to share the same fate, turned back to the vicinity of Council Bluffs, where they wintered.[41] William Clark mentioned other groups of traders on the river that summer,[42] but their activities, successes, or failures have yet to come to light. Even so, the merchants of St. Louis could not have been encouraged by the prospects offered by the Missouri region, at least from the record of those who had returned by the winter of 1807–1808.

The Lisa party, unaware of the activity below them, continued on toward the mountains. They left the Missouri at the mouth of the Yellowstone, turning up the latter stream to its confluence with the Bighorn, where, on the wooded point between the two rivers just above their conjunction,[43] temporary shelters were erected, and the construction of Fort Raymond begun. It was an excellent spot for a post, being in the favorite wintering ground not only of the Crow nation but of game from the surrounding Big Horn and Wind River Mountains. Timber was readily available, as was water, and there was even a small surface deposit of coal in the vicinity for use in winter heating.[44]

It was very late in the season, sometime in early November, 1807, and the men, with the exception of the slacker Bouché, who refused to make wooden pins to help fasten a roof,[45] worked quickly to complete a shelter before the snows moved in. The hunters lost no time in scouting out the near-by country, both for buffalo and other game animals and for likely beaver waters. They found the Yellowstone and the Bighorn, with their many tributaries, teeming with the flat-tailed, furry creatures whose

[41] Chittenden, *American Fur Trade*, I, 160.

[42] Letter, Clark to Dearborn, May 18, 1807, William Clark Collection, MHS.

[43] Drouillard's sketch of the country of the Bighorn and Yellowstone, Aug. 5, 1808, in *ibid.*, photostat of original in National Archives.

[44] Deposition of Manuel Lisa, Mar. 18, 1811, Lisa Papers, MHS. This may have been an apparatus for the manufacture of charcoal as well as a surface deposit of coal.

[45] *Ibid.*

skins satisfied the demands of London society by furnishing the raw material for their tall felt hats. The prospects were such to justify a good deal of optimism on the part of all hands.

The delays in transit which had caused the company to arrive so late in the year Lisa attributed to Bouché, blaming him for the loss of the valuable fall hunt.[46] In order to mitigate this loss, Manuel determined to notify the Indians of his arrival in the area, and to ask them to come to his post to trade.

To accomplish this mission, he dispatched John Colter on one of the most grueling winter odysseys ever accomplished by man. Carrying a pack weighing thirty pounds,[47] containing a few supplies and presents for the Indians, his rifle and ammunition, Colter set out to find as many tribes as he could and send them to Fort Raymond to trade. He found the Crows at the upper end of the valley, and then struck west, crossing the massive Wind River range of mountains, a difficult climb in the best of weather but almost impossible at that time of year. Continuing into Jackson's Hole, a lovely valley entirely surrounded by tall mountains, the lone messenger noted the sublime points of *Les Trois Tetons*, the peaks which became the most important landmark for trappers in the area. Crossing the Tetons into Pierre's Hole, Colter began a large circle back to the fort. Skirting the present Yellowstone Park area, he ran into some thermal activity on the upper Shoshone, his description of which the skeptical trappers derisively dubbed "Colter's Hell."[48] Returning to the post, Colter joined the rest of the hunters, making short forays for food, and trapping a few beaver close to the fort.

In the spring of 1808 this experienced mountaineer was again

[46] *Ibid.*

[47] Brackenridge, *Views of Louisiana*, 92.

[48] A detailed description of Colter's route is given in Harris, *Colter*, 73ff. Merrill J. Mattes, "Behind the Legend of Colter's Hell: The Early Exploration of Yellowstone Park," *Mississippi Valley Historical Review*, Vol. XXXVI (Sept., 1949), 251–82, clearly demonstrates that Colter did not view the geysers of present-day Yellowstone Park.

sent to call in the Indians.[49] While in company with a party of Crows, Colter was forced, in order to keep his "hair," to join his hosts in resisting a Blackfoot attack. He so distinguished himself in action that many attributed the subsequent hostility of the Blackfeet toward the whites as stemming from that incident.[50] The event certainly did not help relations, but the Blackfeet had other, deeper causes for their implacable hatred.

Historians have always assumed that the Lisa expedition had for its original destination the Three Forks vicinity,[51] and had for its purpose the opening of intercourse with the Blackfeet, nominal possessors of that territory. This is a logical assumption in view of the fact that the boats were pointed for the "headwaters of the Missouri," and because, in the opinion of the former members of the Lewis and Clark group, the Three Forks country was the richest in furs of any section of the Northwest. They have also assumed, no doubt correctly, that Drouillard and the others advised against going into Blackfoot lands for fear of reprisals by that tribe for the incident in which Meriwether Lewis had killed two members of their confederation. To this, John Colter may have added an even stronger argument. He had probably discovered the winter previous that the Crow nation, into whose territory they would penetrate if they went up the Yellowstone, were a trading people, already apprised of the white man's predilection for the skin of the beaver. Moreover, they were already adept in the trapping and preserving of skins in the

---

[49] Harris, *Colter*, 121.

[50] The Blackfeet had come to that country to gain revenge for the deaths of the two Piegans killed by Meriwether Lewis. David Thompson, *David Thompson's Narrative of His Explorations in Western America, 1784–1812*, ed. by J. B. Tyrrell, 375.

[51] Captain Reuben Holmes, "The Five Scalps," St. Louis *Reville* (July 17 and 24, 1848). In this biography of Edward Rose, Holmes says that Rose "bargained with Manuel Lisa, in the spring of 1807, to ascend the Missouri to the mouth of the Yellow Stone river," indicating that the party may have had this destination from the beginning.

white man's way, having been instructed in the art by Antoine Larocque,[52] a French member of the British North West Company who had appeared among them several years before on a trading and exploring mission. In addition, the lateness of the season may have made it impossible to reach the Three Forks before meeting the full force of winter.

It is a tribute to Lisa's sagacity that he took the advice of his subordinates, read well the signs of approaching winter, and decided to build his post in Crow country. This alone made possible the success of that first commercial venture. The Blackfeet were not then, nor did they ever become, trappers of beaver and traders of skins to the white man, either British or American.[53] The Blackfeet were true Plains Indians, strong, warlike, and self-sufficient. They roamed a vast hunting ground stretching northward from the Three Forks of the Missouri to beyond the Saskatchewan River, following the migrations of the buffalo, and being supplied with all the necessities of life by that animal. So while their neighbors took to trapping and trading skins with the British for blankets, guns, and beads, as well as the other accompaniments of trade, the Blackfeet remained disdainfully aloof. What need had a Blackfoot, wrapped in a buffalo robe, for a Hudson's Bay blanket; what need had he for guns when the Blackfeet could easily defeat any of their neighbors without them?

Relations were friendly, if not profitable for the British, and remained so until about 1806–1807. By that time trade with the tribal foes of the Blackfeet had increased to the point where those tribes were well enough supplied with British weapons to stand

[52] Antoine Larocque, "Journal of Larocque: From the Assiniboine to the Yellowstone, 1805," ed. by Lawrence J. Burpee, *Publications of Canadian Archives*, No. 3 (1910), 28.

[53] Oscar Lewis, *The Effects of White Contact upon Blackfoot Culture with Special Reference to the Rôle of the Fur Trade*, 28. Only one small band of Piegans ever did any trapping.

up to their haughty antagonists and defeat them in battle. Then the Blackfeet became hostile to all whites, British and Americans alike, and jealously guarded their frontiers against any intrusion.[54] When they learned of American trappers in their lands to the south, they came down on the warpath to drive the hated whites out, and to gather the rich booty of furs and equipment which they could trade with the British for the now desirable guns and ammunition. It is entirely possible that had Lisa's party moved on to the Three Forks in 1807, they would have met the same fate which befell the expedition of the Missouri Fur Company two years later. Thus Colter's aid to the Crows only added fuel to an already burning fire, the flames of which would scorch the next party in the area.[55]

Life went on in a normal manner during the cold winter months at Fort Raymond. The hunters roamed the countryside, bringing their kill to a scaffold which had been erected about a mile distant from the post. From there it would be brought to camp by some of the *engagés*. The irrepressible Bouché refused to bring in the meat on November 29,[56] and a great feast was held at the scaffold by grizzly bears and, after they had eaten their fill, wolves. This could have been a serious loss to the company had game become scarce, and Lisa later placed an excessive valuation of one thousand dollars on the destroyed meat.[57] Étienne Brandt, one of the more trusted *engagés*, being privileged to distribute goods to the men along with Lisa, Drouillard,

[54] *Ibid.*, 23; Thompson, *Narrative*, 375.

[55] Letter, Thomas Biddle to Secretary of War Atkinson, Oct. 29, 1819, *American State Papers*, 6, Indian Affairs, II, 201, indicates that Lisa had a meeting with the Blackfeet before building Fort Raymond, and that the meeting was peaceful. He discounts the idea that Lewis had anything to do with their later hostility. As Chittenden, in his *American Fur Trade*, points out, however, the early trappers confused the Blackfeet with the Gros Ventres, as does Chittenden himself, and it is entirely possible that Lisa had a meeting with the latter tribe rather than one with any member of the Blackfoot confederation.

[56] Deposition of Manuel Lisa, Mar. 18, 1811, Lisa Papers, MHS.

[57] *Ibid.*

and Benito Vasquez, Lisa's second in command, took his cue from Bouché and began to steal from the storeroom. He was caught, and Lisa called him a scoundrel and a thief, among other things, and threatened him with a knife.[58] Brandt deserted shortly thereafter and went to live with the Indians. He turned up in St. Louis in 1809 and attempted to sue Lisa for what amounted to defamation of character. Lisa and Drouillard countersued to collect damages and won, although Brandt took refuge in the Law for the Benefit of Insolvent Debtors.[59]

By the time spring came the trappers had their guns and traps well oiled and were anxious to break the confines of the garrison to get to the business at hand. Trappers were not gregarious by nature, and a long confinement with a large number of people always made them restless for the open spaces. All, that is, except Bouché. On May 1, Benito Vasquez finally had to order him to lay his traps.[60] The others had long been out, and the returns of those close to the post were beginning to come in. Predictably, Bouché refused, and made himself a total loss to the company by never catching a beaver while he was in the mountains. He then tried to foment a mutiny by spreading the rumor that Lisa had given his men poor powder,[61] but the cooler heads knew that that would be the last place any bourgeois would cheat them. If it had been Bouché's object to wreck the expedition, the fact that he did not was caused by no lack of effort on his part.

For the rest, they seemed well satisfied with their lot. Beaver were plentiful and there was a good chance of making a profit. Colter still wandered in the mountains searching out Indian tribes

[58] Depositions of Jean Baptiste Mayette and George Drouillard, Apr. 5, 1809, Lisa Papers, MHS.

[59] This statute, passed mainly to relieve the pressure on the local jail, served well many of Lisa's men, and even his former antagonist, Robert McClellan. As was the case in most frontier communities, bankruptcy was a common thing.

[60] Deposition of Manuel Lisa, Mar. 18, 1811, Lisa Papers, MHS.

[61] *Ibid.*

for trade. George Drouillard also pursued a solitary course in the wilderness, in part retracing the steps made by Colter the previous winter but keeping more to the south, always on the lookout for any contact with the Spaniards, who were reputed to have a mine in the area.[62] Intercourse with the Spanish was never far from Lisa's thoughts, and he would make efforts in the future to open a trade with Santa Fe from the upper Missouri. The Crows probably told him of the Snake Indians, from across the continental divide, who traded directly with the Spanish, and may even have had Spanish articles to show him, further stimulating his already active imagination. The information brought back to St. Louis by Drouillard and Colter was incorporated into the maps which William Clark was preparing for the government, and became the basis for much of the geographical knowledge of the area for many years.[63]

On June 4, 1808, Baptiste Tibeau took an outfit[64] amounting to $1,922.05,[65] probably destined for trade with the Crows in order to acquire the pelts of their spring hunt. Tibeau, with Baptiste Marie, also incurred a debt of $51.00 on that date, indicating that Marie was going with him, and the two would do a little trading for themselves. So sanguine of success was Lisa that the debt of $51.00 was payable by seventeen beaver skins, or $3.00 per skin.[66] This was a fantastic price for skins in the mountains, for there were many times when beaverpelts did not bring that much in the markets of Montreal, New Orleans, or New York, let alone St. Louis. Thus it is not strange that the majority of the men stayed in the mountains after Lisa left for St. Louis, for it was entirely possible that each one of them would

[62] For a description of Drouillard's wanderings, see Harris, *Colter*, 85ff.

[63] *Ibid.*, 97.

[64] An "outfit," at least as I use the term, means the sum of trade goods, guns, powder, lead, tobacco, alcohol, etc., to be used in trading with the Indians.

[65] Pierre Menard "Notes," Menard Family Papers, Illinois State Historical Society, Springfield, Illinois.

[66] *Ibid.*

make his fortune. A talented trapper could handle a string of ten or more traps, and could, with any sort of luck, pay for his stake in the course of a single hunt. This fair treatment also accounts for the recurrence of many names on Lisa's list of *engagés* from year to year.

Only one incident marred the accomplishments of the spring. Edward Rose, a part-Negro trapper-interpreter who had lived for years with the Osages, and had probably become known to Lisa while there, had been sent to the Crows shortly after the arrival of the party at the site of their winter encampment. He was given an outfit with which to trade for beaver and horses, and he spent the winter with the Indians. Rose, who later became one of the most notorious of the mountain men, fancied himself an Indian and dedicated his life to proving it to Indian and white alike. Perceiving that the native custom was to respect that man most who unselfishly gave away all of his possessions, Rose, by spring, became the best-loved man in the Crow camp by giving away all of his trade goods. Returning to the post sometime after the weather broke, and unable to account for the loss of the goods, Rose got into a bitter argument with his employer. Words ceased abruptly as Rose leaped upon Lisa, starting a fight. Manuel probably would have been killed by the muscular mulatto had not John Potts happened on the scene. As Potts pulled off the struggling Rose, Lisa, whose boat was waiting to take him to St. Louis, left the two men grappling, climbed aboard the boat, and headed out into the current.

Rose freed himself from Potts, dashed outside, and saw the boat swinging slowly into the stream.

Infuriated with passion, and almost blind with rage, he ran to a swivel pointed towards the river, and quickly directing its line of fire, "touched it off" with his pipe, just as a man was passing in front of its muzzle. He happened to be a long-legged man, and in the act of stepping, so that a canister of bullets passed harmlessly between his legs, and only caused him to jump a few feet

61

in the air and fall directly in front of the piece, from which place he roared out that he was dead. The Boat's crew was . . . on their benches, and it was well they were, for every ball went through the cargo box of the boat, and almost in a raking line; they could have been safe in no other position; as it was they all escaped unhurt.

Rose was then restrained from reloading and getting off another shot at the fast disappearing boat. A few days later Rose left the fort with all the goods he could beg, borrow, or frighten away from the men, and headed back to the Crows.[67] Bad as this incident was, Rose was destined to turn up again and again in Lisa's employ, for the trader forgave him and used his services on several occasions as a trader and interpreter. Evidently his worth was such that Lisa could afford to overlook the loss of goods which his employment inevitably entailed. This is quite a tribute to Rose, for Lisa was not a man to give up a penny if there was any way to avoid it. The name of Edward Rose is conspicuously missing from the long list of accounts due Lisa at the latter's death, so Rose either made up the losses or Manuel wrote them off as business expense.[68]

Had it not been for the murder trial that Lisa and Drouillard had to face in St. Louis, their return would have been a triumph. Carrying the proceeds of the winter and spring hunts at Fort Raymond, and whatever they had been able to obtain by trade along the river, Lisa could well have been proud of the results of that first voyage. Not only did he bring in a handsome profit, but it was done in only two-thirds of a hunting season. Even as he re-

[67] The description of this incident, including the quotation, is taken from Holmes, "Five Scalps," loc. cit.

[68] This list of accounts formed part of Lisa's estate at the time of his death, and seems to be a compilation of all the debts owed him at that time. It covers the entire period of his residence in St. Louis, and includes such names as Benito Vasquez, George Drouillard, Pierre Menard, and numerous engagés, most of whom, in 1820, were either dead or insolvent. Very little of this money was ever collected.

turned, the major portion of his men, who had remained upriver, were preparing for the fall hunt of 1808, operating in excellent beaver country from a substantial post. They were about to spread out into all of the good beaver waters of the northern Rockies. Contact had been established with the Crows, and could be expected with the other tribes of the area. Certainly the future of the association of Lisa, Morrison, and Menard looked bright.

Manuel's successful return cast the gauntlet to the St. Louis merchants. The choice would be theirs to make: to enter into competition for the riches of the upper Missouri, with the distinct possibility of great loss; or continue present practices and be satisfied with second rank behind the brash Spaniard and the Americans who surely would be attracted to St. Louis by the promise of great wealth. The threat of American rivals was not an idle one. Already John Jacob Astor's American Fur Company was moving into the Great Lakes region, and could easily push across the Mississippi into the West. Charles Gratiot, Chouteau's son-in-law, and a man with great business acumen, was always counseling merger with Astor, and the latter had made overtures in that direction as early as 1800.[69] This was an extremely difficult decision to make, although with excellent hindsight the choice seems an obvious one. The Lisa voyage demonstrated the great risks involved in such an undertaking, emphasized the role of chance in making an expedition such as that a success or a failure, and also proved that great profits were available to the fortunate and daring.

It was well for these merchants that Lisa had a greater vision than the continuation of his small association. He had seen for himself the vast fortune to be gained from the fur trade of the Northwest, and knew that a handful of men and a sixteen-thousand-dollar outfit could never harvest that wealth. Lisa envisioned an expedition of hundreds of men ascending the Missouri,

[69] Letter, John Jacob Astor to Auguste Chouteau, 1800, Chouteau Collection, MHS.

breaking into groups large enough for self-protection against the Indians in case of attack, and able to trap with impunity the country they chose. They would move into Blackfoot country, head southward to make contact with the Spaniards and the Indian tribes between, even cross the mountains into the Columbia drainage basin, theretofore the exclusive prerogative of the British. This vision haunted Lisa for the rest of his life. Unfortunately, he was able to show it to very few.

III

The Missouri Fur Company
Great Expectations

THE St. Louis to which Manuel Lisa returned had scarcely changed during his absence. A petition for incorporation into a city had been circulated on July 5, 1808, and among the signatories was *"Madam Manuel De Lisa por su Mari,"*[1] but more than a change in nomenclature was necessary to effect any great difference in the place. The influx of a few Americans had not altered either the structure or the character of the town. There was a new air of expectancy about it now, though, with the dynamic Meriwether Lewis as governor, and Lisa's return seemed to usher in an era which promised to turn St. Louis into the metropolis of the West, the fur capital of the world.

After the completion of the trial, the partners wasted little time settling accounts and preparing for the coming year. Each of the three claimed furs worth $2,667.50, with Lisa taking an extra $985.00 for leading the expedition.[2] It is not clear from the rec-

---

[1] Petition, July 5, 1808, St. Louis History Envelope, MHS.

[2] Bryan and Morrison Store, Kaskaskia Ledger D, 267, 438, William Morrison Records, Reel One, Microfilm in Illinois Historical Survey, Lincoln Hall, University of Illinois, Urbana, Illinois; Pierre Menard Journal, No. 5, 90, Illinois State Historical Society, Springfield, Illinois; and the complete summary of Morrison's connection with the fur trade in John L. Tevebaugh, "Merchant on the Western Frontier," *loc. cit.*, 131.

ords whether these sums are the total receipts of the voyage or profits after costs were deducted, but the company was reorganized to allow Drouillard equal status as partner, and plans were formulated for another trip in the coming spring.[3] Lisa then made a hurried trip to Louisville, perhaps to arrange for the disposition of his furs with his friend, and one of the leading merchants of that city, Dennis Fitzhugh. He returned to St. Louis about the middle of November, 1808,[4] and bent to the task of arranging for an outfit for the men at work high above. In addition, the canny trader, hoping to implement the extensive plans he envisioned for the upper country, began to cast about for more financing.

For possible investors, Manuel was able to provide truly promising prospects, the same outlook which was motivating Lisa, Morrison, Menard, and Drouillard to continue their association. In addition to the profits already achieved, the group had a strong trading post at the base of the mountains and had opened a profitable trade with the Crows. But further than that, and due primarily to Lisa's enterprise, daring, and breadth of vision, the skeleton crew at work above, numbering about forty men under the leadership of Benito Vasquez, was engaged in traversing and trapping virtually all the rich beaver areas in American territory, and perhaps beyond. Divided into small parties, the majority of the men, in the summer and early autumn of 1808, had gone to the Three Forks of the Missouri, reputed to be abounding in beaver, and were trapping the Madison, Jefferson, and Gallatin rivers and their many tributaries in addition to all of the surrounding country. If they had no trouble with the Blackfeet, Manuel could count on having upward of one hundred packs of beaver waiting for him in the spring. In addi-

[3] Kaskaskia Ledger D, 438, Illinois Historical Survey.

[4] "Your letter from Louisville of the 2nd of Nov by Mr Manuel I received a few days ago." Letter, William Clark to Benjamin O'Fallon, Nov. 22, 1808, O'Fallon Papers, MHS.

Missouri Historical Society

MANUEL LISA

AUGUSTE CHOUTEAU

tion, a small party of three had headed southward to trap "the River of the Spaniards," and perhaps meet representatives of that nation to begin negotiations for opening a trade to Santa Fe.[5] The time to invest in the operation was immediately, before the returns of the hunt then in progress arrived in St. Louis and enabled Lisa, Morrison, Menard, and Drouillard to continue their progress without the need of assistance.

Investment capital in St. Louis meant, primarily, the Chouteaus, and no one more fully understood the urgency of the situation than they. Well aware of the riches of the upper Missouri, and desirous of acquiring a share of it, the Chouteaus exhaustively explored the possibilities of the situation before acting. To enter into competition with Lisa at that time was dangerous at best. That knowing entrepreneur had treated both his men and the Indians fairly, and, being the initial trader into the area, would command the first allegiance, and the pick of the pelts of the various tribes. Considerable expenditure of cash would be necessary over a long period of time to break his hold on the territory. Some sort of working agreement seemed to be called for, particularly if Lisa had opened contact with Santa Fe. With trade open in that direction, it was conceivable that Lisa could circumvent entirely the St. Louis merchants, and not even so much as purchase supplies from them.

The possibilities of agreement seemed to resolve themselves into two: a corporation, the leadership of which would naturally fall to Lisa because of his experience and prior investment; or a partnership, in which the individuals involved would share equally the burdens of work, the risks inherent, and the profits earned. The first offered the virtues of efficiency, directness of purpose, and quick action, but these were not necessarily beneficial to cautious men bent on controlling as much as possible their investment in a risky business. Too much might depend upon

[5] These operations are noted in Letter, Pierre Menard to Adrien Langlois, Oct. 7, 1809, Kaskaskia Papers, MHS.

the judgment of one man, and, if he made a mistake, the whole corporation might be wiped out. The partnership, while not possessing the advantage of single direction, seemed, at least to the Chouteaus, much better suited to a venture of this nature. With several partners the risk would be spread out, with less likelihood that an error on the part of one could ruin all. There would be more opportunity for joint control of policy, with each man to have a vote on matters of importance. This would tend to slow down operations, to allow full discussion of the various questions which inevitably would arise and the possible avenues of trade to be pursued. Lisa, after all, was a headstrong individual, prone to taking the bit in his teeth and forging ahead regardless of obstacles. Such a man could dash the hopes of a company in one ill-timed adventure. All of this speculation depended, of course, upon the willingness of the partners to expand their operation to include others.

Lisa and company were quite willing. Although they had done very well, and were prepared to continue on their own, all the risks still remained. Dame Fortune continued to control their destiny. Not only would they like to spread the risk, but with new capital the trading monopoly of the upper Missouri held all sorts of possibilities.

Out of the many meetings and discussions over the winter of 1808–1809 came the Articles of Association and Co-partnership of the group of merchants known as the St. Louis Missouri Fur Company,[6] which name was soon popularly shortened to simply

[6] I have seen three copies of the Articles of Agreement, no two of which are alike in naming the members, although they do not differ in the body of the agreement. One is in the St. Louis Missouri Fur Company Ledger Book, 1809–12, MHS, apparently kept in St. Louis by Clark, and into which he had copied the communications received from the partners upstream. The second is in the Missouri Fur Company Ledger Book, 1812–14, Vol. XXX, William Clark MSS, Kansas State Historical Society, Topeka, Kansas. The third copy is in French: Articles of Agreement, Mar. 3, 1809, Chouteau Collection, MHS. The second contains the inter-

the Missouri Fur Company. The members, aside from Lisa, Menard, and Morrison, all of whom remained in the new company—Drouillard did not become a partner—comprised most of the important merchants of St. Louis. There was Benjamin Wilkinson, brother of the former Governor, but apparently not possessed of his more famous kinsman's talent for intrigue. An active trader and excellent businessman, his untimely death cut short what could have been a profitable career. Pierre Chouteau, an old rival of Lisa, brought to the company not only the most individual wealth of any member but a thorough knowledge of Indian trading based on longer experience than any of his partners. Sylvestre Labbadie, well-educated member of an old St. Louis family who had dabbled in trade before, joined more out of a spirit of adventure than anything else, although he was not the less concerned with making a profit.

The brother of the then Governor, Reuben Lewis brought his youthful vigor and considerable competence to the company, in addition to his function of keeping Governor Meriwether Lewis apprised of its activities and sympathetic to its objects. Both Lewis and Labbadie had served their wilderness apprenticeships under another of the partners, William Clark, when he had built Fort Osage for the government in 1808. Clark, former companion of Meriwether Lewis on their voyage of discovery to the Pacific Ocean, and now Indian agent for the territory, was included as much for his unquestioned honesty and unbiased judgment as for his investment and the possible benefits he might be able to bestow in his official capacity. Auguste Chouteau, Jr., was involved for himself, although probably financed by his father,

lineation of the name Dennis Fitzhugh, but has no signature for him. The first nowhere contains the name of Andrew Henry, but has the interlineation of Dennis Fitzhugh, and his copied signature as well. The French copy is unsigned, and contains neither the name of Dennis Fitzhugh nor that of Andrew Henry. This indicates that Henry was a late-comer to the deliberations, but was certainly one of the partners.

while Andrew Henry, a young man from the mining district, invested what must have been most of his savings in the venture. He proved to be one of the ablest field captains the Missouri Fur Company had, and later lent his skills to William Ashley, when that gentleman made his successful entry into the trade in 1822. The name of Dennis Fitzhugh, close friend of William Clark, prominent businessman of Louisville, Kentucky, who had done business in the past with Lisa and others of the partners, was also interlined in the Articles of Agreement, but apparently he took no part in the actual operations of the company.

The most noteworthy feature of the Articles of Agreement was the way in which it concretely delineated the aura of distrust which hung about this heterogeneous collection of merchants banded together to exploit the riches of the Northwest.[7] The document, signed on March 3, 1809, contained twenty articles, an inordinate number of which were concerned not with the positive aspects of company operation but with negative prohibitions imposed upon the members and the penalties which could be incurred for various breaches of the Articles. Although the business *mores* of that day were no better, or worse, than our own, the lengths to which these men went to insure each other's honesty not only were absurd but were partly the cause of the company's failure to take full advantage of its prospects.

The objects of the organization as set forth in the Articles of Agreement were "trading and hunting up the river Missouri and to the headwaters thereof or at such place or places as a majority of the subscribing co-partners may elect." Being a true copartnership, the members were "to generally pay equal proportions of all and every expense whatsoever, which may be

---

[7] Douglas, "Manuel Lisa," *loc. cit.*, 257, thinks that the presence of Lisa's "enemies" Chouteau and Wilkinson indicates that Manuel was forced into the Missouri Fur Company, although it is difficult to see Lisa being forced to do anything, while Brackenridge, *Views of Louisiana*, 92, indicates that Lisa formed the company. In any case, the bedfellows were not happy with each other.

deemed expedient by the aforesaid majority of the company."[8]
But the members did not trust each other out of sight. No one
was willing to go upriver while his partners remained in St.
Louis, and, conversely, no one was willing to remain in St. Louis
while his partners went upriver to do heaven-knew-what while
unobserved in the wilderness. As a result, the second article required each member, or a designated representative acceptable
to the inescapable majority of the partners, to accompany the
expedition of the company to the mountains in the spring of 1809,
and, with specific exceptions, to remain there for the three-year
duration of the articles. Furthermore, when the expedition
reached the Mandan villages, the majority was to decide the
posts and duties of the various members, and they were to comply
with the decisions and instructions under pain of a $1,000 per
year fine. Fortunately, the founders were able to agree that the
most respected member of the group, William Clark, should be
designated as agent in St. Louis, to reside there and accept and
store goods sent down-river by the company.

As might be expected, the matter of spending and receiving
money was given a great deal of consideration, with the partners
bestowing the most attention to income. Making no provision for
payment of operating expenses, and having appointed no one
to take care of such, the partners nonetheless declared, "Whenever any Peltries, furs or other property belonging to the company shall be sent down to the said agent [Clark], the same shall
be (as speedily thereafter as may be) divided equally between
all the partners, and their representative proportions paid to them
or their agents on demand."[9] In other words, there was to be no
reinvestment of profits, no sinking fund for current or future
use. Whenever the company earned a few dollars, they were to
be taken out immediately as the property of the separate partners.

[8] Missouri Fur Company Ledger Book, 1812–14, MHS.

[9] *Ibid.*

This ridiculous system was modified to a degree when, on September 20, 1809, the founders added to their agreement an article stating: "Previous to the division of the Peltry, fur and other property mentioned in article 15 all expenditures of whatever nature incurred by the Company previous to the said Division shall first be deducted from the gross amount of Property to be divided as specified in said article." At the same time, Pierre Chouteau and William Clark were "authorized by the Company to sign and execute all notes, bills, obligations, receipts discharges & acquittances for and in behalf of the Company."[10]

On the expenditure side of the ledger, Lisa and Wilkinson were designated factors "to trade with the Indians or men employed by the Company," and "to make purchases of peltry and merchandise, to engage men and draw bills of exchange . . . ," all of which was subject to the condition that "No purchases of Merchandise are to be made without the consent and approbation of a majority of the Company."[11] Such an incredibly constricting system must have found some modification in actual practice to have been able to operate at all. It was fine to call for the concurrence of a majority in the purchase of merchandise or the payment of bills, and to have all members pay equal shares of each bill as it fell due, as long as there was a majority of the membership collected in St. Louis, but after the commencement of the first voyage in the spring of 1809, such would not be the case. Clark would remain in St. Louis while the rest of the partners went upriver. Once at their destination, the stockholders would separate to go their various ways in the mountains. Chouteau, Lisa, and Menard would all return to St. Louis within about a year, while Wilkinson and Chouteau, Jr., were to follow down in another year. It was impossible to get a majority together on short notice, and, although most of the partners had designated acceptable agents to act in their absence, it was not a very satis-

10 *Ibid.*
11 *Ibid.*

factory way of conducting a business, and did nothing to dispell the distrust the members felt for one another.

Although the honest and plain-dealing men like Menard and Henry were appalled at the duplicity and double-dealing encouraged by the Articles and practiced by certain of the members, Lisa's legal mind seems to have accepted this method of operation as a matter of course. His only complaints centered on the lack of capital, said to amount to not more than forty thousand dollars,[12] and the rather limited scope of operations. Certainly he, Menard, and Morrison had no cause for complaint in the way their old partnership was treated by new company. The partners agreed that the Missouri Fur Company should purchase, at 100 per cent of the first cost, all the merchandise and horses on hand at Fort Raymond. This must have added considerably to the profits made by the original three from that first voyage, for there were over twelve hundred dollars worth of horses at the post when Lisa left it, and no doubt more had been traded for since. The arrangement was beneficial to the new group as well, for it did not have to assume the cost of transporting the merchandise upriver, and the agreed price of thirty dollars per head for the horses in the mountains was cheap considering their price ranged as high as eighty dollars from time to time.

Although the final agreement was not signed until March 3, 1809, the company had been formed and in operation for nearly

---

[12] Brackenridge, *Views of Louisiana*, 92. A receipt in the Chouteau Collection, MHS, reads:

> Received of Mr. Pierre Chouteau his note amounting to two thousand fourteen Piastres & twenty eight sols silver of the United States for his share in the Missouri Fur Company
>
> St. Louis 12 June 1809
>
> $2014–28   PIERRE MENARD

If this was Chouteau's complete share, the capitalization would have amounted to a little over twenty thousand dollars. It is doubtful that Lisa, Menard, and Morrison would have entered such a partnership, because they would have been able to furnish almost that themselves.

a month. Lisa and Menard took inventory of the goods on hand in Kaskaskia,[13] and commissioned Adrien Langlois, Menard's trusted agent, to go to Vincennes and purchase more from Touissant Dubois.[14] If Dubois could not furnish the requisite commodities, then Langlois was to continue on to Detroit, at which place he was to buy goods and recruit some men for the coming voyage. In addition, Langlois was to attempt to commit some of the Detroit merchants to furnish the company with twelve or fifteen thousand dollars worth of merchandise for the following year. The partners hoped to have the returns of the first season's hunt in hand by then and be able to pay for the goods on receipt.

According to Joseph Charless, editor of the *Missouri Gazette:*

> The Missouri Fur Company, lately formed here, has every prospect of becoming a force of incalculable advantage, not only to the individuals engaged in the enterprise, but the community at large. Their extensive preparations, and the respectable force they intend to ascend the Misouri with, may bid defiance to any hostile band they may meet with:—The streams which descend from the Rocky Mountains afford the finest hunting, and here we learn they intend to build their fort. They have engaged to convey Shehakah, the Mandan chief to his nation.[15]

The last sentence of this article, added as sort of an afterthought by the editor, was the key to the expected success of the Missouri Fur Company. Should the returns of the hunt then in progress not meet expectations, or the initial effort of the company be less than anticipated, they were still assured of seven thousand dollars for safely conveying the Mandan chief to his home.

On February 24, the company, although not yet a legal entity signed a contract with Governor Lewis, binding themselves

---

[13] Inventory, Feb. 10, 1809, Kaskaskia Papers, MHS.

[14] Instructions, Manuel Lisa and Pierre Menard to Adrien Langlois, Feb. 10, 1809, Kaskaskia Papers, MHS.

[15] *Missouri Gazette* (Mar. 8, 1809).

to return Shahaka to his village.[16] Taking into consideration the failure of the previous attempt under Ensign Pryor, the government required the company to provide 120 men, 40 of whom had to be Americans and expert riflemen, which would form a body of militia, under the command of Pierre Chouteau, to escort the chief past the Arikara villages.[17] In addition, the company was to provide at least fifty rifles, and ammunition to supply them. According to the terms of the contract, the voyage was to commence on or before April 20, 1809, and in no case later than May 10, or the company would forfeit three thousand dollars of the stipulated fee.[18] To reward the company even further for its services, Governor Lewis promised not to license any other traders above the Platte River before the last date set for departure, giving them a welcome headstart into the upper country.[19]

Certainly the company, in order not to lose the three thousand dollars, either had part of the expedition under way before May 10, or had made some arrangement with the Governor, for the military detachment did not leave St. Louis until May 17,[20] and the main trading party left exactly a month later. The first group to leave consisted of 160 men, among whom were "a few Delawares and Shawonies, employed for hunting."[21] The trading section must have numbered close to 190,[22] about one-half of whom

[16] Articles of Agreement between Meriwether Lewis, Governor, and the St. Louis Missouri Fur Company, Feb. 24, 1809, Chouteau Collection, MHS.

[17] *Ibid.*

[18] *Ibid.*

[19] *Ibid.*

[20] Dr. Thomas, "Journal of a Voyage . . . Missouri," *Missouri Gazette* (Nov. 30, 1809). I have nowhere found a reference to the first name of Dr. Thomas, who apparently was the surgeon of the trip, and the promised continuation of this article never appeared in subsequent issues of the *Gazette.*

[21] *Ibid.*

[22] Thomas James states that there were 350, probably in the entire party, including Chouteau's militia. This figure agrees reasonably well with the number of deserters and the final number who left Fort Mandan for the mountains. Thomas James, *Three Years among the Indians and Mexicans,* 2.

were Americans, and the rest experienced French and Creole hunters and boatmen who had been recruited from as far as Detroit and Louisville as well as St. Louis and Kaskaskia. A group of 80 hunters left ahead of the main party[23] and waited for them at Côte Sans Dessein, across from the mouth of the Osage. It is impossible to determine the extent of the outfit carried by the company, but the few facts available indicate that it was appreciably larger than the one taken upriver by Lisa in 1807. F. Regnier and Company provided goods to the amount of $6,171.14¼ on May 3,[24] while Pierre Chouteau had furnished merchandise valued at £6,861/98/6.[25] The price in pounds sterling implies that the goods came from Montreal, perhaps imported before the Embargo Act became effective. There is no notation of the amount contributed by Lisa and Menard through Langlois, nor is there any indication of the quantity of merchandise and horses purchased from the supply at Fort Raymond. As far as committing the Detroit merchants to supply the next season's articles, Langlois' trip was a failure. At any rate, the entire party consisted of thirteen keelboats and barges, a flotilla designed to carry them unmolested past any bands of marauding Indians.[26]

To those partners who accompanied the military expedition, the early part of the voyage must have been a pleasant one, particularly for those who never before had ascended the Missouri. They went ahead at a leisurely pace, with the men gradually becoming accustomed to their tasks, and to the prodigious amount of work required to propel a boat against the strong current of the river. Rolling hills fell away from either bank, densely

[23] "We found here about 80 men." Letter, Pierre Menard to Adrien Langlois, June 23, 1809, Kaskaskia Papers, MHS.

[24] St. Louis Missouri Fur Company Ledger Book, 1809–12, MHS.

[25] List of goods furnished by Pierre Chouteau to the Missouri Fur Company, June, 1809, Chouteau Collection, MHS.

[26] Thomas James, *Three Years*, 3.

wooded and dressed in the new green of spring growth. Wild-
flowers bloomed in profusion, game was to be seen on every hand,
and the brilliant plumage of the parakeets flashed in the sun-
light as they flitted from tree to tree. The beautiful bottom land
of the principal tributaries, such as the winding Gasconade, beckoned to prospective farmers, and a number of the Americans,
finding the labor demanded of them to be more than they had
bargained for, heeded that call at once.

Those who remained in St. Louis with Lisa and Menard did
not have so pleasant an introduction to the Missouri. Manuel was
issued his license to trade "with the *several nations and tribes
residing on the Missouri and its branches, above the entrance of
the river Plate, with the exception of the Arickara Nation*" on
June 7,[27] and on June 16 he appeared before Justice of the Peace
M. P. LeDuc, claiming a bill due from one John Sherman.[28]
The next day the final contingent left St. Louis.[29] The season was
extremely late and Lisa drove his men unmercifully in order to
make up time. The party set some sort of short-haul record on
the Missouri, arriving at the mouth of the Osage, some 120 miles
upstream, in six days. The pace was too much for many of the
Americans, who were not used to the backbreaking toil of moving
a boat against the roiling current, especially when the work day
was from dawn to very late at night. Upon their arrival at the
Côte, Menard wrote that they found "about 80 men, of which
one half are American hunters and almost all revolted. It was
necessary to make new arrangements with them, but I hope all
will be better in the future."[30] Lisa, writing to Clark the same

---

27 License, June 7, 1809, Lisa Papers, MHS.

28 Notice, June 16, 1809, Menard Family Papers, Illinois State Historical Society.

29 Menard wrote from Fort Mandan on October 7, 1809: "We arrived here fifteen days ago after a navigation of 97 days." That would make the date of departure June 17. Letter, Pierre Menard to Adrien Langlois, Oct. 7, 1809, Kaskaskia
Papers, MHS.

30 Letter, Pierre Menard to Adrien Langlois, June 23, 1809, in *ibid.*

day, enclosed the contracts of four deserters, whose accounts totaled over eight hundred dollars, which sum he hoped Clark would be able to collect, and, in order to save him from some of the brutal facts, said only that he had found "all the American hunters badly disposed."[31]

All was not better in the future, for the next day Lisa wrote again, this time mentioning three more deserters, and one man who had been disengaged. The company was obliged to send back a boat and a pirogue[32] for lack of men to operate them, and Clark was asked to sell them for the account of the company. As they left the mouth of the Osage, Lisa's force consisted of "172 men. nine barges and a canoe."[33] Even if Chouteau had maintained his complete roster of 160 men, which is doubtful, Lisa's figure indicates that approximately 18 men had deserted by that point. The traders joined with the militia at the Osage villages, and departed from there on June 28,[34] with the next stop to be Fort Osage, where the commander of the post, Captain Denison, was to give the militia a final inspection. On July 2, Lisa again wrote to Clark, this time while on the Missouri about five leagues below the mouth of the Grand River. Unable to hide his growing discouragement over the snail's pace maintained by the joint expedition, he mentioned 2 more deserters who had cost the company over one hundred dollars, and went on to say:

We are going very slow, we left a barge. the same that Mr. Ben

[31] Letter, St. Louis Missouri Fur Company Ledger Book, 1809–12, MHS.

[32] A pirogue was a wooden canoe hollowed out of a log, usually cottonwood, sometimes reaching sixty or seventy feet in length and four feet across. They were used extensively near the trading posts, and two such vessels lashed together and boarded across were sometimes used to transport cargoes downstream. They could, in this condition, carry from ten to fifteen tons. Franklin G. Adams, "Reminiscences of Frederick Chouteau," *Kansas State Historical Society Collections*, Vol. VIII (1903–1904), 423–34.

[33] Letter, Manuel Lisa to William Clark, June 24, 1809, St. Louis Missouri Fur Company Ledger Book, 1809–12, MHS.

[34] Thomas, "Journal," *loc. cit.*

Wilkinson had from Louisville, the Boat is sent to Mr. Cadet Chouteau's son. I beg you to sell it for the Interest of the Company.

Reuben Lewis commands the Boat in which the americans are together, two men for each oar and still they complain. I am fearful that more will desert and that we shall be obliged to leave another Boat, I am distracted. I will write you more very soon. we have four or five men sick.[35]

The slowness of the voyage was exasperating to Lisa, who was anxious for news of his men at Fort Raymond, and also to the hunters, who surely would lose the fall hunt if the present pace was maintained. On July 8 the party reached Fort Osage, firing off guns in salute, and having them properly returned by the cannon of the fort.[36] The expedition remained at the government station for three days, during which time the militia was put through its paces while the traders tried to reorganize their depleted company. Lisa had had good cause to be distracted. A group of deserters stole a canoe loaded with supplies and successfully made their escape in it. These men, six in number, were later apprehended and admitted their crime.[37] Unfortunately, their arrest did the company little good, for such men rarely had any money to pay their debts or make restitution, and merely joined the always lengthening list of insolvent debtors.

Lisa sent down a statement of the debts of all of the deserters to that time, and it amounted to slightly more than $1,750.[38] By the time the voyage was completed to the Mandan villages, the list of deserters amounted to thirty-two, with accounts totaling $3,712.54.[39] The debts of those discharged and disabled brought the total to over $4,000, little of which could ever be collected.

[35] Letter, Manuel Lisa to William Clark, July 2, 1809, St. Louis Missouri Fur Company Ledger Book, 1809–12, MHS.

[36] Thomas, "Journal," *loc cit.*

[37] Deposition of Joseph Lebeau, July 12, 1809, Fur Trade Papers, MHS.

[38] Letter, Manuel Lisa to William Clark, July 10, 1809, St. Louis Missouri Fur Company Ledger Book, 1809–12, MHS.

[39] St. Louis Missouri Fur Company Ledger Book, 1809–12, MHS.

Losses of this nature were one of the reasons the company had to charge "mountain prices," even to its own *engagés*. By this time Manuel was thoroughly disgusted with some of the boatmen, and he wrote to Clark, "I have sent eight Americans with a man named ——— to make two canoes, and as soon as they return I will send them to make two more that we may put those Americans and Indians that do not rowe together in those canoes."[40] He also mentioned meeting Ramsay Crooks at Fort Osage, and told of the latter's rapid departure to meet his partner, Robert McClellan, at their old winter quarters near Council Bluffs. These two traders were still attempting to develop a business for themselves on the Missouri, after having been turned back by the Rees in 1807. Manuel was worried that Crooks and McClellan would get the jump on him, even though Crooks had given his promise to await the passage of the Missouri Fur Company at the Bluffs. Lisa made provision to take an assortment in his own boat, "which is the fastest going boat we have,"[41] to overtake them. But that precaution proved unnecessary, for Crooks was re-encountered at the prescribed meeting place, and the threat of another organization's getting ahead of the Missouri Fur Company was dismissed. Crooks and McClellan gathered their men and made an attempt to follow the Lisa party a little later in the season.[42]

As the expedition was finally to leave Fort Osage, Lisa wrote:

> We have been compeled to leave a McKinac boat, a quantity of Corn, for want of men we find ourselves more and more in trouble first, by the deserters & secondly by sickness but we expect by the manner we are now fixed that we will go on well. . . . we are altogether started from this place 153 men all armed, Bourgeoise Indians, Engages & Mullattoes. . . . I have calculated that the

---

[40] Letter, Manuel Lisa to William Clark, July 10, 1809, St. Louis Missouri Fur Company Ledger Book, 1809–12, MHS. The blank is in the original.
[41] *Ibid.*
[42] Thomas, "Journal."

Pork, flower and other provisions we have, will last one month, by that time we will be where we shall be able to kill plenty provisions, we have besides that Corn enough to last us up to the Arickaras.[43]

Menard, however, was not so optimistic. Writing to Langlois, he said:

I hasten to tell you that after a very long passage for the distance of the road, we have finally reached 120 miles in the Missouri. We have heard nothing new except that we are assured that we will handle 30 packs of Beaver at the Maas [Omahas] and the high piles [Council Bluffs] which are a little above the river Plate.[44]

The rest of the letter betrayed his distraught state, as he implored Langlois to look after the Menard family, to do his best to pay Menard's debts, and gave every indication that he was sorry he had ever decided to embark on such a venture, and wished he was back home. Menard finished his epistle by remarking, "But I suppose that everything will come out better than even I can forsee, and work always for the best."[45] The party had turned its back on civilization, and was now fairly started for the upper Missouri. If Menard was homesick, he was not the first nor the last to reach that state on a voyage to the mountains.

The bargeload of Americans which was commanded by Reuben Lewis, and about which Lisa had made his deprecatory remarks in the letter to Clark on July 2, was steered by Thomas James, an American soldier of fortune whose main distinction was that he became the unofficial chronicler of the voyage.[46] As an American, and as adverse to work as the next man, he sympathized with the plight of his crew, whom he described as "light hearted, jovial

[43] Letter, Manuel Lisa to William Clark, St. Louis Missouri Fur Company Ledger Book, 1809–12, MHS.

[44] July 10, 1809, Kaskaskia Papers, MHS.

[45] *Ibid.*

[46] Thomas James, *Three Years.*

men, with no care or anxiety for the future, and little fear of any danger."[47] Lisa, who, at least by James, "was suspected of having invited the Rickarees to attack the Government troops under Capt. Prior, with Shehaka the year before, for the purpose of preventing the traders and trappers who were with the troops from getting to the upper country," was held in very low esteem by the Americans, and the feeling, obviously, was reciprocated. As James described it, the partners traveled in the forward barge, "and there Liza and some of his colleagues lorded it over the poor fellows most arrogantly, and made them work as if their lives depended on their getting forward, with the greatest possible speed."[48] It is to James's everlasting discredit that he never realized that in the north country a man's life and fortune very often did depend on getting forward with the greatest possible speed, even when no danger was apparent. The Americans were capable of keeping up with their French counterparts over a short distance, but were unable, or unwilling, to put forth a sustained effort. As a consequence, they usually were dragging into camp long after the rest, and this nightly occurrence did tempers on either side no good.

Two weeks out of Fort Osage, James's crew ran out of provisions and was forced to subsist on "Boiled corn, without salt. At the same time the other boats were well supplied and the gentlemen proprietors in the leading barge were faring in the most sumptuous and luxurious manner. The French hands were much better treated on all occasions than the Americans."[49] This indicated that the Americans had refused to ration themselves to make the supplies stretch out a month as Lisa had calculated they should, and when they did run out of pork, they were not enterprising enough to send one of their number to hunt up some fresh meat. Such men were a constant trial to the partners as well

[47] *Ibid.*, 3.
[48] *Ibid.*, 4.
[49] *Ibid.*, 4.

Portrait by Gilbert Stuart
From William Clark Kennerly, Persimmon Hill

WILLIAM CLARK

Missouri Historical Society

SYLVESTRE LABBADIE

Missouri Historical Society

PIERRE CHOUTEAU

as a source of embarrassment to John Dougherty and the other Americans who performed their allotted tasks without complaining and later became leaders in the mountains. The food situation became unbearable for the Americans shortly after the party passed the Platte, and, led by James Cheek, a tall, raw-boned Tennessean, they staged a mutiny.[50] For the sake of harmony, Lisa acceded to their demands for more food, but the incident rankled, and he did not forget it.

At the Au Jacques, or James River, the party was met by a large band of Teton Sioux,[51] who treated the men to a great feast of the supreme Indian delicacy, roast dog. James could not stand the sight of the steaming bowls, each of which had the paw of a dog dangling over the edge to identify positively the main ingredient, and excused himself from the dinner. The company left an outfit with the Tetons before moving on. The rest of the Sioux bands were not so friendly. Flying the British flag, they confronted the boats in a hostile manner, and only the size and martial bearing of the fleet kept them from doing some mischief. The Sioux complained that they had been promised a trader who would come and live with them, but he had never appeared.[52] They were now tired of waiting. To somewhat assuage their injured feelings, another outfit was detached and trade opened, with the traders probably using Loisel's old post at Cedar Island.[53]

Just below the Arikara villages the body of militia was put ashore opposite the boats. Dragging their cannon, this soldierly array marched along in line with the flotilla as they approached the palisaded Ree towns. The Arikaras were thoroughly intimidated by this show of strength, and made great protestations of

[50] *Ibid.*, 5.

[51] *Ibid.*, 5.

[52] Letter, Pierre Chouteau to William Eustis, Dec. 14, 1809, Pierre Chouteau Letterbook, 142, MHS.

[53] Letter, Pierre Menard to Adrien Langlois, Oct. 7, 1809, Kaskaskia Papers, MHS.

friendship. Chouteau took the occasion to lecture them on their past conduct, and the Indians piously promised, no doubt with straight faces, to mend their ways and be friendly with the whites in the future.[54] After leaving an outfit with the Rees,[55] the expedition once more moved on toward the Mandan villages. The return of the old chief, whom the Mandans had just about given up for lost, occasioned wild rejoicing on the part of the nation, and they had little time to give to the whites while the celebration continued. This disappointed James, who thought the Indians should always show great deference to white men.[56] At the Mandan towns the party received some disheartening news. Chouteau had, two days before arriving at the Mandan towns, been informed that three agents of the British North West Company were there. He sent ahead a dispatch, asking them to await the arrival of the Americans, but they had gone on. Before leaving, however, the British had informed a white man residing among the Indians that the North West Company had erected a fort at the Three Forks of the Missouri. This news was made more credible by the fact that thirty American hunters, who had been accustomed to visit the Mandans, had not been seen or heard of for almost eighteen months.[57] If this information was true, the Missouri Fur Company was destined for trouble, for the British had more resources closer at hand than did the Americans.

Moving on, the company passed through the village of the Gros Ventres, where they were hospitably received. About ten or twelve miles above the Gros Ventres the company halted to begin construction of its main outpost, which would be the jumping-off point for an overland expedition to trapping country, and also the trading post for the Gros Ventres and Mandans.[58]

[54] Thomas James, *Three Years*, 9.

[55] Letter, Pierre Menard to Adrien Langlois, October 7, 1809, Kaskaskia Papers, MHS.

[56] Thomas James, *Three Years*, 9.

[57] Letter, Pierre Chouteau to William Eustis, Dec. 14, 1809, Pierre Chouteau Letterbook, 142, MHS.

The season was well advanced, the date being September 22, and there was much still to be accomplished. Benito Vasquez had been waiting for them at the Mandan villages, and his report of the past year's activities was not encouraging. The optimism which pervaded the atmosphere at Fort Raymond at Lisa's departure in 1808 had given way to disappointment in the face of difficult odds. The hostile Blackfeet had driven out most of the men who had gone to trap in the Three Forks country, stealing their beaver, horses, traps, guns, and ammunition in the process. Only one party of four men, led by Casé Fortin, was still in that area. When last heard from in October, 1808, this party had in cache at Three Forks twenty packs of beaver, and could be expected to have at least fifty by the present. Vasquez theorized that they had crossed the divide to winter with the peaceful Flathead nation, and was confident of finding them during the next winter's hunt.[59] It was doubtful, then, that the British had a post in Blackfoot country.

The men who had returned from Three Forks to Fort Raymond had been re-equipped, and formed a party, headed by Beauvais and Sanguinet, to trap the "River of the Spaniards," where the existence of many beaver was reported. Jean Baptiste Champlain, a young man of great promise as a trader and trapper, but more importantly as a leader of men, had an outfit with the Crows, and, when last reported, had three or four packs of beaver. No doubt by this time he, too, would have considerably more. After watching the departure of all the hunters, Vasquez had then closed up the fort, cached its effects, and journeyed to the Mandans to await Lisa and the expedition. He brought with him only fifteen beaver skins and ten buffalo robes—a miserable showing for the new partners who expected so much.[60]

[58] Letter, Pierre Menard to Adrien Langlois, Oct. 7, 1809, Kaskaskia Papers, MHS.

[59] *Ibid.*

[60] *Ibid.*

Of all the returnees from Blackfoot country, John Colter had the most harrowing tale to tell. In company with his old comrade John Potts, Colter had gone directly to Three Forks in the fall of 1808, feeling that was the most profitable place to float his stick.

They were examining their traps early one morning, in a creek about six miles from that branch of the Missouri called Jefferson's Fork, and were ascending in a canoe, when they suddenly heard a great noise, resembling the trampling of animals; but they could not ascertain the fact, as the high perpendicular banks on each side of the river impeded their view. Colter immediately pronounced it to be occasioned by Indians, and advised an instant retreat, but was accused of cowardice by Potts, who insisted that the noise was caused by buffalo, and they proceeded on. In a few minutes afterwards their doubts were removed, by a party of Indians making their appearance on both sides of the creek, to the amount of five or six hundred, who beckoned them to come ashore. As retreat was now impossible, Colter turned the head of the canoe toward shore; and at the moment of its touching, an Indian seized the rifle belonging to Potts; but Colter, who is a remarkably strong man, immediately retook it, and handed it to Potts, who remained in the canoe, and on receiving it pushed off into the river. He had scarcely quitted the shore when an arrow was shot at him, and he cried out, "*Colter, I am wounded.*" Colter remonstrated with him on the folly of attempting to escape, and urged him to come ashore. Instead of complying, he instantly leveled his rifle at an Indian, and shot him dead on the spot. This conduct, situated as he was, may appear to have been an act of madness; but it was doubtless the effect of sudden, but sound reasoning; for if taken alive, he must have expected to be tortured to death, according to their custom. He was instantly pierced with arrows so numerous, to use the language of Colter, "*he was made a riddle of.*" They now seized Colter, stripped him entirely naked, and began to consult on the manner in which he should be put to death. They were first inclined to set him up a mark to shoot at; but the chief interfered, and seizing him by the shoulder, asked him if he could run fast? Colter, who had been some time among the Kee-hat-sa, or Crow Indians, had in considerable degree acquired the Blackfoot language, and was also well acquainted with Indian customs, he knew that he now had to run for his life, with the dreadful odds of five or six hundred against him, and those armed Indians; therefore cunningly replied that he was a very bad runner, although he was considered by the hunters as remarkably swift. The chief now commanded the party to remain stationary, and led Colter out on the prairie three or four hundred yards and released him, bidding him *to save himself if he could*. At that instant the horrid war whoop sounded in the ears of poor Colter, who, urged with the hope of preserving life, ran with a speed at which he was himself surprised. He proceeded toward the Jefferson fork, having to traverse a plain six miles in breadth, abounding with prickly pear, on which he was every instant treading with his naked feet. He ran nearly half way across the plain before he ventured to look over his shoulder, when he perceived that the Indians were very much scattered, and that he had gained ground to a considerable distance from the main body; but one Indian, who carried a spear was much before all the rest, and not more than a hundred yards from him. A faint gleam of hope now cheered the heart of Colter; he derived confidence from the belief that escape was within the bounds of possibility, but that confidence was nearly being fatal to him, for he exerted himself to such a degree that the blood gushed from his nostrils, and soon almost covered the fore part of his body. He had now arrived within a mile of the river, when he distinctly heard the appalling sound of footsteps behind him, and every instant expected to feel the spear of his pursuer. Again he turned his head, and saw the savage not twenty yards from him. Determined if possible to avoid the expected blow, he suddenly stopped, turned round, and spread out his arms. The Indian, surprised by the suddenness of the action, and perhaps the bloody appearance of Colter, also attempted to stop, but exhausted with his running, he fell whilst endeavouring to throw his spear, which stuck in the ground, and broke in his hand. Colter instantly snatched up the pointed part, with which he pinned him to the earth, and then continued his flight. The foremost of the Indians, on arriving at the place, stopped till others came up to join them, when they set up a hideous yell. Every moment of this time was improved by Colter, who, although fainting and exhausted, succeeded in gaining the skirting of cotton wood trees, on the borders of the fork, through which he ran, and plunged into the river. Fortunately for him, a little below this place there was an island, against the upper point of which a raft of drift timber had lodged, he dived under the raft, and after several efforts, got his head above water amongst the trunks of the trees, covered over with smaller wood to a depth of several feet. Scarcely had he hid himself, when the Indians arrived on the river, screeching and yelling, as Colter expressed it, "like so many divils." They were frequently on the raft during the day, and were seen through the chinks by Colter, who was congratu-lating himself on his escape, until the idea arose that they might set the raft on fire. In horrible suspense he remained until night, when hearing no more of the Indians, he dived from under the raft, and swam silently down the river to a considerable distance, when he landed and travelled all night. Although happy in hav-ing escaped from the Indians, his situation was still dreadful: he was completely naked, under a burning sun: the soles of his feet were entirely filled with the thorns of the prickly pear; he was hungry, and had no means of killing game, although he saw abundance around him, and was at least seven days journey from Lisa's Fort, on the Bighorn branch of the Roche Jaune river. These were circumstances under which almost any man but an American hunter would have despaired. He arrived at the fort in seven days, having subsisted on a root much esteemed by the Indians of the Missouri, now known by naturalists as *Psoralea esculente*.[61]

[61] John Bradbury, *Travels in the Interior of America*, 17–20. Of all the extant versions of this tale, this one seems the most reliable. Bradbury was not given to excessive embellishment, and he got the story directly from Colter, himself noted for his veracity.

The news of Blackfoot hostility did little to dampen the enthusiasm of the hunters for the Three Forks area. If four men could collect fifty packs of beaver, which might be worth as much as $25,000, in a single season, they could all become rich. Even the *engagés* who did not have the favorable contracts of Alexis Doza[62] and some of the others were eager to get to beaver water. While the post was being built and supplies and equipment doled out to the hunters and trappers, James's Americans received some rough treatment. Ostensibly to make a complete inventory of all goods and equipment, the company took back all of the guns and ammunition it had furnished the Americans, and, at the end of three weeks, it had not returned them. This probably was designed as a none too gentle hint that the company did not want the obstreperous Americans around, and an indication that they should avail themselves of the opportunity to return to St. Louis with Lisa and Chouteau. Whatever the reason for this action, the Americans feared that the company was about to turn them out into the wilderness without weapons, which would have been the equivalent, according to James, "of a cat in hell without claws."[63] Not to be outdone, James purchased from John Colter some traps, a gun, and ammunition. "Seeing me thus equipped, Liza the most active, the meanest and most rascally of the whole offered me new and good traps, a gun and ammunition."[64] Lisa was obviously trying to protect the company from the inevitable lawsuit, for they were required by contract to furnish James with necessary equipment. Disgusted, James, in company with two other Americans, Miller and McDaniel, headed upriver to hunt and trap on his own. Relieved to be rid of one of the major troublemakers, the company settled down to direct its forces for the coming hunt.

[62] According to the terms of his three-year contract, Doza was to be outfitted by the company, and, in return, was to remit one-half of his catch to them. See Appendix I in this volume.

[63] Thomas James, *Three Years*, 11.

[64] *Ibid.*, 11.

In a council of the partners it was reaffirmed that Lisa and Chouteau would return to St. Louis to prepare the outfit for the following spring, while Andrew Henry would take forty men and horses overland to Fort Raymond, to reopen the post and make it fit for habitation again. Pierre Menard would command the boats the rest of the way to the same destination, and the combined parties would winter there preparatory to starting to Three Forks in the spring.[65] Menard was to return to St. Louis in the summer of 1810, leaving the mountains on June 15, and bring his report of the progress made together with the returns of the hunt. Menard was not pleased with the accomplishments to that point, for he wrote Langlois:

> We have left 2 equipments with the Sioux, one with the Rickaras and one which we leave here for the Mandans and the Gros Ventre which is the most extensive. I would tell you that I do not have a good opinion of the equipments at all. I do not believe one loses [money] here, but again I do not believe that one will make great profits for the reason that one makes only [buffalo] robes. Very little beaver although the country produces quite a lot, but the savages do not hunt at all and are lazy, if one can get them to hunt for beaver.[66]

Menard could not see the reason for so large an investment in goods for trade with the Missouri natives when the returns were so low, but it was precisely this investment in friendship, more than anything else, which allowed the Missouri Fur Company to use the great highway of the Missouri without fear of being blocked or cut off by hostile Indians. Concerning the conduct of the partners and their relations with the men, Menard was even more unhappy:

> It is not long since I became resigned to suffer in order to gain

[65] Letter, Pierre Menard to Adrien Langlois, Oct. 7, 1809, Kaskaskia Papers, MHS.

[66] Ibid.

money, but the manner of some of my associates displeases me. I love to see things done frankly, which is not at all the case here and often causes small difficulties. All this displeases me and makes me suffer almost as much as my absence from my family and my friends, and with all these little difficulties one gains nothing, to the contrary, one thus loses a lot and I am angry to be obliged and forced to say that we are wrong at least three times out of four with the engagés and the hunters. Thank God this is about to end. I am almost certain not to have anything to do with the parties I commanded. I perceive that all the difficulties are onerous for us and thus we lose a lot for one must always come to that which is right. I have a lot of confidence in the party of Mr. Henery. He admits everything perfectly with his humor as well as his honesty and his frank manner and without beating about the bush. I will also say to you despite the fact that I do not have the highest opinion of our expedition, nobody sees clearer than I the advantages and resources of the Missouri. There is no doubt that if one finds the means to exploit it, it will make him a great fortune. All depends on the direction that one will take. If taken well one will succeed, but if one makes mistakes, one will ruin himself.[67]

Well said, but Menard could offer no better direction himself.

While Henry's party hurried overland, apprehensive of what they might find on the Yellowstone, and Menard and his crew struggled on against the fast-icing Missouri, James and his two companions were having a taste of the life of trappers in the wilds. After some desultory trapping which produced indifferent results, the three decided to "hole up" for the winter, building a log hut to ward off the cold. They still had not come to the realization that hard work and privation were the lot of those who chose the life of the wilderness to gain their fortune. The food situation soon became difficult, and James agreed to stay and guard the goods while Miller and McDaniel went for help. James was visited shortly thereafter by friendly Indians who

[67] *Ibid.*

91

gave him a bit of food to tide him over, but he was in poor condition when visited by three of Lisa's men, bound with dispatches from Fort Mandan to Fort Raymond in February, 1810. They told James that his partners had reached the fort but had been in no great hurry to leave, and had later been killed by the Rees while out trapping. James decided to accompany the men to Raymond, and, after suffering starvation and near death, they ultimately reached their destination.[68]

James was surprised to find Menard at the post, and attributed the fact of Lisa's return to St. Louis to a conversation which allegedly took place shortly after the arrival of the expedition at Fort Mandan, in which Lisa was again confronted by his antagonist of the mutiny:

> Chouteau's name was mentioned in the course of the conversation when Cheek coolly remarked that if he caught Chouteau a hundred yards from camp he would shoot him. "Cheek! Cheek!" exclaimed Liza, "mind what you say." "I do that," said Cheek, "and Liza, I have heard some of our boys say that if they ever caught you two hundred yards from camp they would shoot you, and if they don't I will. You ought not to expect anything better from the Americans after having treated them with so much meanness, treachery and cruelty as you have. Now Liza," continued he, "you are going to the forks of the Missouri, mark my words, you will never come back alive." Liza's cheeks blanched at this bold and reckless speech from a man who always performed his promises, whether good or evil.[69]

Whatever the reason for Lisa's absence, James, who thought more highly of Menard, decided to stay with the company and to try his luck at Three Forks with the party which was going to depart for that point within a few days of his arrival.

Among the dispatches brought to Fort Raymond was a letter from Sylvestre Labbadie, the partner who had remained in

[68] Thomas James, *Three Years*, 17.
[69] *Ibid.*, 17.

charge of Fort Mandan, addressed to Menard. In it Labbadie, who was probably suffering from the same pangs of homesickness that had bothered Menard on the river, enriched, no doubt, by the winter's boredom, confessed that he had only joined the company out of a sense of ennui with life in St. Louis, had cured this malady, and was now ready to return to his family in St. Louis, even at the cost of the prescribed penalty in the Articles of Agreement. Further, he was struck by the shortsightedness of the article requiring all the partners to go upriver. Using his own position as an example, he said a common clerk, worth a salary of three hundred dollars per year, could do his job. The partners, by requiring themselves to remain upriver, were only adding to their expenses. He requested Menard to approach Jean Baptiste Champlain, who had accompanied Lisa in 1807, and was perhaps the brightest young prospect among the hunters, to take his place at Fort Mandan.[70]

Menard, who had other things to think about, nonetheless kept the letter, not destroying it as Labbadie had requested. In company with Henry and Lewis, and guided by John Colter, Menard and his party set out for Three Forks.[71] They had the misfortune to be struck by snow blindness, which forced them to remain encamped, and helpless, for two days and nights, during which time a band of thirty Snake Indians rode through their camp, but pitying the condition of the trappers, did them no harm.[72] The group arrived safely at the confluence of the Jefferson, Madison, and Gallatin rivers on April 3, and began at once to construct a fort.

[70] Letter, Sylvestre Labbadie to Pierre Menard, Feb. 3, 1810, Pierre Menard Letterbook, 1785–1818, Illinois State Historical Society.

[71] Thomas James, *Three Years*, 18. James says the party numbered thirty-two, but the figure must have been closer to eighty. William Clark reported that Henry's party across the mountains numbered sixty. Letter, William Clark to William Eustis, July 20, 1810, William Clark Collection, MHS, photostat of original in National Archives.

[72] Thomas James, *Three Years*, 20.

Most of the heavy work was completed within a week, and the party split up to begin the hunt. James, in company with Dougherty, Wier, and Brown, decided to trap the Missouri between the Forks and the Falls, while another group of eighteen moved up the Jefferson. The rest remained with Menard to complete the post.[73] On April 12, while the larger group of trappers was still within ten miles of the camp, the Blackfeet fell upon them, killing two, Cheek and Ayres, and mutilating their bodies. By the time the rescue party arrived, there was no trace of three others, Freeharty, Rucker, and Hull.[74] Wrote Menard, "It would be much better if they were dead than prisoners. So often they are."[75] The company had lost, in addition to the men, their traps, some of which were later recovered, skins, ammunition, and seven horses. Some of the beaver and equipment later turned up in British hands.[76] James's group, which had the misfortune to lose the beginnings of a promising hunt when their canoe overturned, managed to return to the fort in safety. John Colter, who had had two near-miraculous escapes from the Blackfeet in the past, decided that his luck was about to run out, and that it was time for him to leave the mountains. This permitted Menard and Lewis, at least, to get off letters to St. Louis describing the situation at Three Forks.

The beaver were there, and, if the Blackfeet could be placated, the hunt would be a success. To accomplish this, Menard detailed his plan to Chouteau:

> It is true that we shall accomplish nothing this spring, but I trust that we shall next fall. I hope between now and then to see

[73] *Ibid.*, 19.

[74] Letter, Pierre Menard to Pierre Chouteau, Apr. 21, 1810, printed in Chittenden, *American Fur Trade*, II, 897.

[75] Letter, Pierre Menard to Madam Menard, Apr. 21, 1810, Pierre Menard Letterbook, 1785–1818, Illinois State Historical Society.

[76] Alexander Henry and David Thompson, *Journals*, II, 735.

the Snake and Flathead Indians. My plan is to induce them to stay here, if possible, and make war upon the Blackfeet so that we may take some prisoners, and send one back with propositions of peace—which I think can easily be secured by leaving traders among them below the Falls of the Missouri. Unless we can have peace with these [savages] or unless they can be destroyed, it is idle to think of maintaining an establishment at this point.[77]

Lewis was not even that optimistic, for he wrote his brother:

. . . I fear we shall not do so well as we had flattered ourselves we should. My principal hopes are now from the Collumbia, I am confident that the Blackfeet are urged on by the Brittish traders in there Country. . . . By June another Boat will leave this country I am in hopes to be enabled to have it more in my power to forme an opinion on the future prospects of the Company, & should they not mind I shall clearly be of the opinion that it would be for the best interest of General Clark & myself to sell out, if it would be done on living terms, but at the same time I do not relinquish the idea of trade in this Country, & should the New York Company go into operation I should have no doubt but an interest in that would be valuable, and that it would be wise to sell out of the present, the resources of this Country are very great, but why ————— ————— tell you, who knows them so well, Mr. Shamplain tells me that the martin abound in the mountains dividing the waters of the Spanish River as it is called, on what is supposed to be the Rio del nort, from the waters of som of the Southern branches of the Collumbia, on a River falling into the Gulf of California, which he thinks most probable. Beaver abounds in the same country but it is so high that it is allmost perpetual snow, the upper branches of the Collumbia are full of Beaver, and the rout by the middle fork on Madison's River is almost without mountains it is about 5 or 6 days travel to an illigable plan for a fort on that River where the Beavers from

[77] Letter, Pierre Menard to Pierre Chouteau, Apr. 21, 1810, printed in Chittenden, *American Fur Trade*, II, 898.

the account of Peter Wyzer, is as abundant as in our part of the country.[78]

It was obviously wealthy country, and all that was necessary was capital, like Astor's, to be able to develop it.

Not until the twenty-second did another party set out from the fort to trap. This one, numbering thirty men, and carrying only three traps each because Menard did not deem it prudent to risk more, moved up the Jefferson as had the previous one.[79] Originally planning to stick together for protection, the group, meeting no hostile sign, soon split into groups of four, two to trap and two to keep camp. George Drouillard, having a very successful hunt, began to go out by himself, contrary to advice. One inevitable morning they found the body of that brave trapper "mangled in a horrible manner; his head cut off, his entrails torn out and his body hacked to pieces."[80] Near by were the bodies of two Shawnee scouts who had also been trapping, their bodies similarly decorated. This event discouraged even the bravest, and plans were made for those, like James, who wished to quit the mountains to return to St. Louis with Menard, while the remainder, some sixty in number, would cross the divide to the waters of the Columbia with Henry to winter with the peaceful Snakes and Flatheads.[81] On June 5, Henry wrote to Francis Vallé, one of those who had escaped the first onslaught of the Blackfeet, showing how his emotions were torn by the desire for compatible company and the grim logic that a man was not safe in the north country:

> Since you left the fort I was told by Charles Davis that some days past you expressed some regret at going down. If that is the

[78] Letter, Reuben Lewis to Meriwether Lewis, Apr. 21, 1810, Meriwether Lewis Collection, MHS.

[79] Letter, Pierre Menard to Pierre Chouteau, Apr. 21, 1810, printed in Chittenden, *American Fur Trade*, II, 897.

[80] Thomas James, *Three Years*, 37.

[81] *Ibid.*, 38.

case & you have any wish to stay, you shall have the same bargain which Manuel gave you last fall & better should you desire it.

on the other hand. if you have realy a wish to decend I will by no means advise you to stay, but would rather advice you to go home to your family who I know will be extremely glad to see you, altho the pleasure of your company for a year in this wild country would be to me inestimable.[82]

Menard's return to St. Louis in mid-July marked the end of one and one-half years of constant frustration for the partners of the Missouri Fur Company. On May 6, Auguste Chouteau, Jr., had appeared in St. Louis with the crushing news that the post at Cedar Island had burned to the ground, destroying furs valued at from twelve to fifteen thousand dollars.[83] The spring hunt on the headwaters of the Missouri had been frustrated by the machinations of the Blackfeet, eight good men had been killed, considerable amounts of equipment had been lost or stolen, and, Menard reported, as if to pile on final injury, the caches on the Yellowstone had been broken into and plundered by the Gros Ventres.[84] Even worse, the Embargo Act had sharply curtailed the trade in beaver, and the price was considerably depressed.[85] Still, the *Missouri Gazette* was able to report:

Adding all those untoward circumstances, the Fur Company have every prospect of success, although a majority of the season was occupied in distributing the hunting parties and exploring the foot of the mountains: although they have had upwards of $12,000 worth of valuable furs consumed, yet they have been able to send down about fifty packs of Beaver, besides other Furs

[82] Letter, Andrew Henry to Francis Vallé, June 5, 1810, Fur Trade Papers, MHS.

[83] *Missouri Gazette* (May 10, 1810).

[84] Thomas James, *Three Years*, 38.

[85] At the meeting of the partners on July 26, 1810, William Morrison agreed to purchase the beaver at $2.50. The notation does not specify whether this was for the pound or the pelt, although it is presumably the former. In either case it was not much of a price. St. Louis Missouri Fur Company Ledger Book, 1809–12, MHS.

to a considerable amount, and have taken measures to ensure more than double that quantity in the spring.[86]

So the company, through auction sales of surplus merchandise and equipment,[87] the contract for the return of the Mandan chief Shahaka, and the relatively meager returns of the year's hunt, was still able to break a little more than even. And if the credit due William Morrison in July, 1810, of $6,633.25 from the company was his share for the year, they did quite well indeed.[88] Whatever the return, it was not good enough for the partners, for they had expected to bring in nearly three hundred packs of beaver alone that first year.[89] Clearly something would have to be done to tighten the company's operations, particularly until the political situation was eased and the fur market returned to normal, and to ensure future profit. Eyes once more turned to the prime movers, Pierre Chouteau and Manuel Lisa.

[86] *Missouri Gazette* (July 12, 1810).

[87] Auction sales by the company brought in over $2,000. St. Louis Missouri Fur Company Ledger Book, 1809–12, MHS.

[88] Kaskaskia Ledger D, 229, Illinois Historical Survey.

[89] Brackenridge, *Views of Louisiana*, 93.

IV

The Missouri Fur Company
Retrenchment and Reorganization

MANUEL LISA and Pierre Chouteau had returned in the latter part of November, 1809,[1] to a St. Louis shocked and saddened by the death of Governor Meriwether Lewis. As unexpected as it was untimely, the Governor's passing only served to depress further the already gloomy leaders of the Missouri Fur Company. As an observer later put it:

> The hopes of the Fur Company which ascended this River have died with their patron and benefactor *Gov. Lewis* [.] Chouteau and Manuel, two of the Stock holders returned last Fall from the [report] of those Gentlemen the situation of the Compy is critical and the prospects of advantage commence but slender except the Mandan & riccara Nations, all the Missouri Indians were unfriendly & inclined to Commit depredations in the Property of the Company.[2]

The partners were also startled to find a vicious rumor circulating in St. Louis, casting a stigma on their operations. Ramsey Crooks and Robert McClellan, who the company had met and passed at Council Bluffs on their way upstream, had gathered their men and equipment, and had attempted to follow the Mis-

[1] *Missouri Gazette* (Nov. 23, 1809). The *Gazette* indicates that the date was November 20.
[2] Letter, Robert Lucas to Captain House, Jan. 29, 1810, Lucas Papers, MHS.

99

souri Fur Company to the upper river, but were stopped by the combined Sioux tribes, and were forced to build a post to trade with them. The Indians stayed with the traders long enough to see them get construction fairly well under way, and then returned to their camps to gather trade goods. Crooks and McClellan, fearing the consequences of remaining, had quickly packed up and escaped downstream with their men and merchandise. Upon their arrival in St. Louis, the unhappy traders let it be known that they suspected the Missouri Fur Company, and Lisa in particular, of inciting the Sioux against them to keep competition from the upper Missouri.[3]

Lisa and Chouteau had little time for rumor, however damaging, and went on about their business. Chouteau reported the safe return of the Mandan chief, and no doubt hurried to collect the stipulated fee before Washington might decide that the late Governor Lewis had been too generous with the company. Lisa paused long enough to pen a quick note to Madam Menard, informing her that her husband, who had lately left Fort Mandan with fifty-six men to join Henry, Lewis, and Morrison at Fort Raymond, was well, and could be expected in St. Louis sometime during the coming July.[4] After a minimal visit at home with his family, who had long since become used to having Manuel away for most of the year, Lisa set out eastward in an attempt to procure an outfit for the coming season.

Stopping in Vincennes on January 23, 1810,[5] Manuel picked up his old friend Touissant Dubois, and the two immediately started for Detroit. During the long and dangerous ride across country, the travelers suffered greatly from the bitter cold, Lisa more so as a result of having been twice thrown from his recal-

[3] Chittenden, *American Fur Trade*, I, 160–62.

[4] Letter, Manuel Lisa to Madam Menard, Nov. 25, 1809, Pierre Menard Letterbook, 1785–1818, Illinois State Historical Society.

[5] Letter, Manuel Lisa to Pierre Chouteau, Jan. 24, 1810, Chouteau Collection, MHS.

citrant horse into icy waters. Arriving safely, they crossed to the British side of the city, where they stayed in the home of Richard Pattinson, a long-time friend and business associate of Pierre Chouteau. From there Lisa reported the dismal prospects:

> ... generous offers have been made to us, but it is impossible for me to get a needle across due to the embargo. .... If however the war is not declared after all, I shall continue my way to Montreal. I do not abandon my progress, and I will push it until I succeed. ... Mr. Dubois returns to the Poste [Vincennes] by whom I write you, without having made any business at all. This damned embargo hinders all communication of the two sides, guards are all along this river, who watch if one takes anything across, and the fines are very harsh, confiscation of the goods, five hundred dollars fine & twenty five days in prison. I believe that this time I shall go to prison, because I could not bear that one would not let me take over merchandise. If by chance the embargo continues, for the five hundred dollar fine, I would do this in consequence. All that one could do to me would be to put me in prison. (One must joke sometimes.)[6]

Unable to import merchandise through Detroit, Manuel went on to Montreal, but instead of returning by way of Chicago, as he had intended, he circled through Philadelphia, still in hopes of finding an outfit.[7]

His hopes, and the expectations of the company, remained unrealized as Lisa returned empty-handed to St. Louis. This meant that the men in the field would have to shift for themselves during the season of 1810–11, since there would be no expedition to bring them aid, equipment, or trade goods. The only progress, if such it could be called, made by the company that winter was in Washington, where William Clark had found

[6] Letter, Manuel Lisa to Pierre Chouteau, Feb. 14, 1810, Chouteau Collection, MHS.

[7] Jeannette E. Graustein, "Manuel Lisa and Thomas Nuttall," *Missouri Historical Society Bulletin*, Vol. XII (April, 1956), 249–52.

"the Genl. Government were not favorably impressed with the objects and correct intentions of the Company," Congress probably being unhappy with the amount required to return Shahaka. Clark "explained to them the real views of the Company, and . . . obtained their approbation, and some assurances in support of Measures which may be taken by the Co. to keep out foreign intruders."[8] These "foreign intruders," which meant the British, were a constant source of annoyance to the President of the Missouri Fur Company, and he kept up a constant barrage of letters trying to induce the government to do something about their presence on American soil. In this, he was uniformly unsuccessful.

Lisa spent the summer in and about St. Louis attending to his own affairs, taking a good deal of time in court, occupied with cases instituted by the company to recover money from some of the *engagés* and deserters, and also involved in a few instigated by *engagés* and former employees against the company, such as the case of Jean Baptiste Bouché versus Lisa, Morrison, and Menard.[9] Manuel, together with the rest of the partners in St. Louis, waited anxiously for the arrival of Pierre Menard with the proceeds of the hunt, and for his report on the prospects for the future. On June 26, Manuel inserted a notice in the *Missouri Gazette* offering a twenty-five-dollar reward for the return of his wallet, lost near St. Louis, containing the notes of various individuals amounting to over three thousand dollars.[10] On August 11, Lisa became the administrator of the estate of the late George Drouillard, and tried to settle the confusion of that hunter's accounts.[11]

Menard's return and subsequent report to the partners was

[8] Letter, William Clark to Pierre Chouteau, Feb. 20, 1810, Chouteau Collection, MHS.

[9] A large number of these cases are contained in the Lisa Papers, MHS, and the Missouri Minute Book of the Supreme Court, 1809–11, in the same depository.

[10] *Missouri Gazette* (June 28, 1810).

[11] *Ibid.* (Sept. 6, 1810).

something less than encouraging. The failure of the company to send up an expedition in the spring of 1810 had placed Andrew Henry in a most difficult position, and no one was more fully aware of that than Manuel Lisa. While it was true that Henry and his men could live off the land like the Indians, it was equally true that they would find it impossible to replenish their by now meager supply of powder and lead. To use up their ammunition procuring the daily supply of meat would leave them defenseless against the attack of the Blackfeet or any other tribe which found them in such a state. Something would have to be done in the spring to alleviate Henry's condition.

In a meeting of the stockholders on September 10,[12] at which Lisa, Menard, Clark, Labbadie, Auguste Chouteau, Jr., Walter Wilkinson for Benjamin Wilkinson, and M. P. LeDuc for Pierre Chouteau were present, it was voted to send a relief party to aid the hunters and traders under Andrew Henry and Reuben Lewis, but the cost of the goods to be taken upstream was not to exceed $2,000. Further, no more than twenty-one men were to be hired, and their wages, the cost of the boat, provisions, and other necessary equipment could total no more than $4,750. Lisa, Menard, and Clark were designated to organize the expedition. What this meant was that while the Chouteaus and Labbadie were willing to let the company go to the aid of the helpless men, they were not willing to contribute much, if anything, to furthering the business of the organization on the river, and it fell to the three named to finance the major share, indeed probably all, of the relief expedition. The lack of quick profits and the uncertainty that the future held had caused the Chouteaus to lose heart in the enterprise.

In the same meeting the remarks which Labbadie had transmitted to Menard early in the spring found favor with a majority of the company, and the second article of the original agreement, requiring that all of the partners ascend the Missouri, was abol-

[12] St. Louis Missouri Fur Company Ledger Book, 1809–12, MHS.

ished. They decided that only two of the stockholders were needed upriver at any given time, and that these men should be paid a salary of fifteen hundred dollars per year for that service. This was a triumph of common sense, and certainly Lisa was in support of the move, since he would be, in all probability, on the river each year. The members were to remit to William Clark on or before July 1, 1811, five hundred dollars cash to defray this new expenditure.[13]

No doubt there was also a great deal of comment on the latest threat to the prosperity of the Missouri Fur Company, the presence in St. Louis of Wilson Price Hunt, partner in John Jacob Astor's newly formed Pacific Fur Company. Hunt and his motley aggregation of boatmen and hunters, recruited from the leftovers of the Hudson's Bay Company and North West Company in Montreal, Detroit, and Michilimackinac, had arrived only a week before with the intention of picking up more recruits in St. Louis for their journey across the continent to the mouth of the Columbia.[14] There, according to the plan envisioned by Astor, they would meet a party sent by boat from New York, set up a post to prosecute the fur trade of the area, and deal directly with the vast fur markets in the Far East. Although the purpose of Hunt's expedition was clearly beyond the scope of the area encompassed by the Missouri Fur Company, there was apprehension that Astor might be planning to include the upper Missouri in his scheme. The basis for this fear was the presence of Ramsay Crooks and Robert McClellan in the new company as partners. These men were thoroughly familiar with the Missouri and its trade, and had old scores to settle with Lisa and the Missouri Fur Company.

Hunt, afraid of the opposition he might encounter in St. Louis, and desirous of having his men experience a winter in the wilder-

---

[13] *Ibid.*

[14] Kenneth W. Porter, *John Jacob Astor, Business Man*, I, 184; Washington Irving, *Astoria, or Anecdotes of an Enterprise beyond the Rocky Mountains*, I, 140.

ness before finally committing themselves to the venture, left St. Louis on October 21.[15] Making the mouth of the Nadowa, near present-day St. Joseph, Missouri, before the river iced over, Hunt's men, in company with the Oto nation, spent the season inuring themselves to the hardships of the coming voyage. Hunt returned to St. Louis in January to recruit more men, and to out- fit himself for the long journey.[16] In this he was opposed, of course, by the agents of the Missouri Fur Company, who were themselves trying to recruit a crew and get together an outfit. Hunt's presence only served to increase costs, in terms of both the higher wages which had to be offered to experienced men and the higher prices which the merchants demanded for goods.

While Hunt was organizing his men in St. Louis and the mouth of the Nadowa, Lisa addressed himself to a task which had long needed doing. As the head of a group of St. Louis mer- chants and traders, Manuel drew up a petition to be presented to the Territorial Legislature, asking for a revision of the statutes concerning boatmen, calling them inadequate, and pointing out the many abuses which existed, particularly with reference to the fur trade.[17] The legislature concurred, and with unusual alacrity passed, on October 30, 1810, a new act concerning boat- men.[18] Although far from being the ideal sought by the mer- chants, the law did set up a registry for contracts, and allowed either party to a contract to sue for his rights. Deserters were to be jailed, and a stiff fine was to be the penalty for harboring a runaway. Unfortunately for the employers, any boatman jailed had to be supported there at the expense of his prosecutor until the trial was completed, or be freed, since the jails were still too

[15] Porter, *Astor*, I, 184; Irving, *Astoria*, I, 144.

[16] Irving, *Astoria*, I, 147; Chittenden, *American Fur Trade*, I, 183.

[17] Journal of the Territory of Louisiana, entry, Oct. 25, 1810, MSS, Mercantile Library, St. Louis, Missouri.

[18] *Laws of the Territory of Louisiana: Passed by the Governor and Judges Assembled in Legislature, in the Month of October, 1810.*

crowded for comfort.[19] However, it was a beginning, and the merchants were grateful for that.

In November, Lisa became embroiled in an acrimonious debate, in the form of letters published in the *Missouri Gazette*, with William Morrison over some beaver skins purchased from the company for which Morrison had not paid the stipulated price.[20] This was the first public notice of the bad feeling which existed between the two men, and culminated in Morrison's refusal to take part in the reorganization of the company in 1812, and later appeared in the courts in a number of suits and countersuits. The Pacific Fur Company, particularly Crooks and McClellan, must have taken great delight at this falling out among the partners.

Being a newcomer to St. Louis, Hunt, as he scoured the town for crewmen and an outfit, was unaware of the changes which were taking place in the budding metropolis, making it a better place in which to live.[21] Although still plagued by many Indians, who, when drunk, liked nothing better than to burn down the nearest barn, the city was making progress upward from her earlier primitive state. An ordinance was passed authorizing the formation of fire companies to protect the residents against that worst of all frontier scourges. Speed limits were passed on the driving of horses and carts, with a fine of five dollars to be levied for infractions. Other pieces of legislation were adopted providing for such sophisticated measures as the removal of dead animals from the streets, and even the building of privies adjacent to public thoroughfares was forbidden. Culture and education began to become more prominent, with many private schools being opened, including Mrs. Bourne's School for Young Ladies, and meetings were held to determine the feasibility of a public

[19] *Ibid.*

[20] *Missouri Gazette* (Nov. 14 and 21, 1810).

[21] These and other evidences of a growing and maturing St. Louis are contained in the weekly editions of the *Missouri Gazette* for this period.

library. There were, according to the census of 1810, 5,667 souls in St. Louis and its environs, who were catered to by a dozen mercantile establishments, an equal number of distilleries, nine water mills, six sawmills, fifteen horse mills, two shot towers, and many other evidences of a thriving community.[22] Imports to St. Louis were said to amount to $250,000 per year.[23] This was a prospering city and the fur trade had done much to make it so.

Spring came early in 1811, and Hunt, who had been successful in finding both men and equipment, left for the Nadowa with his party on March 12.[24] Lisa, behind in his preparations, and fearful of the growing hostility of the Sioux, actuated by British intrigue which increased in direct proportion to the deterioration of relations between Washington and London, made an attempt to delay Hunt long enough to allow the two parties, neither of which was particularly large, to ascend the river together for protection. Using the same method he had utilized against Pike, Manuel caused a warrant to be issued against Pierre Dorion, a half-blood former employee of the Missouri Fur Company, who had signed on as Hunt's interpreter.[25] Like many another individual in St. Louis who had found life in the wilderness too much after one attempt, Dorion owed a debt to the company for a considerable quantity of alcohol at Fort Mandan, for which he had been charged mountain prices. Incensed at what he considered extortionate rates, including the price of ten dollars per quart for the liquor,[26] Dorion refused to pay.

[22] *Missouri Gazette* (Jan. 16, 1811).

[23] Brackenridge, *Views of Louisiana*, 123.

[24] Chittenden, *American Fur Trade*, I, 184; *Missouri Gazette* (Mar. 14, 1810) gives the date of Hunt's departure as March 11.

[25] Irving, *Astoria*, I, 152.

[26] Bradbury, *Travels*, 103. Dorion was probably exercising the frontiersman's prerogative of exaggeration, for Thomas James, who certainly harbored no love for either Lisa or the Missouri Fur Company, also complained of the exorbitant charges at Fort Mandan, but the price he named was twelve dollars per gallon. Thomas James, *Three Years*, 42.

Lisa was frustrated in this move by John Bradbury and Thomas Nuttall, two English naturalists who were going to accompany Hunt and his expedition as far as the vicinity of the Mandan villages. These two had remained behind their party in St. Louis to await a final mail delivery, and had heard that the sheriff planned to apprehend Dorion at St. Charles. Hurrying overland that night, the naturalists turned counterspies overtook Hunt and warned him of the coming arrest. In company with his Indian woman, the resourceful interpreter took to the woods to bypass the town. Hunt was fearful that Dorion, who already had been advanced two-thirds of a year's salary, would not reappear, but the day after departing from St. Charles and the thwarted sheriff, he was sighted waiting along the riverbank, and a boat stopped to pick him up.[27]

The Missouri Fur Company, meanwhile, held, on March 25, a final meeting prior to Lisa's departure.[28] There the main, if not the only, contributors of supplies to the voyage were noted: Manuel Lisa, $2,322.13¾; William Clark, $1,405.51½; Pierre Menard, $548.00. For his services as company representative at the Mandan villages, where it was agreed he would wait for Henry, Lisa was to receive a stipend of $1,000.00. There was also a further modification of the original Articles of Agreement: the fourteenth and twenty-first articles were strengthened to require all partners in possession of goods belonging to the company to deliver them to William Clark immediately upon their arrival in St. Louis.[29] This was done to prevent another internal dispute such as the one in which Lisa and Morrison had been involved.

The boat which Lisa had procured was a small, well-built keelboat of twenty tons' burden, armed with a swivel and two

[27] Bradbury, *Travels*, 11.
[28] St. Louis Missouri Fur Company Ledger Book, 1809–12, MHS.
[29] *Ibid.*

brass blunderbusses. It also was provided with an ingeniously constructed false cabin designed to hide the limited stock of trade goods, thus keeping temptation away from the prying eyes of any Sioux they might happen to meet.[30] The stipulated twenty-one, several of whom already had been up the Missouri with Lisa, had been engaged as a crew, and the boat, in addition, carried Baptiste Charbonneau, hired as an interpreter, and his wife Sacajawea, the lovely Bird Woman of the Lewis and Clark expedition.[31] Also aboard was Henry Brackenridge, an American traveler who was persuaded by Lisa to embark on the great adventure as a hunter. On the twenty-seventh, Lisa agreed to accept on his own account $313.80 worth of tobacco, and $713.12½ worth of powder from the company, provided it was delivered on or before the thirtieth.[32] This further indicated that despite the qualms of the rest of the company, Lisa was willing to risk his own capital and credit on the expedition to rescue Andrew Henry, and was determined not to neglect the trade of the Missouri entirely in the process. He knew that if the St. Louis traders ignored the Indians of the Missouri at this time, the British would have no difficulty securing their allegiance, and the Missouri would be closed to trade.

The boat set out from St. Charles on April 2,[33] with the intention of moving as rapidly as possible to catch Hunt's four boats and travel in their company through the territory of the Sioux. Lisa was also afraid that Hunt, moved by the entreaties of Crooks and McClellan, might incite the Sioux to attack the tiny contingent of the Missouri Fur Company, as they had claimed Lisa had done to them two years before. A halt had to be called a few miles upstream so that Lisa could perform the

---

[30] Brackenridge, *Views of Louisiana*, 200.
[31] *Ibid.*, 202.
[32] St. Louis Missouri Fur Company Ledger Book, 1809–12, MHS.
[33] Brackenridge, *Views of Louisiana*, 200.

ritual of returning to St. Charles to bring along some of the men who still remained, reluctant to part from their friends, liquid and otherwise. After that, the boat moved along at a rapid pace, the men waking at dawn and working until after dark. Lisa unerringly picked the quietest waters and the proper channels around islands, and by April 11 they had passed the mouth of the Osage, and had gained two days on Hunt.[34]

Despite the desire for all haste, Lisa found time to spend "an hour to relieve a poor ox, which was swamped near the bank. The poor creature had remained there ten or twelve days, and the sand into which he had sunk, was become hard and solid. The wolves had paid him friendly visits from time to time, to inquire after his health, while buzzards, crows, and eagles, tendered their salutations from the boughs of the neighboring trees." This act of selfless kindness apparently pleased the wind gods, for the next day they were able to use the sail and made twenty-eight miles.[35] Fort Osage was passed on April 25, and the crew was heartened to learn that they had gained nearly one hundred miles on Hunt and his expedition. The passing of this last outpost of civilization caused all the men to reflect on their condition, but Lisa, by striking up song after cheering song, did not let them think of homes and families, but rather kept them working with extra vigor.[36]

Thus far the men had borne their Olympian labors without a murmur, strengthened, no doubt, by their fare, consisting of "lied corn hominy for breakfast, a slice of fat pork and biscuit for dinner, and a pot of mush with a pound of tallow in it for supper."[37] This was far better than the ordinary boatman's diet, for Lisa realized the effort that would be necessary on the part of all hands. By May 4, however, the unremitting labor had

[34] *Ibid.*, 216.
[35] *Ibid.*, 210.
[36] *Ibid.*, 219.
[37] *Ibid.*, 202.

taken its toll and there was open talk of discontent, which Brackenridge took upon himself to discourage.[38] On the seventh the
crew pulled ashore to make a new mast from a sturdy white oak,
the old one having been snapped by a low-hanging tree branch,
and Manuel worked the crew late by torchlight to get it completed and stepped.[39] On May 10 the mouth of the Platte was
put behind, and the veteran boatmen indulged themselves in
shaving the heads of the greenhorns unless they could provide
a "treat" in honor of passing the boundary of civilization.[40] Making excellent time, the party, on the eighteenth, was able to espy
the ragged banner atop Blackbird Hill. This landmark was
named for a powerful chief of the Omahas, who, during his lifetime, was venerated as almost a god for his seemingly magical
powers over the lives of his rivals. An unscrupulous trader had
given the chief a supply of arsenic, and had instructed him in its
use, thus literally providing him with the power of life and death,
a power which he used to great advantage. Caught in the smallpox epidemic of 1802, which had decimated his tribe, Blackbird
had been buried in the top of the hill astride his favorite horse,
so that in death he might view his friends, the traders, coming
up the Missouri.[41]

The following day the party reached the Omaha village,
where they discovered that Hunt was only four days ahead. Lisa
sent Charbonneau forward with an Indian guide, to ask Hunt to
wait for them, and exhorted his men ahead with all possible
speed.[42] On May 23 they encountered F. M. Benoît, then company factor at the Mandan villages, making his way downstream
in a small boat loaded with peltry.[43] From him Lisa learned that
all of the Missouri Indians, with the exception of the Arikaras

[38] *Ibid.*, 223.
[39] *Ibid.*, 224.
[40] *Ibid.*, 226.
[41] *Ibid.*, 229.
[42] *Ibid.*, 230.
[43] *Ibid.*, 233.

and Mandans, were antagonistic to the Americans. The Sioux had become openly hostile, and had killed a number of hunters in the vicinity of Fort Mandan. He also informed Lisa that Henry was in great distress over the mountains, but was expected to appear at Fort Mandan sometime during the summer. On the twenty-sixth Charbonneau returned with the message that Hunt had promised to wait for them at the Ponca village. Arriving at that place on May 27, the crew was informed by the natives that Hunt, no doubt fearing that Lisa was trying to pass him in order to turn the Indians against the Astorians, had left in great haste three days before.[44]

Lisa redoubled his efforts, knowing that Hunt was now moving at top speed, and began to travel late at night, guided only by the stars, the moon, the shadows on the bank, and his own knowledge of the river. Aided by a favorable wind, the keelboat, at one stretch, made seventy-five miles in a little over twenty-four hours. On June 1 it suddenly looked as if their massive effort had gone for naught as they were stopped by a small party of Sioux flying the American flag. Lisa and Brackenridge went ashore to parley with them, fearing all the while that the main body of Indians would appear over the high bank at any moment. Manuel made it understood that he was traveling to the rescue of his men far upstream, that he would be the trader to the Sioux, and would return in three months to satisfy their desires by building a post for the purpose of trading with them at Cedar Island.[45] These words, and a handsome present, placated the savages, and the boat was allowed to pass. By eleven o'clock the next morning Hunt had been overtaken, and the little flotilla of five boats sailed on together.

The first meeting of the rivals was peaceful, a remarkable occurrence in view of the reiterated threat of Robert McClellan to shoot Lisa on sight if he ever encountered him in Indian coun-

[44] *Ibid.*, 234.
[45] *Ibid.*, 237.

try. McClellan was fond of making such declarations, voicing a similar one at Edward Rose on one occasion, but both sides apparently recognized that this was sheer bravado and not to be taken seriously. Lisa learned that Hunt had met the main group of Sioux, who had been deterred from attacking the Astorians only by the timely appearance of a war party of three hundred Rees, who had come down to escort the traders to their village. Lisa had apparently missed this group, passing them sometime during the night shortly before joining Hunt. Amicable relations did not continue for long, for Lisa once again became involved with Dorion, this time trying to lure him away from his employers. The incident ballooned completely out of proportion as all of the latent suspicions on both sides were given vent, and it soon became apparent that a duel between the leaders would have to be fought to settle the differences in the wilderness tradition. Bloodshed was prevented only through the good offices of Brackenridge and Bradbury, who interceded and somewhat pacified the combatants.[46] All intercourse between the two groups was severed, however, and there was no contact of any kind for a week; Lisa even traveled the opposite side of the river. By June 11, and the impending arrival at the Arikara villages, some conversation had to take place, so Lisa sent Brackenridge as an emissary to Hunt to arrange the landing. The next day the parties arrived together, and the leaders were immediately to attend a council in the lodge of the principal chief.

Lisa was the first of the whites to speak, and was nervously eyed by Hunt, Crooks, and McClellan as he did so. Far from evincing hostile intent, Manuel told the Rees that the Astorians were his friends, and that any injury done to them he would consider as done to him.[47] With this speech, the men of the Pacific Fur Company relaxed to an extent and informed Manuel that they planned, on the advice of three of Lisa's former em-

[46] *Ibid.*, 241; Bradbury, Travels, 103.
[47] Brackenridge, *Views of Louisiana*, 246; Bradbury, *Travels*, 113.

113

ployees, Edward Robinson, John Hoback, and Jacob Reznor, whom they had picked up on the Missouri and had hired as guides,[48] to strike overland straight west from the Arikara village in order to keep well south of the dangerous Blackfeet. With this in mind, Hunt concluded an agreement with Lisa in which the latter was to purchase Hunt's boats and some of his equipment, part payment of which was to be made in vitally needed horses.[49]

Lisa sent a land party to Fort Mandan[50] to get the horses, and he continued his voyage by water on the nineteenth, leaving one of the men to continue the trade with the Rees. Pessimistic about Hunt's prospects for making the mouth of the Columbia, Lisa never expected to see that group of individuals again. When the boat reached the Mandan villages, the first visitor aboard was old Shahaka, who grumbled his disappointment at having to return to the primitive Indian life after having tasted civilization in Red Head's Town. Most discouraging to him was the fact that no one believed him when he related the wonders he had seen. Reuben Lewis was also there with the welcome report that Andrew Henry was on his way to the Mandans with a rich catch.[51] At the end of July, Lisa dispatched two boats downriver with Brackenridge in charge, twelve men as crew, and Bradbury, anxious to return to civilization to present his findings to the world, as passenger. Much to Bradbury's dismay, for he had hoped to gather more specimens on his way down, these men traveled as fast as possible, in order to protect the valuable cargo of furs they carried, and made St. Louis in fourteen days.[52]

[48] Bradbury, *Travels*, 77.

[49] *Ibid.*, 121; Brackenbridge, *Views of Louisiana*, 264.

[50] This is not, apparently, the Fort Mandan built in 1809 above the Gros Ventre, but another stockade called by the same name at the Mandan villages.

[51] Bradbury, *Travels*, 143.

[52] *Ibid.*, 174; Brackenridge, *Views of Louisiana*, 264.

BLACKFEET INDIANS ON HORSEBACK

INTERIOR OF A MANDAN CHIEF'S HUT

The furs and good news of the Henry party brought down by Brackenridge was heartening to the partners in St. Louis, especially since the beaver market had turned sharply upward, and Joseph Hertzog, a Philadelphia merchant, was writing to his partner in St. Louis, Christian Wilt, "Beaver my boy send me till your back breaks."[53]

Sometime that summer Jean Baptiste Champlain and his party of twenty-three hunters returned to Fort Mandan from their expedition to the Arapaho nation on the headwaters of the Platte. Champlain advised that the "Spaniards of Mexico" sent a party each year to trade with the Arapahoes. Exciting information, and on this basis Lisa determined to make a direct contact with his former countrymen from the upper Missouri by equipping Champlain with some goods suitable for the Spanish trade, hoping that he would meet someone from Santa Fe upon returning to the Platte. If such a connection could be established, perhaps the Missouri Fur Company would be able to succeed even in the event war between Great Britain and the United States became a reality, and perhaps they could put trade between St. Louis and Santa Fe on a permanent basis.[54]

A gaunt and skin-dressed Andrew Henry appeared at the Mandan villages sometime in September, presented Lisa with a number of packs of beaver, and related an appalling tale of adventure in the mountains. His group had been given a violent send-off from the Three Forks when a party of two hundred Blackfeet fell upon nineteen hunters. In the battle which ensued twenty-two Indians had been killed, while the trappers lost only one man before retreating to the confines of the fort.[55] In their

[53] Letter, Joseph Hertzog to Christian Wilt, July 18, 1811, Letters from Joseph Hertzog, 1811–15, MHS.

[54] Herbert E. Bolton, "New Light on Manuel Lisa and the Spanish Fur Trade," *Southwest Historical Quarterly*, XVII (July, 1913), 61–66.

[55] Letter, Henry M. Brackenridge to Joseph Charless, printed in *Missouri Gazette* (Aug. 8, 1811).

journey across the mountains, the most accomplished horse thieves in the West, the Crows, stripped them of their mounts, which were not only valuable as pack animals but could be used for food in times of necessity, many trappers averring a preference for horse meat rather than beef.[56] The group wintered on what has since been called "Henry's Fork" of the Snake River, a beautiful country, well stocked with beaver, but had the misfortune to be involved in a most severe winter, with deep snows and bitter cold keeping game from the area, ultimately forcing the men to subsist a large part of the time on roots, and to dress themselves, Indian style, in the skins of animals.[57] The spring had also been poor, with heavy rains swelling the streams and making trapping difficult. Still, in all, it had been a profitable hunt.

The partners returned downstream in the fall of 1811, stopping to rebuild the trading post at Cedar Island, which had burned out in the spring of 1810, and supplied it for trade,[58] thus redeeming Lisa's promise made to the Sioux during the summer. Manuel was worried about the possibility of an alliance between the Sioux and the British through the agency of Tecumseh and the Prophet, who were organizing the Indians east of the Mississippi, and whose emissaries were appearing along the Missouri, and he was taking great pains to please the Sioux in every way. He was an acute observer of the Indian attitude, and reported to Clark that not only were the Missouri Indians, with few exceptions, hostile to the Americans, but wampum was being carried with British influence all along the banks of the river.[59] Still, the *Missouri Gazette*, in reporting Lisa's return, was moved to comment "that the company has been placed on a better foot-

---

[56] *Ibid.*

[57] *Missouri Gazette* (Oct. 26, 1811).

[58] *Ibid.*

[59] Letter, Manuel Lisa to William Clark, July 1, 1817, printed in *Missouri Gazette* (July 5, 1817).

ing than it was generally supposed it could be; and that there exists the most flattering prospect for future success."[60]

To insure that success, however, it was obvious to the partners that some reorganization was necessary in order to have more efficient operation, and Charles Gratiot was given the job of working out a new and satisfactory partnership with expanded capital.[61] The final meeting of the St. Louis Missouri Fur Company took place on January 23, 1812.[62] Present for the last rites were Lisa, Pierre Chouteau, Clark, Lewis, Pierre Chouteau, Jr., for Menard, Walter Wilkinson for Benjamin Wilkinson and Andrew Henry, Charles Gratiot for Sylvestre Labbadie, and M. P. LeDuc for Auguste Chouteau, Jr. The partners simply decided to let the company expire on March 7, while the members went on to more and, it was hoped, better things. Pierre Chouteau and Manuel Lisa were commissioned to sell off the assets of the company then held by Clark, and Pierre Menard was to assist Lisa and Chouteau in apportioning the proceeds among the several members.

Gratiot, realizing the crying need for capital, proposed, in expanding the worth of the company, to bring John Jacob Astor into the picture by offering him five shares of the new organization, making him a full partner in a nine-man partnership.[63] The members, jealous of their own positions, and fearful that once in the business, Astor would soon dominate, were cold to the proposal, and there is no indication that Astor made any move to change their minds. On January 24 the members of the former company signed a new body of articles creating the president and directors of the Missouri Fur Company.[64] The new arrange-

---

[60] *Missouri Gazette* (Oct. 26, 1811).

[61] Letter, Charles Gratiot to John Jacob Astor, Dec. 14, 1811, Charles Gratiot Letterbook, Mar. 6, 1798, to Jan. 6, 1816, Charles Gratiot Collection, MHS.

[62] St. Louis Missouri Fur Company Ledger Book, 1809–12, MHS.

[63] Letter, Gratiot to Astor, Dec. 14, 1811.

[64] Missouri Fur Company Ledger Book, 1812–14, Kansas State Historical Society. The agreement is also printed in the *Missouri Gazette* (Feb. 2, 1812).

ment, instead of the old copartnership, was instead a limited partnership, with a board of directors of three men who would be entrusted with the operation of the enterprise. The organization was to have a capital stock of not more than $50,000, $23,000 of which was to be subscribed by a public sale of shares, while the rest was formed by "the funds of the former St. Louis Missouri Fur Company, which is now up the Missouri, calculated at twenty nine thousand nine hundred and eighty five dollars, in goods wares and merchandize, and debts due by hunters who are now out."[65] The upper limit was apparently placed to prevent any outsider from buying up a controlling share, although this was a needless precaution. The public shares were priced at $1,000 per share, and the first directors appointed, William Clark, again elected president, Lisa and Labbadie, were commissioned to oversee the sales. There was to be a stockholders' meeting on the first Monday of December, annually, at which time the business of the company would be reviewed, the outfit for the following year decided upon, and, hopefully, the dividends from profits to be declared. At this time, two-thirds of "the whole of those entitled to vote" could initiate a change in the Articles of Agreement. Each of the signing members was to receive three shares of stock for his portion of the goods and equipment of the old company which were taken into the new, so Lisa, Menard, and Morrison were still being carried by their investment in that first enterprise.

The president of the board of directors was to be the general transactor of business for the company in St. Louis, for which he was to be allowed six hundred dollars per year for clerks, storage, and so forth. One other member of the directory was to ascend the river to the highest post below the Falls of the Missouri, there to undertake the company's business, for which he would receive an annual salary of one thousand dollars. A regu-

[65] *Ibid.*

lar system of books was to be kept, and they were to be open to inspection by any and all of the stockholders. The association was to continue in effect until the first Monday in December, 1818, with the provision that two-thirds of the stockholders could dissolve the group at any previous time by calling a general meeting for the purpose, and publishing notice of such meeting for six weeks previous in the *Gazette* or other Louisiana newspaper.

The distrust so evident in the old company remained to plague the new. Again the stockholders were enjoined against trading for their personal interest in the territory encompassed by the organization, this time under penalty of ten thousand dollars. Once more profits were to be divided yearly, and while there was to be a prior arrangement for the subsequent year's outfit, no provision was made for any losses that might be sustained, and there was no fund available to meet temporary emergencies with which they might have to cope. A new precaution was instituted when each director, before assuming his duties, "shall if required, give a bond with two securities to the satisfaction of the stockholders assembled, in such sums as by them may their bye laws order & direct, not exceeding double the amount of compensation allowed them, with a condition for the faithful performance of their duties."[66] Such provisions made the articles sound as if the men making them up had never met each other, or perhaps it was that they knew each other too well.

The articles were published, by agreement, in the *Missouri Gazette* of February 2, and several succeeding issues. On the same day the commissioners of the new company advertised the public sale of stock, and Lisa and Chouteau inserted the notice of a public auction of the remaining assets of the old company, consisting of "Boats, Rifles, Guns, Howitzers, and sundry other articles, also 130 arpents of land near Portage des Sieoux."[67] At a meeting of the board on January 27, where it was decided

[66] *Ibid.*   [67] *Missouri Gazette* (Feb. 2, 1812).

119

to advertise publicly the sale of stock, the following resolution was passed:

> *Resolved* that it is expedient that necessary articles be purchased Soutable for the Hunters and for the Indian Trade up the Missouri, and that in the purchase of said articles, those mentioned in a list furnished by Mr. Manuel Lisa be procured if possible.[68]

This was a tribute to Lisa's sagacity as a trader, an art which required creativity, good luck, and meticulous attention to detail. The successful trader—and Lisa was certainly the most outstanding example—had to have a thorough knowledge of each tribe with which he dealt, for each had differing needs and desires. One tribe would take a three-point blanket of solid red, while another wanted the same blanket with a blue stripe, and still a third might want only blue two-and-one-half-point blankets. The same was true of beads, although blue ones were universally in demand, knives, mirrors, and even tomahawks, with tribes designating various sizes and weights, some even specifying hammer heads or spikes opposite the blade. This meant that a man planning to trade with very many tribes had to carry a fantastic variety of goods. Not only that, but the trader had to know approximately how much of each article to have on hand for each tribe so as not to be overstocked and have to return with unsalable goods, and yet have enough not to run out and lose a whole trade for the want of one article. As a last resort, the trader had to be an excellent salesman, able to convince the natives that the goods he carried they either wanted or needed.

Even if the trader had a perfect outfit, he still had to be a diplomat with the acumen of a seer and the patience of Job. The proper presents to the correct chiefs in a certain sequence were requisite before the opening of any trade, and the merchant had to be careful not to insult or ignore even the least of the chiefs

[68] Missouri Fur Company Ledger Book, 1812–14, Kansas State Historical Society.

lest his traffic be ruined before it was fairly started. Price was another possible bone of contention between the trader and his potential customers, and the knowledgeable individual usually let the chiefs in council decide what should be a fair exchange price for any article and then try to bargain if he thought the price out of line. Since the Indians were no judges of the actual worth of the trade goods, the merchant had little to worry about on this score. Especially, the trader had to have a firm control over his liquor supply, to ration it out in quantities designed to keep the Indians, who always demanded it, placated, but never in quantities large enough to allow them to get drunk, for there was no greater problem for the trader to cope with than inebriated Indians in and around his post. They were unpredictable, violent, and malicious, inclined to destroy rather than increase trade.

Lisa had had, of course, long experience with the tribes of the Missouri, and had dealt fairly with them. They came to know that he always brought good presents, had quality goods, and dealt plainly with everyone. Fearless, strong, and a man who kept his word, Lisa's reputation among the various tribes saved his expeditions from disaster on more than one occasion. It was not by accident that Manuel was chosen to lead every expedition of the company up the Missouri, and was also given the duty of selecting and purchasing the next year's outfit during the winter. An indefatigable worker, Manuel merited the confidence of large numbers of his men, and, although there were always members of his various crews who feared and distrusted him, he always got them to their destination in safety. Those who appreciated that fact came back to serve him again and again, until the names of his crewmen begin to become familiar on his later rosters, and many of those men advanced in importance, becoming steersmen, clerks, and even factors.

It was one thing to be able to select the proper outfit for their projected voyage but quite another to be able to purchase it, as the directors of the Missouri Fur Company soon found. At a directors' meeting on February 8 they recorded the alarming fact that no merchandise could be purchased on the credit of the company.[69] Despite the fact that the old firm had met all of its obligations, and had made a modest profit, St. Louis merchants were unwilling to extend credit. With the threat of war with Great Britain becoming more ominous by the day, these prudent businessmen did not wish to extend themselves very far into the future. If war was declared, the frontier would be in flames immediately, for the Indians, incited by British agents within the boundaries of the United States, would go on the warpath against the Americans. Not only would the trading groups on the upper Missouri be cut off and probably destroyed, but St. Louis itself would be threatened.

Lisa, confident of his own ability to control the natives of the Missouri, was not unduly alarmed at the company's prospects, and Clark, as Indian agent, knew that the presence of an American trading company in the area would be the best insurance against an Indian uprising. But this was not good enough for the general public, and the directors were forced to resolve:

> ... that it is expedient that three thousand six hundred Dollars cash, and Five thousand Dollars Credit, is necessary to be given by the members of this company to complete the necessary outfit, and that the president be authorized to call upon each individual member of the company, for Four hundred dollars Cash, and a credit of Six hundred dollars by there [sic] notes payable in August next.[70]

This was an extremely short note, and the directors must have been confident that the present collection of furs in company posts was enough to cover it. The adoption of this expedient also indicated that the shares of stock offered for public consumption were not being taken up, and in truth they never were. The price

[69] Ibid.
[70] Ibid.

of one thousand dollars per share limited drastically the number of people able to buy, and those wealthy enough to make such a purchase either were already members or were unwilling to invest in so uncertain and dangerous an enterprise.

The response of the company to the appeal of the directors was completely negative, and, to save the company's operations, "Clark and Lisa each put up their notes for over ten thousand dollars and Labbadie for about one thousand."[71] But notes were simply that, and Lisa, desperate for cash, mortgaged three thousand acres of the old grant, originally given to his brother Joaquin and later transferred to himself, to Antoine and Pierre Carraby, New Orleans merchants, for $3,000.00.[72] With these funds the company was enabled to purchase supplies and equipment for the projected voyage. Materials were gathered from many sources, with no very large purchases made from any one firm. Among the largest single procurements was one for $1,269.52 from Christian Wilt,[73] who had become a merchant of great prominence in the few years he had been associated with St. Louis. William Morrison also extended to the company merchandise amounting to $583.56 on the six months' note of Manuel Lisa and William Clark.[74]

On top of these difficulties, the company had to meet competition for the purchase of an outfit in the persons of Robert McKnight and James Baird, who were organizing a group to essay a journey to Santa Fe in the hopes of starting trade in that direction. They did not find a hospitable welcome in St. Louis when the purpose of their mission became known, and they wrote to one of their financial backers, Michael McDonough, "We dis-

[71] Douglas, "Manuel Lisa," *loc. cit.*, 369. Douglas gives no source for this statement.

[72] St. Louis Records, Book C, 561, Office of the Recorder of Deeds, City Hall, St. Louis, Missouri.

[73] St. Louis Missouri Fur Company Ledger Book, 1809–12, MHS.

[74] Statement, William Morrison to Pierre Menard, May 18, 1812, Menard Family Papers, Illinois State Historical Society.

cover at this Early Period a jealousy arising in this place respecting the trade to that country."[75] So little did they know of the Santa Fe trade that they called this an "Early Period." One of those most unhappy over this turn of events was, of course, Manuel Lisa, who had long harbored ambitions in the same direction, and had even made attempts to open the Santa Fe trade himself. However, he was now heading north and would have to put off his southwestern aspirations for another season.

On April 15 the company hired one of the stockholders, Reuben Lewis, as a clerk, with a salary of $525 per annum, plus $75 worth of merchandise, thus insuring the presence of two stockholders on the voyage.[76] James O'Fallon, William Clark's nephew from Louisville, joined the Missouri Fur Company for this voyage, beginning a career which would leave its mark on the history of the Missouri Valley, and raise O'Fallon to a position of affluence in the process.[77] In all, it was one of the best and most experienced crews ever to ascend the river. This was well, for the possibilities of trouble were quite apparent.

With all the problems of financial organization, preparing an expedition, and the ever-present fear of Indian hostility in the upper country, the partners in the company could still indulge themselves in a little cautious optimism. There remained a large number of hunters spread all over the Western country, any group of which was capable of bringing in a fortune in furs. Posts were operating at Cedar Island, with the Sioux, at the Arikara villages, the Mandan towns, and Fort Mandan, above the Gros Ventre. It was expected that Lisa would send down the proceeds from these places and put the company on a sound basis almost immediately. These proceeds would pay for the first out-

[75] May 21, 1812, Santa Fe Papers, MHS. This is a typed copy of an original in the possession of Mr. Everett Graff, Winnetka, Illinois.

[76] St. Louis Missouri Fur Company Ledger Book, 1809–12, MHS.

[77] Letter, Dennis Fitzhugh to James O'Fallon, Mar. 21, 1812, O'Fallon Papers, MHS.

fit and perhaps allow the company to operate on a cash basis in the future. New parties of hunters would be dispatched to the West, and, barring extensive interference from the Blackfeet, would make a profitable hunt to add to the receipts expected from the trading portion of the voyage. Such was the situation as Manuel Lisa prepared to embark on his fourth major ascension of the Missouri.

V

The Missouri Fur Company
Demise

THE expedition which left St. Louis in early May, 1812, was a small one, carrying only $11,000 worth of merchandise in two boats.[1] The partners, justifiably, did not want to risk more, the threat of war with the British being so imminent. John C. Luttig, the clerk and chronicler of the voyage, joined the crew at Bellefontaine on May 8, and Lisa came on board the following day to lead his men once again in the unremitting battle against the mighty Missouri.[2]

Things changed little in that struggle from year to year, for while a man, by long experience, might come to know the basic outlines of the stream-bed and understand its general movements, the unexpected was always present and dangerous. About the only permanent lesson taught by the river was respect. Jean Baptiste Mayette, an *engagé* of 1807, who, by this voyage, had risen to the position of patroon or steersman of the largest of the two boats, was knocked overboard by "a Log shamming against the rudder."[3] The river was denied a conquest as Mayette was

<hr>

[1] Letter, Charles Gratiot to John Jacob Astor, Apr. 25, 1812, Charles Gratiot Letterbook, Mar. 6, 1798, to Jan. 6, 1816, Charles Gratiot Collection, MHS.

[2] John C. Luttig, *Journal of a Fur Trading Expedition on the Upper Missouri*, ed. by Stella M. Drumm, 28.

[3] *Ibid.*, 29.

fished from the muddy torrent, but not so fortunate was Baptiste Latoulipe, another old hand, who was swept over the side on June 26 and was not seen again.[4] Manuel's own Negro boy Charlo, accompanying his master up the river for the first time, perhaps hoping to emulate his illustrious predecessor York, of the Lewis and Clark expedition, was claimed by the Missouri as he fell from a steep bank into the murky water, unperceived by the men, and drowned.[5] So the river continued to take a toll of the brave men who dared to breast its current.

On June 3, after a fairly rapid passage, unencumbered by any major difficulties, the party reached Fort Osage, where two hunters, Caleb Greenwood[6] and Daniel Laurison, were picked up.[7] This indicated that again Lisa was planning to have the trading portion of the voyage keep the river natives friendly, while experienced hunters brought in the real profits from trapping excursions into the mountains. Moving north the next day, they met several pirogues piloted by members of the company coming down from winter quarters, and, presumably, bringing furs.[8] One of these men, Louis Bijou, a trader of some talent, was taken aboard to return to the wilderness, Lisa planning to make him a key figure in this year's operations. Late the same day Michael Immel caught up to the boats and rejoined the crew. This promising young member of the company, already a veteran woodsman, had backtracked to Fort Osage to retrieve his dog, which had inadvertently been left behind. He brought Manuel the disquieting news that the McKnight party, which had been outfitting in St. Louis that spring, was on the road to Santa Fe.[9] This information probably stimulated Lisa to think

[4] *Ibid.*, 42–43.

[5] *Ibid.*, 59.

[6] Caleb Greenwood's biographer is inclined to believe his subject had been on a previous voyage with Lisa. See Charles Kelly, *Old Greenwood.*

[7] Luttig, *Journal,* 35.

[8] *Ibid.*, 34.

[9] *Ibid.*, 35.

about what action to take in that direction, depending, of course, on the success or failure of Champlain's initial attempt to open trade with the Spaniards. What had been a pure speculation on Lisa's part the previous year had now become a vital necessity if Lisa was to be the first into Santa Fe, for he could not, now, hope to catch the McKnight group. In any case, a more direct approach would seem to be called for in the face of earnest competition. The Missouri, at least for the moment, held all of his attention, however.

The Platte was passed on June 26, with the usual highjinks, the greenhorns being subject to all sorts of hazing procedures initiating them into the wilderness fraternity. On July 4 the heavens sent a salute to the day in the form of a tremendous thunderstorm, which caved in the bank under which they had camped for the night, and the resulting shift in the course of the river nearly drowned Lisa in his bedroll.[10] Recovering from this near disaster, the crew proceeded well until July 15, when they "met the Company boat coming from the Rees with peltries, Papin and 5 Men. Mr. Manuel Lisa thought proper to take her back again having not sufficient Loading to defray the expense."[11] Evidently the previous season's trading had been something less than satisfactory, at least with the Rees. If Papin's experience was typical, the company was in for difficulty, and Manuel wanted to make sure before sending in such discouraging information.

The twenty-first brought the expedition face to face with the Sioux. Obviously pleased with the arrangement Lisa had made with them the year before, giving them a specific post and a permanent trader, the Indians put on a great show of friendship and cordiality. Plans were made to erect a new post with the Sioux for trading purposes. The Indians stated that they had nothing to trade at that time but promised to have plenty in the fall. None-

[10] *Ibid.*, 46.
[11] *Ibid.*, 52.

theless, the post was completed and stocked with $4,087.98¾ worth of merchandise,[12] since Manuel wished to take no chances on losing the allegiance of those tribes. There was no better way to forestall British intrigue than having men and goods constantly on the scene. Louis Bijou was left in charge, with three hunters and two *engagés* to man the post.[13] The remaining crew, on August 7, arrived at the Arikara villages, and there met a strange reception. The natives, some twelve hundred of them in all, were in a state of great excitement. Lisa, alarmed, immediately "went to the Village, and held a Council with the Principal Chief, the 2 other Chiefs did not come to the Council and jealousy reigned among them, about 2 P.M. the Women and Children who were about our Boats were called away to the Village, and in a few Minutes the Coast was clear, this was not a friendly Signal, and we prepared for the worst."[14]

Nothing happened before the midday meal, and after a scanty, rapidly consumed repast, Manuel, with ten armed men, marched from the boat to the fort, at the same time sending for the chiefs to come and explain their conduct. The chiefs appeared, Lisa and his ten breathing a little easier at their presence, and outlined specific grievances. One of the chiefs had not received his presents while the others had, thus disrupting the normal course of business and insulting the neglected Indian, but, anticipating Lisa's displeasure over the meager returns of the past season, their more serious concern was that the Americans were planning to remove the merchandise from the Ree village to another post farther up the river. This had been Manuel's intention from the beginning, and the quantity of furs carried by Papin only strengthened his determination to make the move. After hearing the chiefs out, the daring trader reaffirmed his decision to

[12] Missouri Fur Company Ledger Book, April, 1812–July, 1813; 1817, Vol. XXXIII, William Clark MSS, Kansas State Historical Society.

[13] Luttig, *Journal*, 58–59.

[14] *Ibid.*, 66.

move despite their objections, and, after the slighted chief had received his presents, all agreed to have the new post built about twelve miles above the villages, near the mouth of Hunkpapa Creek.[15] Thus, "harmonie was restored, they traded some in the afternoon loaded the Peltries &c and prepared for Morning, set a Volunteer Guard, though guarded, the Indians would pilfer any thing they could lay their hands on."[16] This was proven when the expedition lost two cats to the thieves the next day. Luttig deplored this loss, maintaining that there was no more valuable asset to a trading post than a couple of cats, for they killed from four to ten mice per night, and did a good job of protecting the furs from those destructive rodents.

The new site was reached without incident the next day, the boats were unloaded, and construction of the new fort was commenced at once. While the work was getting under way, Lisa "resolved to go up with a party to the Bigbellies [Gros Ventres] to arrange Matters with them and bring down the Peltries, the Bigbellies having killed 2 hunters and stole 26 Company horses, as also detained the Trader they had with them."[17] Motivated here, no doubt, by concern for his men, furs, and merchandise, Manuel was also anxious to discover why the Gros Ventres, and their perennially friendly chief Le Bourgne had turned against the Americans. He took twenty-six men to accomplish the mission, and soon returned with some pelts and a few horses that he had acquired by trade. Le Bourgne had refused to give up the stolen horses and obviously had been influenced by the counsels of the British, which were more and more being heard in that neighborhood. Shortly thereafter, the outside walls of the new

---

[15] Ray H. Mattison, "Report on the Historical Aspects of the Oahe Reservoir Area, Missouri River, South and North Dakota," *South Dakota Historical Society Collections*, Vol. XXVII (1954), 159, gives the exact location as the East ½. SE¼, Section 1, T22N, R29E, just above the mouth of Hunkpapa Creek.

[16] Luttig, *Journal*, 67.

[17] *Ibid.*, 69.

FUR TRADERS IN A FLATBOAT
Attacked by Indians on the Missouri

MACKINAW OR CORDELLE BOAT
(Note the men on shore pulling the boat by means of a rope.)

post were completed and "the house fur trade was commenced made 36 packs of different Peltries and prepared the Boat which had to go to St. Louis."[18] This vessel, with a thirteen-man crew, left the fort on August 30,[19] and arrived in St. Louis on September 27.[20]

With that necessary bit of business out of the way, Lisa could begin to implement his plans for the coming year's hunt. No word had as yet been received from Champlain, and there was much concern manifested for the safety of him and his crew. In order to get news of this wanderer and to warn him, if possible, of the growing hostility on the part of the Indians, particularly the Gros Ventres, Manuel proposed to send Charles Sanguinet, one of his most trusted lieutenants and a man already familiar with the land of the Arapahoes, to that tribe. With him, in order to introduce formally Manuel Lisa and the Missouri Fur Company to the Spaniards, Lisa sent a letter proposing the opening of trade between the Missouri Fur Company and Santa Fe, explaining that he had been behind Champlain's attempt to do the same thing the past year. Since there had been no news of that individual, Lisa was now sending Sanguinet and two *engagés* to the same territory to reaffirm his trading intentions, and to tell Champlain that the company was setting up a post at the mouth of "the Petite Corne, which empties into the Rio Amarillo."[21] Further:

> I have especially instructed Don Carlos Sanguinet to arrange that this letter of mine should fall into the hands of some Spaniard who may be worthy to communicate with me on those honorable principles, and in no other manner, my desire being to engage in business and open up a new commerce, which might

[18] *Ibid.*, 74.

[19] *Ibid.*, 75.

[20] Letter, Charles Gratiot to John Jacob Astor, Sept. 27, 1812, Charles Gratiot Letterbook, Mar. 6, 1798, to Jan. 6, 1816, Charles Gratiot Collection, MHS.

[21] Bolton, "New Light on Manuel Lisa," *loc cit.*, 61–66.

easily be done. With this in view, and as director of the Missouri Fur Company, I propose to you gentlemen that if you wish to trade and deal with me, for whatever quantity of goods it may be, I will obligate myself to fill each year any bill of goods which shall be given me, and all shall be delivered (as stipulated) both as to quality and as to quantity, at the place nearest and most convenient for both parties, to your satisfaction, after we shall have agreed on the chosen place.

In case any of you should wish to come with Don Carlos Sanguinet to this my establishment to communicate and trade with me, you will be received and treated with great pleasure and satisfaction, and assured of sufficient escort, agreeable to you, up to the time you return to your country. I commend Don Carlos Sanguinet to you as a trustworthy and honorable man, and, if you are agreed, you may confide in him without any fear whatever; and in case you do not come in person, I shall be obliged to you if you will write me. Meanwhile, awaiting you, I beg God to spare you many years.

Your most attentive and faithful servant,
MANUEL LISA[22]

Here was a last-ditch attempt to secure ingress to Santa Fe, with the Spaniards to name their own conditions, and with Sanguinet given almost complete freedom to bargain. Lisa well knew that such privileges were seldom allowed businessmen under the Spanish flag, and calculated to make the inducement to trade with him as enticing as possible. The letter was dated September 8, and on September 11, Sanguinet set off on his mission,[23] taking along $1,019.75 in merchandise to indicate the seriousness of Lisa's appeal.[24] On the same day the rest of the hunters departed for the West, Louis Lorimier taking four men with him to trap the Wind River area and trade with the Crows, and Reuben

[22] *Ibid.*

[23] Luttig, *Journal,* 76.

[24] Missouri Fur Company Ledger Book, April, 1812–July, 1813; 1817, Kansas State Historical Society.

Lewis, with the largest group, eighteen in all, going to the Little Horn to set up a small post for his own hunters, and for the men still spread all over the mountains from the last expedition.[25] The lack of man power probably forced Lisa to abandon any attempt at the Three Forks, particularly in the face of increasing British activity throughout the Northwest. He still retained that area as his goal, no doubt feeling that if he could personally meet in council with the chiefs of the Blackfoot confederation some amicable and mutually profitable arrangement could be worked out, as it had been with every other tribe with which he had dealt in person.

Having seen his men off into the wilderness, Manuel turned to the task of maintaining peaceful relations between the various Indian tribes which were beginning to frequent his post, particularly between the Arikaras and the Gros Ventres, as well as trying to counteract British maneuvering among the tribes. Personally mediating between the Gros Ventres and Arikaras, Lisa was able to prevent an outbreak of hostility, and saved himself a good deal of grief. He wisely did not trust the natives surrounding his post, and took care to keep as few furs on hand as possible. On September 29 four men set out in a canoe for St. Louis "with a few Peltries," and probably with orders to stop at Bijou's post and pick up his furs as well.[26] There was no sense in taking excessive chances with the receipts, especially since they were as small as they were.

Work still progressed on the fort, and it was not until October 19 that they "hung the great Door of the Entrance of the fort, which ceremony was saluted by 7 Guns and 3 rounds of Musquetry, made the Tour—around the Fort and Baptized the

25 Luttig, *Journal*, 76. Luttig calls the river simply the Little Horn, while Lisa, in his letter to the Spaniards, refers to the "Petite Corne, which empties into the Rio Amarillo." The Little Horn, or Little Bighorn of Custer fame, empties into the Bighorn rather than the Yellowstone.

26 *Ibid.*, 88–89.

same MANUEL."[27] Trade had been continuing while the post was being completed, but it was not particularly brisk considering the large number of Indians constantly in and around the fort. This was cause for concern on the part of all hands, everyone fearful that some small incident would serve to turn the prairies red with blood, and knowing that if blood was to be let, theirs would be the first to go. Lisa was also anxiously awaiting word from Sanguinet to the south, and from Lewis regarding progress in Crow country.

News began to trickle in, all bad. On December 12, "Baptist Antoine alias Machecou, arrived express from Mr Lewis and brought the displeasing news, that the hunters that were equipped by the Company and which had been on the Spanish Waters trapping, had been robbed by the Crows, one of them Danis was killed by some Indians supposed Grosventres."[28] Displeasing indeed, but only hearsay. The following day, however, "Cadet Chevalier arrived express from Mr. Charles Sanguinette with a Letter dated the 3rd instant in the Prairie on his Return from the Arepaos, in which he confirmed the sad news of the hunters, he found none and was informed by the Arepaos, that 3 of them were Killed by the Blackfeet, supposed Champlain and 2 others, Lafargue and 5 others had run off to the ———— Spaniards, 8 of them had gone to the Crows which are now with Mr Lewis, and 3 or 4 others they know nothing of at all, they the hunters had much Beaver cached and the Remainder plundered with all other things."[29]

The loss of Champlain hurt Lisa deeply, for a number of reasons. It was always difficult to be indifferent to the loss of an old friend, particularly one who had shared the beginning of this great adventure. Champlain had grown under Lisa's eyes into an excellent trader, a fine hunter, and a capable leader of

[27] *Ibid.*, 94.
[28] *Ibid.*, 100.
[29] *Ibid.*, 101–103.

men. No one had known more about the area to the south of Three Forks, nor had anyone been more qualified to essay the opening of the Santa Fe trade. With him died the hopes of opening a connection between the upper Missouri and the Spanish provinces, leaving the field open for McKnight and Baird. The Missouri Fur Company would hereafter be bound to its fate in the upper Missouri country. Lisa probably did not learn the actual details of the disaster which befell Champlain's crew until the next summer, when, in St. Louis, he was contacted by Ezekiel Williams, one of the hunters who had been with that body, and had been fortunate enough to escape. Williams told of the harrassment they had suffered from the Indians, the agreement of the men to separate in the hope that in dispersion they might all escape, and of his leaving Champlain with the Arapahoes, Champlain preferring to try to get back north to the Missouri while Williams headed east toward civilization.[30] The hostility of the Indians in that area only underscored the impossibility of approaching Santa Fe from the Missouri.

On top of the disheartening intelligence sent in by Sanguinet, the Arikaras, on December 16, "came and told us a dreadful History which they had been informed by the Sioux, as they sayeth, that the Sioux had Killed Bijou, and plundered the trading house."[31] If this was true, the company faced near calamity for the season. Sioux hostility meant that these strong warriors had accepted the British wampum, and would make it difficult, if not impossible, for the Americans to get the proceeds of their hunt downstream to St. Louis. Lisa immediately dispatched a letter to Bijou, sending as courier one of the Sioux loiterers around the fort, and promised the Indian a horse if he brought

---

[30] Letter, Ezekiel Williams to Joseph Charless, printed in the *Missouri Gazette*, (Sept. 14, 1816). Williams' letter is the basis of David H. Coyner, *The Lost Trappers; A Collection of Interesting Scenes and Events in the Rocky Mountains*. The scenes he depicts are interesting, even if fictitious.

[31] Luttig, *Journal*, 104.

back an answer.[32] The eager brave assured his generous employer that he would bring in a reply, evincing such confidence that the men took heart that the Ree story was a fabrication. One small bit of good news served to buoy the sagging prospects of the company, when, on the sixteenth, letters from Lewis and Lorimier indicated that they had been able, in their journey across country to the Little Horn, to pick up twelve packs of beaver by trading and trapping.[33] With such an auspicious beginning, these groups might have an extremely profitable hunt, and pull the company out of the red. But as Lisa was pondering his difficulties at Fort Manuel, even greater troubles were developing for him in St. Louis.

The arrival of the boat from Fort Manuel on September 27, with the returns, such as they were, for the past year, could not have been encouraging to the partners. The price of beaver was quite low in St. Louis in the fall of 1812. It had stood at $2.50 per pound in May,[34] and certainly had not gone up after the declaration of war between Great Britain and the United States. If the company boat carried only the thirty-six packs mentioned by Luttig, the proceeds would have amounted to $9,000.00, although since Luttig said they were mixed furs, the net worth may have been less, not nearly enough to pay for the outfit taken up by Lisa. At the annual meeting on December 7 the partners in St. Louis examined the books and found "a ballance appears due to Sundries by the Compy of Seventeen thousand ninety dollars 28 cents."[35] The stockholders then went on to the annual election for office, and, apparently blaming Lisa for the lack of profits, especially because he was not there to defend himself, replaced the industrious Spaniard on the board of direc-

---

[32] *Ibid.*, 105.

[33] *Ibid.*, 105.

[34] *Missouri Gazette* (May 2, 1812).

[35] Missouri Fur Company Ledger Book, 1812–14, Vol. XXX, William Clark MSS, Kansas State Historical Society.

tors with Pierre Chouteau. Those voting were William Clark, Sylvestre Labbadie, Pierre Chouteau, A. P. Chouteau, Jr., Andrew Henry, and Reuben Lewis, through his appointed representative Clark.[36] The Chouteaus had always been chary of their investment, and Labbadie could be counted on to vote with them in this matter. Clark, knowing that Lisa was essential to good Indian relations, and that the presence of the company was necessary on the Missouri to protect American interests, probably voted to retain Lisa. Lewis, despite his forebodings in 1810, had not only remained with the company but was now leading a group of hunters in the mountains. Since control by the Chouteau faction would mean cutting back company activities, Lewis' vote probably went along with Clark's. That left the decision up to Andrew Henry. No doubt discouraged by his own experience, certainly enough to dampen the enthusiasm of the most optimistic, and fearing that his investment was unsafe in the face of war, to say nothing of not receiving a satisfactory return for that investment over the years, it was natural for Henry to vote conservatively.

Having removed Manuel from the directory, the members then went on to make it possible to keep him as the head of the river expeditions, should there be any more, by altering the sixth article to read, instead of one member of the board's being required to ascend the river: "One of the Directors, or Stockholders, or Such other Soutable person . . . ."[37] There was still no one who could compare with Lisa as a trader. On this matter Clark did not cast Lewis' vote, and Charles Gratiot, acting for Pierre Menard, made up the two-thirds of the stockholders necessary to effect such a change.[38] This majority was unwilling to invest anything further in the company's operations, and so directed that all funds coming into the hands of the president

[36] *Ibid.*
[37] *Ibid.*
[38] *Ibid.*

be used to pay off the debts, and any surplus, and only the surplus, be used for making up the outfit for the following spring. With the war on and St. Louis in a distracted state due to the threat of Indian attack, retrenchment measures were, they felt, in order.

St. Louisans had good cause to be worried about their town in the spring of 1813, as the British stepped up their efforts to incite the Indians against the Americans. The threat of Indian attack brought back unpleasant memories to too many citizens, and preparations were organized, in some cases, in near panic. There was talk of rebuilding the old Spanish wall and taking refuge behind it, but of more practical value were the several volunteer militia companies which were organized. Close watch was kept on British schemers, particularly their most active representative, Robert Dickson, who the *Gazette* liked to call "the celebrated English trader." Dickson was given a commission from British authorities in Montreal as Indian agent, with the job of securing the Indians of Illinois, Indiana, and the trans-Mississippi area to the Union Jack.[39] James Calloway, a prominent resident of the St. Louis area, wrote back to his wife from Portage des Sioux in May that he had heard from a very high source that Dickson had traveled all through American territory, giving presents to the Indians in return for their promise to fight for the British against St. Louis.[40] Issue after issue of the *Gazette* chronicled the movements of British agents, particularly Dickson, relating these movements to changes in the Indian situation. While the people of the city observed the machinations of the British and Indians, Manuel Lisa was in the center of their activities.

The hostility of the Indians around Fort Manuel was grow-

[39] Louis A. Tohill, "Robert Dickson, British Fur Trader on the Upper Mississippi: A Story of Trade, War, and Diplomacy," Ph.D. Thesis, University of Minnesota, 1926.

[40] May 9, 1813, Maher Collection, MHS.

ing more apparent every day, and this had its effect on the men. Three *engagés* were sent out to meet Sanguinet and escort him to the post, but these three worthies quickly returned without accomplishing their assignment, claiming to have run across the track of a party of Indians, which had frightened them back to the safety of the fort. December 29 brought Bijou's long-awaited reply and injected a little cheer into the holiday season, which had been rendered more gloomy by the death of Sacajawea on December 20.[41] Bijou still had a full crop of hair and was in fine health, but better than that, he had "traded very well more than expected." A week later Sanguinet and his two *engagés*, Latour and Lange, arrived, bringing along thirty-one horses for which they had traded.[42] The following day Lisa sent out three men with powder and tobacco to Reuben Lewis and his men on the Little Horn, but they, like their predecessors, speedily returned, reporting "they had seen something like Men and got scared, they would not go on, returned the Goods, but kept their Equipments for the Voyage which made their tale doubtful, and it seemed they had no Idea to go, and cheat the Company out of their Goods."[43] There were more than enough Bouchés along on this voyage.

Lisa had had enough, and two of these men, and two other *engagés*, including Latour, who had gone out to the Arapahoes with Sanguinet, were, on January 21, "ordered out of the fort, they had made a complot against the Adopted Principles of the Company Mr Manuel tried every way to gett them in Employment but they would neither engage nor hunt nor pay their Debts . . . the Company looses considerable by them, say about 4000 dollars."[44] That would more than take care of the twelve packs Reuben Lewis had on hand. Not even mountain prices could support losses of that magnitude.

[41] Luttig, *Journal*, 106.
[42] *Ibid.*, 110.
[43] *Ibid.*, 111–12.
[44] *Ibid.*, 114–15.

Conditions were appreciably worsened when Charbonneau returned from the Gros Ventre village on February 21, after having traded only 168 out of a possible 492 skins, and told of how British influence had grown there. Le Bourgne had been dethroned, and was living in disgrace, and the Gros Ventres were now completely hostile to the United States.[45] The next day Archambeau, one of the hunters, was killed in close proximity to the fort, and the men were worried to see camped outside their walls representatives of the Arikara, Mandan, and Cheyenne nations. The Cheyennes were the most restless and seemed to pose the greatest threat, while, as Luttig put it, "as to the Rees we fear nothing, they are a sett of lying and good for nothing fellows."[46] Luttig's journal comes to an abrupt end on March 5, the termination probably provided by an attack by one of the tribes, or by all acting in conjunction.

Lisa, with his knowledge of the Indians, must have been able to evacuate the post with a minimum of loss, and dropped downstream to Bijou's trading house to await word from Lewis. No communications were forthcoming, although Lisa waited until late in May. On the twentieth of that month Manuel paid Edward Rose $250 to guide Lorimier, who apparently had come in sometime during the spring, to the Crows and Reuben Lewis, to apprise the latter and his men of the events at Fort Manuel, and warn them to look to their lives.[47] The crew then loaded the proceeds and sailed directly to St. Louis, arriving either on or shortly before May 29.[48]

Considering everything, Manuel had done amazingly well for the interests of the company. He brought down forty packs of beaver, which, even at the depressed price current, were worth

[45] *Ibid.*, 121–24.

[46] *Ibid.*, 126.

[47] Missouri Fur Company Ledger Book, April, 1812–July, 1813; 1817, Kansas State Historical Society.

[48] Letter, Christian Wilt to Andrew Wilt, May 29, 1813, Christian Wilt Letterbook, 1812–15, MHS.

$10,000, and about three hundred packs of buffalo robes, worth another $12,000 to $15,000.[49] The company was still operating Bijou's post with the Sioux, another one at the Omaha village in the charge of Michael Immel,[50] and the party of Reuben Lewis had yet to be accounted for. But it was the future of the company which seemed depressing to the stockholders. Fifteen men had been lost over the past year, and, worse for trade, "the Aricaras, Chyans, Grosventre, Crows and Aropahays are or may be considered at war with the Americans."[51] The proximity of the British posts to these Indians gave America's antagonists an insurmountable advantage in competion for the red man's allegiance. Significantly, the Sioux, potentially most dangerous to the American cause, were not included on this list.

That summer, in addition to joining in the defensive preparations of the city by becoming a captain in the volunteer militia,[52] Lisa took part in the activities leading to the demise of the Missouri Fur Company. Apparently, the skins brought down that season were not quite sufficient to cover the operating expenses of the organization, for, in a meeting on July 22, the stockholders resolved to sell a sufficient amount of the goods then upriver to cover the debts of the company.[53] They further resolved "that the Directors be authorized to advertise in the Missouri Gazette . . . for a meeting of the Members at St. Louis on friday the 10th of September 1813, for the express purpose of Dissolving the said Company."[54] So five years before the company was to expire, and scarcely two years since the reorganization, the Missouri Fur Company was consigned to oblivion. Only one expedition was sent out, and that was not exactly a failure given existing conditions, but the desired high profits were not

[49] *Ibid.*

[50] Missouri Fur Company Ledger Book, 1812–14, Kansas State Historical Society.

[51] *Missouri Gazette* (June 5, 1813).

[52] Thomas M. Marshall, *The Life and Papers of Frederick Bates*, II, 261.

[53] Missouri Fur Company Ledger Book, 1812–14, Kansas State Historical Society.

[54] *Ibid.*

forthcoming, and a majority had had enough. The resolutions were signed by those present, Clark, Labbadie, the two Chouteaus, Menard, Henry, Lewis, and Lisa, with Lisa's signature last, as though in protest against the destruction of an enterprise in which he retained so much faith.

The dismantling process went about at a rapid pace, with notices of auctions of company merchandise and equipment appearing in the *Gazette* on August 7, evidently preparing for what was already an accomplished fact, and November 10.[55] That the company was definitely going out of business was obvious from the lists of goods for sale, which included traps, guns, axes, and tools of all kinds, and even some beaver musk, which was nearly as valuable as the pelts themselves. The notice for the meeting formally to dissolve the company was duly published, but there was no meeting on September 10. Not only were the necessary two-thirds of the stockholders not present, but there was a new development in the financial life of the city which may have caused the company members to hold off.

The most pressing problem the Missouri Fur Company had had to face from its inception was the lack of available long-term credit. The old Spanish official who had replied to Lisa's memorial for free trade had been quite correct. No one of the partners, indeed not even the combination of partners, had enough ready cash to put the company on a sound basis from the beginning of operations. The only source of credit was the particular merchant or merchants from whom the company purchased its supplies. While such credit was obtainable, it was on an extremely short-term basis—six months, usually, with twelve being found occasionally. The businessmen, of course, were working under the same handicap as the traders, since they, too, dealt in credit with their suppliers. There simply was no fluid capital on the frontier. What was needed most to alleviate this problem was

----

[55] *Missouri Gazette* (Aug. 7 and Nov. 10, 1813).

a bank, and, on August 21, 1813, the Territorial Legislature incorporated the Bank of St. Louis.[56]

Among the commissioners of the new institution were Auguste Chouteau, formalizing his already accepted role, Manuel Lisa, who needed the institution more than anyone, and Moses Austin, a long-time resident of Missouri who had made a small fortune in mining. Unfortunately, this enterprise had a short, stormy, and unprofitable career. Not until July 11, 1816, was enough stock subscribed for the bank to open its doors, and not until September 2 of that year were directors elected. Conspicuously missing from the published list of directors were both Chouteau and Lisa, who had lost interest long before. Chouteau had, by this time, been active in setting up a rival bank, which was chartered as the Bank of Missouri in January, 1817, although it had earlier been conducting business. Moses Austin lost most of his fortune in the speculation, which caused him to look elsewhere for his livelihood, Texas being the place that caught his eye. Manuel Lisa, after that first experiment, and probable loss, did not again become involved in the founding of a bank. But in 1813 the prospective lending institution must have held out some promise of being the source of credit so necessary for the fur traders.

Lisa was not one to sit idly by awaiting developments, and, in company with his agent, Hyacinte Egliz, the trader without a company negotiated a contract with William Clark, in the latter's capacity as Indian agent, to deliver the yearly proceeds of the United States Indian Factory at Fort Osage to Brownsville, Pennsylvania, on the Monongahela.[57] It was a fine occasion, not only to earn a few dollars in a simple transport voyage in com-

[56] Brackenridge Jones, "One Hundred Years of Banking in Missouri," *Missouri Historical Review*, Vol. XV (Jan., 1921), 345–92, is an excellent summary of early banking attempts in St. Louis and Missouri.

[57] Contract between William Clark and Manuel Lisa and Hyacinte Egliz, Sept. 14, 1813, William Clark Collection, MHS, photostat of original in National Archives.

pletely pacified country but to renew old acquaintances and contacts along the Ohio. Two boats and six men were needed to make the trip, and Lisa undoubtedly took along some company goods to be disposed of along the way. Christian Wilt, who was sending some buffalo robes to markets along the Ohio, was worried about Lisa's competition, for he wrote the captain of his boat, "beat Manuel my boy, tis one of your first objects."[58] With the prevailing price ranging from $4.00 to $5.00 per robe, beating Manuel was well worth the effort, particularly as Wilt had only paid $2.50 for his shipment. Lisa, Wilt well knew, would be hard to beat, not only on the river, although Wilt's boat had a good head start, but along the banks of the Ohio, where the energetic Spaniard had contacts of long standing. Indeed, Manuel had such a reputation for disposing of buffalo robes that Samuel Fitzhugh of Louisville had, earlier in the year when the market had dropped in Kentucky, consigned a number of his robes to Lisa in St. Louis for sale.[59] Because the market had reversed, and there was once again a demand for robes along the Ohio, Lisa may have planned to use Fitzhugh as his outlet. The voyage proved a difficult one for Manuel; he had to send one of the boats back as unseaworthy, and this delay may have caused him to miss the annual meeting of the company which took place on December 6.

At that meeting the books were examined, a surplus noted, and a dividend declared, so the members had made a profit after all, which was logical since Lisa had sent down or brought down at least $31,000 in beaver and buffalo skins, and the auctions of equipment and merchandise added to the total. The members also generously permitted the president to keep the remaining

[58] Letter, Christian Wilt to Joseph Hertzog, Sept. 18, 1813, Christian Wilt Letterbook, 1812-15, MHS.

[59] Letter, Manuel Lisa to Samuel Fitzhugh, July 3, 1813, Dennis Fitzhugh Papers, Filson Club, Louisville, Kentucky, courtesy of Mrs. Dorothy Thomas Cullen, curator.

unsold assets of the organization, a few pelts, a small tract of land, and two notes due from *engagés*.[60] Going through all the formalities of corporation procedure even though they were all but out of business, the stockholders elected the same men as president and directors, who did not present a list of articles for the following year's expedition because "it was the wish of a great proportion of the Stockholders that a dissolution of Company take place."[61] Since just five members were voting, with only Clark of all the partners actually present, and the other four acting through their representatives, the company could not be dissolved, so the meeting was adjourned until the following day in the hopes of rounding up a quorum. At that meeting William Morrison was admitted to membership upon his letter of application.[62] Why he should want to become a member at the time the company was going out of business, or why the partners should have accepted him, unless to make a substantial majority for dissolution, are matters for conjecture.

At any rate, the company was not dissolved on either December 6 or 7. Lisa was in St. Louis on December 10, for on that date he submitted an advertisement to the Gazette for publication the next day. In that same issue a notice of another meeting of the stockholders for January 16 was printed. The long-put-off meeting finally took place on January 17. Thomas James, still smarting over his alleged mistreatment, had applied to the company for $150.00, which he claimed was owed him. The company graciously accepted his petition, crediting the sum to his account, which continued to retain a balance in favor of the Missouri Fur Company. Lisa was given a credit of $35.38, for equipment, and another $11.50, the balance of an *engagé*'s account, and, "having unanimously agreed that the interest of the several members requires a dissolution of the said Company,"

[60] Missouri Fur Company Ledger Book, 1812–14, Kansas State Historical Society.
[61] *Ibid.*
[62] *Ibid.*

they proceeded to dissolve it, with Lisa again the last to sign.[63]
Thus the stormy partnership came to a close, and Lisa was once
again thrown on his own resources to try to make something
concrete out of his vision of the northwest.

That this heterogeneous combination of competitors should
fall apart could have been predicted by an acute observer long
before 1814. Only Manuel Lisa, of all the partners, had consistently adhered to the true interest of the company, the development of the animal and human resources of the Northwest for
the advantage and profit of the Missouri Fur Company, though
that he did so in what was not always the most efficacious manner
certainly helped to divide the group. While others, notably William Clark, Andrew Henry, and Reuben Lewis, shared this no-
tion, they had not the burning desire for success that possessed
the Spaniard, or the wherewithal to withstand the reverses which
immediately were encountered. Nor did they grasp the principle
of trade which Lisa seemed to have intuitively: the most important part of the business was in dealing with the human,
rather than the animal, side of the business. From the beginning
he understood that the Indians, particularly those on the Missouri, had to be placated and kept that way if the company was
to survive. This meant that a considerable expenditure for gifts
and trade goods, which would do little more than pay for themselves and have a little profit left over, had to be made. This
most of the other partners were unwilling to do. They realized
that the real profits were in trapping the upper country, and were
interested only in that. William Clark was persuaded of the
necessity of having friendly Indians on the Missouri, not so much
for trade as to further the policies of the United States as Indian
agent, but Henry and Lewis were, principally, trappers. When
costs seemed to be taking too great a share of the profits, they
preferred to withdraw.

The rest of the partners all felt that they had been compelled

[63] *Ibid.*

BEAVER BUILDING A HUT

HERDS OF BUFFALO AND ELK
on the Upper Missouri

to join for various reasons. Sylvestre Labbadie, by his own admission, had associated because he was bored with life in St. Louis
and desired adventure, soon finding that this particular adventure could be expensive and entail much hard work. Pierre
Menard and William Morrison simply continued a partnership
with Lisa which had been profitable in the past, and when profits
were not immediately forthcoming in the new corporation, they
both lost interest, Morrison concentrating on his stores in Illinois, and Menard finding that politics offered a way to make his
fortune without the sacrifices demanded by the fur-trading business. But the Chouteaus, whose unstinting support was necessary
for complete success, had no share of the vision of a northwestern
trading empire, nor any stomach for the tribulations necessary
to achieve it. Immediate and certain gain, continued control of
the economic life of St. Louis, and the protection of their social
status in the city seemed to be their paramount objectives, and
when those conflicted with the goals of the company, the company suffered in consequence. There were profits to be made in
the Missouri Fur Company, but the sure gain was not in the
prosecuting of trapping and trading but in the supplying of merchandise and credit, and the subsequent purchase and resale of
the proceeds brought down from the upper Missouri.

Pierre Chouteau had been the largest single supplier of merchandise to the company from its inception. His supplies in 1809
amounted to at least $35,000,[64] and, in 1810–11, another $3,000
or more.[65] Pierre Chouteau and Auguste Chouteau were suppliers to the company of that necessity of the trade, liquor, as
well, distilling the raw spirits, kegging it, and, after throwing a
handful of tobacco in the bottom of the barrel to provide color
and flavor, happily labeling the lethal concoction brandy. These

---

[64] This is an approximation of the dollar value of the £6,861 plus (see note 25,
Chapter III, in this volume.) There is, in addition, an account totaling $1,251.79⅔
in the Pierre Chouteau Ledger Account, 1802–17, MHS.

[65] *Ibid.*

goods were, of course, sold to the company at retail and paid for in fur at the going rate, or at a rate specified by the practices of short-term credit then prevalent. These furs were held for a favorable advance in price or sent to markets elsewhere, wherever the price was highest, thus cutting the company out of much potential profit from the direct sale of its own furs. As long as this short-term credit system existed, and the company did not get itself on a cash basis to be able to go far afield in its search for merchandise suitable for trade, the Chouteaus could, and no doubt did, dispose of all their excess merchandise to the company. This allowed them to reap a profit from both ends of each expedition, plus a share of the expedition itself, while only sharing a portion of the risk as members. To maintain this favorable position, it was necessary to keep the man most vitally concerned with the success of the company away from St. Louis and the nerve center of control.

This was easily accomplished. None of the partners was as well equipped, either in temperament or talent, to head the yearly expeditions of the company upriver as was Manuel Lisa. They knew it, and he knew it, and it was thus assured that Lisa would be away from St. Louis at least six months out of the year, during which time he would have no control of company policy. The attitude of the Chouteaus is best evidenced in 1811, when Lisa and Clark, with slight support from Labbadie, had to save the company from bankruptcy, when none of the others responded to the call for funds, Lisa going irretrievably into debt in the process. With such internal obstructions, coupled with the normal difficulties of prosecuting trade with the always mercurial savages, compounded by the outbreak of hostilities between the United States and Great Britain in 1812, it is surprising that the company held together as long as it did.

Not the least of the forces motivating the Chouteaus, or at least the active member, Pierre, was social prestige. Auguste and Pierre Chouteau had always been the social as well as the economic leaders of St. Louis, and considered it pretty much their own town. When Lisa returned from the Missouri in 1808, his threat was not only economic but social. Here was a new hero for the citizenry, an upstart, a man who, as it were, had gone from "rags to riches," a social force to be reckoned with. While it might be economically feasible to form a partnership with Lisa, would this not also be an admission of social equality? Certainly, unless some means could be devised to keep an equal partner in a subordinate status. What better way than to put him in personal charge of the expeditions? Pay him a salary, if necessary, above his share of the profits, but relegate him to the simple status of field captain, not business partner. Let him demean himself working with his hands while the executives operated in the office in St. Louis.

This was shrewd logic on the part of the Chouteaus, and inescapable as far as Lisa was concerned. He was the obvious man for the position, and perhaps Manuel knew that better than his partners. Besides, the actual doing was the part of the business he loved; the struggle against the river, the battle of wits against the various tribes, the constant gamble against nature and nature's children, where the stakes were a man's life and fortune, drew him, as they drew countless others, with an inexorable and fatal attraction. So the Chouteaus accomplished their goals, at least until 1814 and the demise of the company. Lisa might continue, but he was now heavily in debt and there were few who either could or would share his vision of the Northwest to the extent of backing his proposals with hard cash. But St. Louis was growing rapidly, with new people moving in every day, people willing, indeed searching, to open new enterprises. Perhaps . . . .

VI

War and Trade
One Last Attempt

NEW support for Lisa's project quickly materialized in the person of Theodore Hunt, a young and ambitious former sailor and citizen of Lexington, Kentucky. Hunt, like many another of his age and temperament, saw in burgeoning St. Louis unlimited opportunity for investment and development. His brother, Wilson Price Hunt, had already gained a modicum of fame in the Mound City by leading the Astorians to the mouth of the Columbia. Early in 1814, perhaps even before the Missouri Fur Company was dissolved, Hunt had been in contact with Lisa, investigating business possibilities, and preparing to take up residence in St. Louis. He purchased a house and lot from Manuel and Polly Lisa on February 3, 1814, and the next day the firm of Hunt and Bright, tanners and curriers, moved in next door to Lisa's residence—down-wind, it is hoped.[1] Late in March, Hunt, still in Lexington, formed a partnership with J. and D. Maccoun, wholesale merchants of that city, to supply the Missouri trade in which he and Lisa were about to embark.[2]

---

[1] Deed, Manuel Lisa and Polly Lisa to Theodore Hunt, Feb. 3, 1814, Hunt Papers, MHS. This land was part of that mortgaged to Antoine and Pierre Carraby in 1812, and Manuel agreed to pay off the rest of the mortgage as listed in the deed.

[2] Letter, Theodore Hunt to J. C. B. Lucas, Mar. 24, 1814, in *ibid*.

On July 14 the new partners submitted a notice to the *Gazette*, printed two days later, announcing their appointment as commissioners to oversee the construction of a bridge over the creek south of town, and calling for bids on the job.[3] But fur trading, not bridge building, was Lisa's forte, and very little time elapsed before he was once again pursuing that elusive empire of the Northwest.

At the dissolution of the Missouri Fur Company, Manuel had either taken the existing posts as his part of the proceeds, purchased them from the company, or simply appropriated the deserted forts for his own use, for the *Missouri Gazette* noted on August 13, 1814:

> A few days ago, a barge belonging to Messrs M. Lisa and Co. which was ascending the Missouri, to their trading establishment, were induced to stop at Mackey's Saline, (commonly called Boons Lick) as the country was overrun by the indians and all the inhabitants in Forts. The crew which arrived here on Saturday night last, in a three day passage, report, that on the south side of the Missouri, the indians had taken all the horses and were killing the cattle for food; that on their arrival at the Saline. The people at Coles' fort were interring a man just shot by the indians.[4]

So Lisa had a post upriver, probably at the Omaha village, but the *engagés* were unable to reach it because of the Indian menace, and that scarcely three days out of St. Louis. The city itself was pessimistic about the Indian situation during 1814, with the *Gazette* calling upon the government to "Jacksonize" the northern as well as the southern Indians.[5]

William Clark, in his capacity as Indian agent, decided, in the face of growing native hostility, upon a bold maneuver to alleviate the strain upon the town, and turn the natives against their

[3] *Missouri Gazette* (July 16, 1814).
[4] *Ibid.* (Aug. 13, 1814).
[5] *Ibid.* (May 28, 1814).

British benefactors. On August 20 he "appointed August P. Chouteau Sub Indian Agent for the Osages—and Manuel Lisa Esq. Agent for the Tribes on the Missouri above the Kanzes."[6] In addition to his munificent salary of $548 per year, Lisa was provided with $1,335 worth of trading merchandise "for the purpose of engaging those tribes in offensive operations against the Enemies of the United States, particularly on the Mississippi who are too numerous for our thin population to oppose."[7]

In both cases the choice was excellent. Chouteau had been associated with the Osages for twenty years as a trader and friend; he was the one who had brought that numerous and warlike people into friendly relations with the white man, and could be counted upon to keep them in that condition. And no one, of course, had more influence with the Indians of the upper Missouri than Manuel Lisa. The American cause could have no better advocate, for the Indians, in recognition of his years of fair dealing with them, his reputation for honesty and integrity among them, and his sincere concern for their welfare, guaranteed that the United States would have its desires heeded at the very least, and probably accepted. Thus the government could not only count on the friendship of the Missouri tribes, particularly the Sioux, but would be able to set them on the warpath against those tribes, the Iowas, Santees, Sac and Foxes, which already had declared themselves in opposition to the United States. To have the Indians fighting among themselves would block British designs and allow the frontier respite from repeated depredations.

Lisa left St. Louis with a boat and the merchandise given him by the government late in the fall of 1814, on or after August 27, so late that he was unable to get beyond Council Bluffs prior to the icing of the river, and was forced to winter at his post

[6] Letter, William Clark to John Armstrong, Aug. 20, 1814, William Clark Collection, MHS, photostat of original in National Archives.
[7] *Ibid.*

there, a fort which he now called Fort Hunt.[8] While there, he lost no time in busying himself in promoting his mission, sending out couriers among the various Sioux tribes, calling them to a spring council at the usual Sioux gathering place, the mouth of the Au Jacques, or James, River.[9] One of these messengers, apparently, was Tamaha, one-eyed chief of the Teton Sioux, a close friend of Lisa and the Americans. Tamaha was instrumental, that winter, in keeping the Santees from disturbing the American frontier by maintaining close contact with his brethren to the east, and continually threatening them with an attack from the rear if they should make a foray against the United States.[10] Robert Dickson, working furiously to incite the Santees, found that every time he had roused them to the point of motion, Tamaha would appear with a reminder of what would happen to their homes and hunting grounds if they should leave. Dickson finally caught his Indian tormentor and threw him in prison, but the damage had been done to the British cause. The Santees made no extensive move with the Tetons menacing their rear.

That season Lisa literally wedded the Omaha nation to the American cause, and, incidentally, their yearly catch of beaver and buffalo to his trading establishment, by taking to wife Mitain,

[8] Letter, Manuel Lisa to William Clark, Nov. 23, 1815, William Clark Collection, MHS, photostat of original in National Archives.

[9] *Ibid.*

[10] Tamaha apparently accompanied Lisa up from St. Louis. See Tohill, "Robert Dickson," *loc. cit.*; Rev. Edward D. Neill, *The History of Minnesota: From the Earliest French Explorations to the Present Time;* Thomas Forsyth, "Journal of a Voyage from St. Louis to the Falls of St. Anthony, in 1819," ed. by Lyman C. Draper, *Wisconsin Historical Collections,* Vol. VI (1869–72), 188–219; Doane Robinson, "South Dakota and the War of 1812," *South Dakota Historical Collections,* Vol. XII (1924), 85–89; and Doane Robinson, "A Sioux Indian View of the Last War with England," *South Dakota Historical Collections,* Vol. V (1910), 397–401. The latter is the publication of an interview between the author and the grandson of Joseph Renville, Sioux interpreter in the employ of Robert Dickson during the War of 1812. Renville gave Lisa all the credit for keeping the Teton Sioux loyal to the United States, and for keeping the Santees from being worth anything to the British.

lovely (were not they all?) daughter of one of the principal families of the tribe.[11] This was good policy, both diplomatically and economically, and was followed by a number of traders and trappers who worked with the various Indian tribes. Some had several wives spread all over the Western countryside, assuring themselves of a home practically anywhere in the wilderness, and, more importantly, obtaining immunity for travel wherever members of their tribes were sovereign. At any rate, Lisa dispensed a few of the government goods to his now fellow tribesmen. The Indians had been just as eager as Lisa for the match, knowing that it meant many presents would be given by the trader, who enlisted a war party to march against the Iowas. The Omahas set out at once for the Des Moines, met a party of Iowas coming down for the express purpose of attacking Fort Hunt, defeated, or rather annihilated, them, and brought home to their white brother by marriage two scalps as proof of their prowess. Having therefore demonstrated their zeal for the cause, the Omahas settled down for the winter to await further developments. Similarly, Manuel made presents to the Otos, exhorting them to join their American brothers against the common enemy. This tribe, having no stomach for winter fighting, politely declined, promising war in the spring. The Poncas also were contacted, and the wishes of the Great White Father in Washington were made known to them. Like the Otos, the Poncas preferred war in the spring, when, true to their word, they sent out a party of from two to three hundred braves against the luckless Iowas.[12]

More crucial to the United States, and particularly St. Louis, was the attitude of the Sioux. With the exception of the Santees, the various Sioux bands had been friendly, or at least noncommittal, preferring to get the best out of both sides in the war of

---

[11] Edwin James, *Account of an Expedition from Pittsburgh to the Rocky Mountains, Performed in the Years 1819 and '20*, I, 244–49, tells the story complete with romantic love, narrow escapes, and triumphant righteousness.

[12] Letter, Lisa to Clark, Nov. 23, 1815, William Clark Collection, MHS.

presents, and were certainly willing to listen to Lisa before binding themselves to anything. The river opened at Fort Hunt on April 4, and by the April 15, Lisa was at the appointed rendezvous, where large numbers of the Yankton and Teton Sioux were assembled in reply to his invitation, with more arriving daily. Manuel held council for the assemblage on April 28, and made plain to them what their course must be. Explaining that the United States had wished to leave them alone during this conflict, which had nothing to do with the red man, but that the British, "Envying their happy and peaceful Situation in with the rest of the Americans, would not on their part consent to this Course of Conduct,"[13] Manuel pointed out that it had been the British who had sown dissension between the Americans and their Indian friends. The time had come, therefore, for the Sioux to make their choice, whether they would make common cause with the Americans in their midst, now offering them the hand of friendship, or whether the armies of the United States, and Lisa personally, could expect to meet them on the field of battle. Lisa pointed out that if they chose friendship and went to war against the natives of the Mississippi, they could go assured that if they chanced to be slain in battle, the Great White Father would take care of their wives and children. This was strong talk on Lisa's part, for while the Great White Father might want to do much for his red charges, his loyal subjects in Congress did not always go along with him, and those same loyal subjects had to pay the bills which Lisa was promising to accumulate.

The rest of the government's presents were then distributed, with the inference that they were but a small token of the bounty of the United States which would be dispensed provided the Sioux acted in amity. This was an amazing act of courage and forthrightness which appealed to the Sioux. A lone trader with but a single boat and a skeleton crew coming among them with presents was fair game for a quick coup, but the trader was

[13] *Ibid.*

Manuel Lisa, the man who had finally satisfied the desires of the Sioux by building a special post for their trade, and he got away with it. The Indians accepted his proffered hand as well as his presents, although probably in reverse order, and promised to go to war as soon as a sufficient force had gathered to make a grand attack. In accordance with instructions, Lisa then departed, taking with him thirty-three chiefs and important men of the tribes for a formal meeting with William Clark in St. Louis. The entourage stopped at Fort Hunt, where they were obliged to wait for Big Elk, principal chief of the Omahas, before taking aboard thirteen of the leaders of that nation. The party arrived in St. Louis on June 7.[14]

While Lisa and the chiefs moved downstream, the rest of the Sioux, preferring, like all Indians, to have overwhelming numbers before beginning a fight, assembled a large war party, consisting of 742 men and 92 women, and set out to wreak havoc among their new enemies on the Mississippi. On the way they met a small party of 26 Iowas, which they totally destroyed, keeping only 2 prisoners to present to Lisa as proof of their exploit. They also brought in the hair trophies of conquest to recount the number of the slain.[15] Heady with this initial success, the Sioux proceeded to lay waste the fields of corn planted by the Iowas along the Chariton River, assuring that hapless tribe of another lean year. Unfortunately, all of the northern tribes had suffered greatly the preceding winter from starvation, and the Sioux were no exception. For lack of food, they turned back short of their goal, many moving south to the Omaha village, in hopes that they would find enough food there to keep them while they awaited their chiefs. While they accomplished no great victories, the knowledge on the part of the natives of the Mississippi that the Sioux were on the move was enough to temper their hostility.

[14] *Ibid.*; also *Missouri Gazette* (June 10, 1815).
[15] Letter, Lisa to Clark, Nov. 23, 1815, William Clark Collection, MHS.

The deputation of Indians was met in St. Louis by William Clark, who, in company with Lisa and Auguste Chouteau, took them to Prairie du Chien. There, in late July, a series of treaties of friendship were signed between the United States and the various tribes present.[16] Lisa signed, as witness, the treaties with the Tetons, Yanktons, Omahas, Sioux of the Lakes, and Sioux of the River St. Peters, indicating the extent of the territory covered by his messengers the previous winter. It was made plain to the tribes that the war between the United States and Great Britain had been concluded. This the natives had a hard time comprehending, for nothing had changed as far as they could see, and they did not know about the capture of Dolly Madison's wash or the Battle of New Orleans. The boundaries of the United States were shown, clearly demonstrating that the Indians were residents on American territory, and therefore subject to American jurisdiction. The group then returned to St. Louis, where another council was held, this one giving the Indians a chance to set forth their own desires, and to lodge a few complaints with the American government.

All of the major chiefs were present in St. Louis—Partizan, fiery leader of the Teton Sioux, already notorious for his attempt to stop the Lewis and Clark expedition; Little Dish, brave warrior of the Yankton branch of the large Sioux family; Big Elk, oratorical chief of the Omahas; and others—and expressed themselves on various particulars of the intercourse between the red and white men. Big Elk, particularly, was able to voice the feelings of the Indians about the unfortunate occurrences which somehow always marked the initial contact between the natives and the whites, to recite the alleged wrongs perpetrated upon the Indians by the whites, and to point out the different philosophies of the Indian and American concerning nature's bounty.

[16] Richard Peters, ed., *The Public Statutes at Large of the United States of America*, VII, gives all of these treaties. For a typical one, see Appendix II in this volume.

In addressing William Clark, upon whose shoulders the burden of blame for the conduct of all white men in Indian country fell, the eloquent chief of the Omahas remarked:

> My Father you have made my heart glad by telling me that you would send traders among us—but I do not want hunters to kill those animals the great spirit gave us to subsist on. I wish to preserve these animals for food for my people—so that we shall be able to make your traders glad, and they will come down and make you glad.[17]

Big Elk considered those who hunted on Indian lands nothing less than poachers, but he could do little about them because they were, at least nominally, under the protection of the government, and would claim that immunity whenever threatened. The worst offenders in this respect, as well as in many others, were the whites who had taken Indian wives, and had chosen to reside with the natives. They were constantly slipping out of the village to hunt and trap whenever the chief was not on hand to stop them. These were the individuals undermining the authority of the chiefs, playing on the jealousies of the younger men of the tribes, constantly counseling friendship with the British, and extolling the virtues of British over American goods. Even worse were their relations with Indian women. As the Omaha put it, "What would you think to see me take your women in the streets and violate them? The whites at our village take the women of the braves and violate them in open day—I myself have run to save them, and appease the injured."[18] Such a description of savagery would fit perfectly the redoubtable Edward Rose, who Lisa had forcibly brought out of Indian country the year before,[19] or Baptiste Dorion, the man used as an illustration by Big Elk. Certainly something would have to be done

---

[17] *Missouri Gazette* (Aug. 5, 1815).

[18] *Ibid.*

[19] Letter, Lisa to Clark, Nov. 23, 1815, William Clark Collection, MHS.

about Dorion and his kind, but Clark had little more authority over them than Big Elk himself.

Mutual statements completed, a huge celebration was undertaken so that everyone would go home in good spirits. Predictably, the festivities ended with the Indians getting deliriously drunk on "strong water," and by the time the ceremonial closed, the alcohol was not much more than plain water. The pious Timothy Flint, visiting in St. Louis at the time, asked the Indians where they had gotten their whisky. "They held their bottles up in the air, and informed him, that the 'great Kentucky captain,' pointing up to the clouds, had rained the whiskey into their bottles."[20]

All involved were able to travel by August 5, and on that day Lisa set out on what was to prove a dangerous and expensive voyage.[21] Smallpox, decimator of many an Indian tribe, found its way aboard the boat, taking the lives of five of the Sioux and one of the Omahas. These dead Lisa took care to inter with fitting honors so as to assuage the feelings of the remaining Indians, and to show the esteem in which the deceased were held by the United States. It was also a good idea to demonstrate, by proper burial, that this was not just another plot on the part of the whites to eliminate the Indian. Burial was a very serious business with the Indian, for if the chief did not receive honors commensurate with his position, he might not be admitted to the happy hunting ground. So Lisa had to bury these chiefs with food and presents enough to carry them through to their ultimate goal—an expensive proposition, and one which Lisa had to stand from his own pocket.

Upon his arrival at the Omaha village, Lisa was greeted by the assembled Omahas and Sioux. The latter recounted their campaign against the Iowas, bringing out eight scalps and saying that Lisa would be presented with the rest of the evidence in the

[20] Flint, *Recollections of the Last Ten Years*, 159.
[21] Letter, Lisa to Clark, Nov. 23, 1815, William Clark Collection, MHS.

spring, and told of another foray they had made against the
Sac and Foxes. The Sioux apologized for not doing more, plead-
ing lack of provisions as the reason, but their appearance spoke
more eloquently than their words, and Lisa was moved to provide corn for forty-two lodges of Sioux. He also paid them for
the scalps produced—paying for scalps was not a British monopoly—and remunerated them for the loss of a man and a woman
on their campaigns, but could do nothing about their request
for guns to protect themselves against the expected retaliatory
blow.[22] For all of these expenses, which Lisa made on his own
authority and paid out of his own pocket, he submitted a bill
to William Clark, amounting to nearly $4,000, which that agent
dutifully sent on to Washington for disposition.[23] There is no
record indicating whether or not Lisa was ever reimbursed for
the expense, but since there is no further mention of it, he probably was.

Manuel immediately returned to St. Louis to prepare for the
next trading season, and planned to embark upriver again on
February 15. His own establishments having suffered from
lack of attention during the time he was actively engaged in government service, he had much to do. What his activities were
that spring remains unknown, although there may be some indication in the writings of one John Dunne Hunter,[24] who
claimed to have been recruited with a band of Osages to trap

[22] *Ibid.*

[23] Letter, William Clark to William H. Crawford, Dec. 11, 1815, William
Clark Collection, MHS.

[24] John Dunne Hunter, *Memoirs of a Captivity among the Indians of North
America*. This is a fanciful tale of the Indian adventures of a white man brought
up by the Osage and Kansa Indians. Like all of these fictions, this one may contain
a germ of truth. Hunter claimed to have gone on an expedition in or about 1816.
His description of Lisa tallies very closely with that of Thomas James, and he may
have gotten his information from that source. The book was considered a fraud
shortly after its publication, but Hunter died in 1827, killed by Indians while involved in a Texas revolutionary plot, without ever knowing that he was believed
to be an imposter. *Arkansas Gazette* (May 29, 1827).

the upper Missouri for Lisa and Company. In any case, Lisa was back in St. Louis on June 22,[25] face to face with slanderous rumors that his conduct as subagent had been something less than honorable. Always quick to defend "the most precious of all jewels, my reputation," Lisa wrote a public letter outlining his activities and defending his actions.[26] In this letter Manuel indicated that he was the employer of "nearly an hundred American citizens," demonstrating that despite his preoccupation with his work as subagent, the trade certainly was sustaining the partnership of Lisa and Hunt.

More serious than the threat to his reputation was the menace of competition in the form of the American Fur Company, which had undergone a reorganization, and, under the leadership of Ramsay Crooks, was prosecuting the trade of the Great Lakes with a new vigor, aided not only by the Astor fortune but also by all means at the disposal of the government Indian agents in the area.[27] The threat to the Missouri trade was evident, for Astor, if he chose, had the capital to drive the St. Louis traders under. To combat this threat, the *Gazette* published the following notice on June 29:

> NOTICE—Those gentlemen desirous of hearing Proposals for a Company for trading up the waters of the Mississippi and Missouri, will attend at 5 o'Clock this evening at the Union Hall
> Jun 29   MANUEL LISA[28]

The appeal fell upon deaf ears, and the combination of Lisa and Hunt continued for another year. Sometime that summer Lisa again headed upriver, and certainly found much to do in addition to trading.

---

[25] Letter, Manuel Lisa to William Clark, July 2, 1817, printed in the *Missouri Gazette* (July 5, 1817).

[26] Letter, Manuel Lisa to Public, *Missouri Gazette* (July 6, 1816).

[27] Letter, George Graham to Richard Graham, June 11, 1816, Richard Graham Papers, MHS.

[28] *Missouri Gazette* (June 29, 1816).

The British, peace treaty notwithstanding, were still making a great show of competition for the trade of the American Indians, and Robert Dickson was remaining active.[29] Lisa, in addition to contending with this, had two posts to care for, one with the Omahas at Council Bluffs, and another farther up with the Sioux,[30] to say nothing of becoming reacquainted with Mitain after so long an absence.

The hunting season of 1816–17 was a busy and profitable one, marred only by one untoward incident. A wandering band of Sioux killed Pedro Antonio, one of Lisa's hunters, within nine miles of the Omaha post. Manuel "took 192 warriors of the *Mahas* tribe and went to the spot. Those who did the mischief had fled. The *Mahas*, impatient for blood, were eager to follow." This was a difficult situation, and Lisa handled it in a most judicious manner:

> I stopped them [the Omahas] with my own presents and my own influence, and I take honor to myself for having done it. The body of Antonio was not mutilated, it was covered with a blanket, and his face with a hat; his comrades might have been killed; they were not hurt. The death of Antonio then was a case of simple murder, and not an act of national hostility on the part of the *Sioux*. For one guilty act, must I turn loose two hundred warriors upon the innocent? Forget all moral principle, and turn barbarian myself, because in a country called *savage?* Besides, I had among the Sioux, at my upper establishment, two Americans and a Creole, who must have felt a tomahawk, if I had revenged upon the innocent, the death of *Pedro Antonio*.[31]

This was true forebearance on Lisa's part, since Antonio's death

---

[29] Letter, Thomas Forsyth to William Clark, June 3, 1817, Thomas Forsyth Papers, MHS.

[30] Letter, Manuel Lisa to William Clark, July 1, 1817, printed in the *Missouri Gazette* (July 5, 1817).

[31] Letter, Lisa to Clark, July 2, 1817, printed in the *Missouri Gazette* (July 5, 1817).

THE STONE WALLS
on the Upper Missouri

From A. E. Mathews, Pencil Sketches of Montana

THE GREAT FALLS OF THE MISSOURI

left him saddled with a debt of $260.92.[32] A difficult business this, with human life one of the cheapest commodities.

Manuel arrived in St. Louis from the north on June 13, 1817, "with a valuable cargo of furs and peltries, said to be worth 35 000 dollars,"[33] and brought with him his daughter Rosalie, first-born of his union with Mitain. What Polly's reaction was to this—indeed to the whole business of Lisa's extra-curricular marriage to an Indian—must be left to the imagination, although Polly, well versed in frontier ways, probably accepted this as a more or less normal state of affairs. Included in his return party was a deputation of Indians, including representatives "from the *Ottoes, Missouries,* and *Poncarars* tribes of Indians accompanied by the first Chief of the Pania Republic. and two chiefs of the Upper Tribe of Seoux."[34] These were the nations which had failed to respond to the call to council at Prairie du Chien; "the cause of their not attending our General Invitation earlier than at the present time, was (as they state) owing to an indirect warfare which had existed between them and the other tribes inhabiting the Country immediately between them and the White Settlers."[35] To get around this danger, and after seeing that nothing drastic had happened to those tribes signing treaties, they had appealed to Lisa, and, as subagent, he had given them safe conduct to St. Louis. William Clark gratified their desire for a treaty, with Lisa signing as witness.[36] This meant that all the tribes of the Missouri south of the Arikaras had now formally declared their friendship for the Americans, and since both the Arikaras and the Mandans had remained friendly to Lisa during the hostilities, the river, at least in theory, was perfectly safe for travel and trade.

[32] Missouri Fur Company Ledger Book, April, 1812, to July, 1813; 1817, Kansas State Historical Society.

[33] *Missouri Gazette* (June 14, 1817).

[34] Letter, William Clark and Auguste Chouteau to Secretary of War, July 1, 1817, William Clark Collection, MHS.

[35] *Ibid.*

[36] Peters, *Public Statutes,* VII.

However good the $35,000 looked to the readers of the *Gazette*, it was not enough to sustain the partnership of Lisa and Hunt, which terminated on the previously decided date, June 22, 1817.[37] The partners separated on amicable terms, indeed may even have remained together for another year, for they were again associated in a major undertaking in 1818. Whatever their connection, or lack of one, it was plain that such a small combination did not have the resources to utilize effectively the potentialities of the fur trade, particularly that of the Rocky Mountains, to which Lisa hoped to return. What arrangements were made, if any, for the next season are unknown. The *Gazette* of August 9 noted that Lisa had sent eastward for a steam engine to run a grist- and sawmill, a fine addition to the St. Louis manufacturing community,[38] but this was only a sidelight as he once again ascended the Missouri for the hunting and trading season.

Manuel was still trading under the name of Missouri Fur Company, but the old designation was undergoing a transformation into Cabanné and Company, another partnership arrangement which would not fully materialize until the spring of 1818, and would never develop into a cohesive organization. Negotiations leading to the formation of the new combine, which, apparently, had been going on for some months, reached an impasse over the question of a just evaluation of the stock and good name being provided the new combination by the Lisa-Hunt company. Lisa was seemingly determined that he should get some monetary recompense for the good reputation—there was none better—earned through hard work, long experience, and much suffering, which he carried among the Missouri Indians, and Cabanné was unwilling that he should get anything of the sort.[39]

---

[37] *Missouri Gazette* (June 28, 1817).

[38] *Ibid.* (Aug. 9, 1817).

[39] Letter, Cabanné and Company to Michael Immel, Feb. 1819, Charles Gratiot Letterbook, Sept. 9, 1812, to June 20, 1819, Charles Gratiot Collection, MHS.

The fiery Spaniard must have been feeling a little better about his personal finances, if not his company resources, as he again moved upriver in the fall of 1817. The courts had gradually been deciding in his favor in the several suits and counter-suits involving himself and William Morrison, dating back to the debate published in the *Gazette*. On March 27, 1816, the court had awarded him $2,492.59 and costs,[40] and on August 29, 1817, he received another $1,847.89 and costs,[41] giving him a little cash to begin paying off some of his various mortgages. Such sums ten years before would have gone a long way toward financing a trading company, but they would now pale into insignificance beside the amounts about to be poured into the Missouri trade.

Moving inexorably toward the foreground in the business affairs of rapidly expanding St. Louis in the fall of 1817 was the dreaded competition of the American Fur Company. Only an exploratory venture, it nonetheless sent the merchants of the Missouri metropolis scurrying to protect their interests. On October 6, Ramsay Crooks, now leading Astor's field operations, applied for a license for two of his employees, Russell Farnham and Pierre Lapeche, to trade on the Mississippi below Prairie du Chien. The request was granted by William Clark.[42] This was precisely the move Lisa had sought to block by asking for all those interested in a company to trade on the Mississippi as well as the Missouri. To move from the Mississippi to the Missouri would be no trick at all, since the natural outlet for the trade contemplated by Crooks was St. Louis. So the threat to the St. Louis monopoly of the Missouri trade was obvious, but, as yet, only a threat. The season of 1817–18 was as successful as the preceding one, and Lisa sent word down that they were doing

[40] Missouri Minute Book of the Supreme Court, 1812–21, MHS.

[41] *Ibid.*

[42] License Application, Ramsay Crooks to William Clark, Oct. 6, 1817, William Clark MSS, Vol. II, Kansas State Historical Society.

better than anyone on the river that winter.[43] This, however, was simply trade, and not the sort of business Lisa had envisioned for the Northwest. He was about to make another attempt to expand the scope of his operations.

The *Missouri Gazette* dutifully mentioned Lisa's return to civilization in early June, 1818, noting that he was accompanied by "valuable cargoes of furs, peltries, &c., &c."[44] His yearly arrivals with rich catches seemingly were becoming too commonplace to recount in any detail. Joseph Charless also significantly noted that "this enterprising gentleman is anxious to again extend our Indian trade to and beyond the Rocky Mountains." Not content with the ordinary trade with the Indians of the Missouri, Manuel was interested in getting to the good beaver country at the headwaters of the river, and sending out trapping parties as he had done in 1807 and 1809. There the real profits were to be made, and with the river now relatively safe for travel, the attainment of this objective should have been possible. Perhaps Cabanné and Company would be the means.

Lisa had also brought with him a new addition to his growing family, a Spanish lad of about ten years, ransomed from the Pawnees. That tribe had captured the boy from a party of Spaniards, and were preparing to offer him as a sacrifice "to the Great Star" when the traders put up goods to purchase his life. Lisa brought him to St. Louis to enable him to be educated, and earn his way through life.[45] It could not have been a very happy homecoming, for, in the midst of the cold season, and February 10, Polly Lisa had passed away.[46] Very little is known of the former Polly Charles, as she kept pretty much out of Manuel's affairs. She

[43] Letter, Ann L. Hunt to J. C. B. Lucas, Jan. 4 and 5, 1818, Lucas Papers, MHS. Her husband, Theodore Hunt, got the information in a letter from Lisa.

[44] *Missouri Gazette* (June 19, 1818).

[45] *Ibid.*; also Edwin James, *Account*, I, 359.

[46] *Missouri Gazette* (Feb. 13, 1818). She was buried on February 11. Oscar Collet, "Index to the St. Louis Cathedral and Carondelet Church Baptism, Marriage, and Deaths," 3 Vols., typescript, MHS, Burial Volume, 68.

bore him three children, none of whom lived to adulthood, and Manuel's only descendants came through his offspring by Mitain.

Lisa, in the manner of the frontier, did not mourn her passing for long, what with the young family and company reorganization pressing for his attention. Somehow he found time for a new and successful courtship, and on August 5, 1818, Manuel Lisa was married to Mrs. Mary Hempstead Keeney, widowed daughter of Stephen Hempstead.[47] Stephen Hempstead, with his family, had come to the wilds of Missouri from civilized Connecticut only a few years before, and had rapidly risen to a place of prominence and respect in the community. The wedding was presided over by the Reverend Salmon Giddings, leader of the Presbyterian group in and around St. Louis, and was witnessed by the bride's brother Charles Hempstead, a young and upcoming attorney, William Clark, Lisa's old partner in the Missouri Fur Company, Bernard Pratte, member of an old St. Louis family and one of Lisa's new partners in Cabanné and Company, and his old antagonist as well as former partner, Pierre Chouteau.[48] The strange combination of the Roman Catholic Lisa and the Presbyterian Mary Keeney, the dark, volatile Spaniard and the quiet and unassuming New Englander, was the cause of much speculation[49] and wonderment, but it was a union based on a deep and abiding emotion which lasted far beyond Manuel's lifetime.[50] The honeymoon, such as it could be in St. Louis in

[47] *Missouri Gazette* (Aug. 8, 1818); St. Louis Marriage Record, 1808–36, MHS; Stephen Hempstead Diary, Aug. 5, 1818, MHS.

[48] St. Louis Marriage Record, 1808–36, MHS.

[49] There was even a story that the new Mrs. Lisa could speak neither French nor Spanish, and Manuel could speak no English, so the two were unable to communicate through the medium of the spoken word. This, so ran the story, was why they were able to live so happily together. Walter B. Stevens, *St. Louis: The Fourth City, 1764–1909*, I, 369.

[50] Mrs. Lisa lived on to the age of eighty-seven, passing away at Galena, Illinois, in 1869. Ambrose P. Smith, *Memorials to the Life and Character of Mary Manuel Lisa*.

August, was shortened and saddened when Mary Lisa, aged five, followed her mother to the grave.[51]

With all of this activity, Lisa was still able to take part in the formation of the new partnership and the preparations for the fall expedition. The previous summer the parties involved in the new enterprise had attempted to set up a board of neutral examiners to determine the value of the goods and equipment brought into the organization by Lisa and Hunt, but they were unable to agree. Lisa had brought down his own estimate of $10,218.89¾, which proved unsatisfactory to the new partners. A set of arbitrators, Ridson Price and Michel Lacroix, cut that estimate to about $5,174.00, which was, of course, unacceptable to Manuel.[52] The situation remained unresolved as the partners prepared for the coming season.

The new combination included Jean Pierre Cabanné, long an Indian trader out of St. Louis, having been involved in the breaking up of Clamorgan's monopoly shortly after Lisa arrived in the Spanish outpost. He was the proprietor of a substantial mercantile company which had been gaining in importance for some time, and which had some connection with Astor in the East.[53] Other members were the firm of Berthold and Chouteau (it was impossible to form any worthwhile enterprise without the inclusion of the name Chouteau), the outfit which later became the western department of the American Fur Company; Bernard Pratte, prominent St. Louis merchant; Theodore Hunt, in part because of his share of the Lisa-Hunt partnership which was, or would be, purchased by the new group as soon as an equitable price could be established; John O'Fallon, William Clark's

[51] Stephen Hempstead Diary, Aug. 16, 1818, MHS.

[52] Letter, Cabanné to Immel, Feb., 1819, Charles Gratiot Letterbook, Sept. 9, 1812, to June 20, 1819, Charles Gratiot Collection, MHS.

[53] The Charles Gratiot Letterbook, Mar. 6, 1798, to Jan. 6, 1816, contains a series of letters between Gratiot and Astor in which the writer asked Astor to take care of the Cabanné accounts in the East. The company grew rapidly from 1814 to 1816.

nephew, up from Louisville and eager to get back on the Missouri to pursue his search for wealth and fame; and Manuel Lisa. Apparently the company was worth about $60,000, a larger resource than Lisa had ever had behind him.[54] Unfortunately, it was a decidedly temporary affair, O'Fallon already having made arrangements to drop out in April, 1819, to go out on his own.[55]

A large trading expedition, under Lisa's direction, set out for the upper river that season, with O'Fallon waiting in St. Louis for the last boat, which departed on September 12.[56] According to him, the merchandise was an assortment "well selected amtg to 21,000 dollars and a Indian assortment just received from London via Mackinaw of about 5,000 dollars."[57] Business was excellent, if one can believe a young man writing home to impress his mother with his ability and success, for O'Fallon stated, on December 14, that he was making money at the rate of $1,000 per month.[58] While O'Fallon was pleased with the situation, Lisa was not. The company was making no attempt to reach the mountains, and the question of the value of the Lisa-Hunt partnership still rankled. He returned to St. Louis in mid-February, contrary, in all likelihood, to the rules of the company, and itemized his reasons for returning in a note to Cabanné on February 13.[59]

[54] Letter, Cabanné to Immel, Feb., 1819, in *ibid*.

[55] Letter, John O'Fallon to Dennis Fitzhugh, Sept. 13, 1818, O'Fallon Papers, MHS.

[56] *Ibid*.

[57] *Ibid*.

[58] Letter, John O'Fallon to Mrs. O'Fallon, Dec. 14, 1819, O'Fallon Papers, MHS.

[59] Unfortunately, this letter has not been found. Perhaps it is lying in some dusty attic along with the papers of Cabanné and Company, which, if they ever come to light, will be a great addition to the knowledge of early St. Louis. Lisa's letter is mentioned in the reply to it: Letter, Cabanné and Company to Manuel Lisa, Charles Gratiot Letterbook, Sept. 9, 1812, to June 20, 1819, Charles Gratiot Collection, MHS.

Lisa feared that the partners were planning to do him some harm, and were keeping him from possessing his share of the goods. Whatever his arguments, they were not considered sufficient by the partners. Cabanné wrote to Lisa assuring him that his suspicions were false, and reprimanding him for returning to St. Louis.[60] At the same time, Cabanné and the others had decided to divest Lisa of his command, and to make concerted efforts to hold the company together without him. A long letter was dispatched to Michael Immel, since he seemed most likely to succeed to Lisa's position, notifying him of Manuel's dismissal, and giving him the details of the make-up of the partnership. According to that statement, Cabanné had furnished $15,925.00; Berthold and Chouteau, $22,286.45; Bernard Pratte, $11,-241.22; Manuel Lisa, $5,596.51; and Theodore Hunt, $4,-718.87; with John O'Fallon due to pay in $12,000.00.[61] There was no mention of the share provided by the Lisa-Hunt partnership, nor was there any indication of the fact, later clarified in a letter to Berthold and Immel on April 16,[62] that Lisa had paid a draft to the company of $5,000.00, and had deposited another draft for the same sum payable on June 10, 1821, which fulfilled his obligations under the partnership. Manuel was also to have provided a share for Immel, which, up to that point, he had not done, and Cabanné proposed that Immel, in return for taking over the field leadership, be entitled to that share, even though unpaid, and the dividend which would accrue.[63] Another letter was sent to the other important men upriver, John Dougherty, Joseph Brazeau, Alex Papin, Joseph Pratte, Jean Baptiste Bouvet, and Moses B. Carson, notifying them of Lisa's removal, and the appointment of "Michael Immell, George Kennerly,

[60] *Ibid.*

[61] Letter, Cabanné to Immel, Feb., 1819, in *ibid.*

[62] Letter, Cabanné and Company to Mr. B. Berthold & Jimmell, Apr. 16, 1819, in *ibid.*

[63] Letter, Cabanné to Immel, Feb., 1819, in *ibid.*

and ——— Richard" to take command.[64] Many of these men were old Lisa hands, having been through all of his vicissitudes, the changes of companies, and the like, and Cabanné did not want to lose them.

There must have been a good deal of justice in Manuel's claims, whatever they were, for Immel and the rest did not remain with Cabanné but chose to follow Lisa into whatever new project he promoted, and the firm of Cabanné and Company dissolved by mutual consent on June 1, 1819. Lisa wasted no time in attempting to obtain supplies for the next season, and with good cause. Prices were extremely high in St. Louis, as shinplasters abounded and the panic of 1819 approached. Included on the list of commodities drawing a better price was beaver—$3.50 per pound.[65] On February 15, Lisa sent off a letter to, of all people, Ramsay Crooks, asking if the American Fur Company might not be able to supply him with commodities usable in the Missouri trade for the coming season.[66]

Crooks was quite astonished that Cabanné and Company had folded so soon, but was no doubt delighted that it should do so. American Fur had long been trying to draw Berthold and Chouteau into an agreement, allowing them access to the Missouri, but had been unsuccessful. Perhaps this was their opening. Crooks wrote a very apologetic reply to the man who had twice put a crimp in his earlier ventures on the river with Robert McClellan, stating that he had not anticipated the dissolution of the partnership, and had ordered no extra goods. The American Fur Company could, regrettably, be of no help.[67] Crooks could scarcely hide his jubilation in a letter to Michel Lacroix on the same date,

[64] Letter, Cabanné and Company to J. Dougherty, Jos. Brazeau, Alex Papin, J. Pratte, J. B. Bouvet, ——— Carson, Feb., 1819, in *ibid.*

[65] Letter, Ramsay Crooks to John Jacob Astor, June 19, 1818, Ramsay Crooks Letterbook, 1816–20, MHS.

[66] Letter, Ramsay Crooks to Manuel Lisa, Mar. 19, 1819, in *ibid.*

[67] *Ibid.*

indicating that he thought all of the former partners would continue to trade individually and probably ruin each other in the ensuing competition.[68] The American Fur Company could then move into the Missouri by default.

But Lisa had other plans as well. In 1819 there took place the ill-fated Yellowstone expedition of the federal government, which planned to move up the Missouri to establish the authority of the United States, and Lisa had a quasi-official position with that group. As early as October, 1818, it was indicated that Lisa was to precede the expedition, "to prepare the Indians for its reception. He will quiet their apprehensions by shewing the benevolent and humane intentions of the American government; and will silence the British emisaries who shall represent the expedition as an act of war against the Indian nations."[69] No small task, convincing the Indians of the "benevolent and humane intentions" of the government.

More to the point, Lisa was instrumental in the formation of a new Missouri Fur Company sometime during the spring and summer of 1819. Another partnership, this one of four years' duration,[70] the new organization consisted of a number of individuals not hitherto associated with the fur trade. Manuel Lisa was the president, and the partners were Joshua Pilcher, a St. Louis merchant and banker of some prominence, Andrew Woods, Moses B. Carson, late of Cabanné and Company, John B. Zenoni, Joseph Perkins, and Thomas Hempstead, Lisa's brother-in-law,[71] with Andrew Drips, later to leave his own mark on the

[68] In *ibid.*

[69] *Niles' Weekly Register,* XV (Oct. 17, 1818), 329-30.

[70] Letter, Joshua Pilcher to Ramsay Crooks, June 16, 1822, Chouteau Collection, MHS.

[71] Deposition of Thomas Hempstead, Nov. 9, 1824, in the case of David Stone, Josiah Bellows, and Oliver Bostwick vs. Mary Lisa, Executrix, and Charles S. Hempstead, Executor, of Manuel Lisa, deceased, St. Louis Records, Book I, 447, Office of the Recorder of Deeds, City Hall, St. Louis, Missouri. There is a similar deposition, giving the same information on the same subject, in the St. Louis Circuit Court File,

trade, added sometime after the original agreement.[72] This Missouri Fur Company was reputed to have a working capital of $70,000.[73] They purchased what supplies were available, and utilized whatever remained of Lisa's equipment to begin trade in the fall of 1819, but made provision to be fully prepared to embark the following year by applying to the firm of David Stone and Company of Boston, Massachusetts, to supply them with the necessary goods.

Lisa wrote to Boston, describing the new company and its prospects, and proposing terms to Stone. Thomas Hempstead went east in the fall of 1819 to close the agreement in person, meeting Oliver Bostwick, acting partner for Stone and Company, in Washington, where the final details were completed. Stone was to deliver the merchandise requested by the Missouri Fur Company to St. Louis by the following May or June, the amount totaling $25,910.98. In return, the company was to market through Stone and Company all of its furs and peltries. Credit, the bane of the early trade, was on a twelve-month basis—not good, but better than the six months' credit under which Lisa had been forced to work previously. Bostwick came to St. Louis in the summer of 1820 to deliver the goods and meet with the president of the Missouri Fur Company. When Bostwick evinced some qualms about the amount which had been advanced to the company, Lisa, supremely confident that the company would be able to discharge its debts within the year, offered to mortgage all of his property in St. Louis as security for the $25,910.98

Oct. Term, 1824, No. 35, Office of the Clerk of the Circuit Court, Civil Courts Building, St. Louis, Missouri, which is conveniently reprinted in Charles E. Peterson, "Manuel Lisa's Warehouse," *Missouri Historical Society Bulletin*, Vol. IV (January, 1948), 81–84.

[72] Deposition of Michael Immel in the case of William Easdale vs. Thomas Hempstead, St. Louis Circuit Court File, Apr. Term, 1821, No. 71, also reprinted in Peterson, "Warehouse," *loc. cit.*, 80.

[73] Beck, *Gazetteer*, 329–30.

debt. The offer was quickly accepted.[74] While these negotiations were under way, Lisa started off for his post at Council Bluffs, now called "Fort Lisa," accompanied by his bride of a year, the first white woman to ascend the Missouri. "Aunt Manuel," as Mrs. Lisa came to be known, was accompanied by another woman, who has remained nameless, and the two were objects of the greatest curiosity on the part of the natives. Upon arriving at Fort Lisa, the party was forced to spend the night in a tipi, since their quarters in the fort had not been completed. Aunt Manuel awakened early in the morning to face a circle of black eyes peering at her from under the edges of the tent, and from then on her life was completely public. Crowds of Indians followed her everywhere, hoping for a chance to touch her fair, wavy hair and her pink cheeks. The Indians demanded that she be the one to make the trades for their pelts, and with Manuel's expert coaching, she did a creditable job. Her courage was put to the strongest test at an Indian feast in her honor, where roast dog was the main course. Like Thomas James before her, Aunt Manuel could not bear the thought of eating the repast, yet she knew she must, since the meal was in her honor. Somehow, under the ever watchful eyes of her hosts, the fastidious New England matron managed to appear to be eating while slipping the meat into a handbag concealed in her lap.[75] The military establishment, which wintered only a few miles above Fort Lisa, provided a civilized touch, holding formal dinners, dances, and the like. The traders replied in kind, and were able to outdo their army neighbors by providing hostesses. This was a far cry from that first winter in the Missouri country, at rough-hewn Fort Raymond in 1807–1808, but advancing civilization was getting

[74] Thomas Hempstead Deposition, Nov. 9, 1824, St. Louis Records, Book I, 447, office of the Recorder of Deeds, City Hall, St. Louis, Missouri.

[75] Mrs. Eliza Hempstead Cooke, "Account of Mrs. Manuel's Trip up the Missouri," typescript, Lisa Papers, MHS. This was written from memory by one who heard the story from the lips of Aunt Manuel.

pretty close to Council Bluffs. While social life bloomed, trading went on apace. The several partners reported in from various points throughout the winter. Joshua Pilcher, who seemed to have caught Lisa's enthusiasm for the business—and some of his trading talent to go along with it—went to the Omaha village to bargain for furs. Although Mitain had been sent away, Manuel did not wish to take any chances on a possible meeting. Pilcher returned with "one hundred and thirty beaver skins, besides raccoon and deer skins."[76] John Zenoni and Joseph Perkins established a small post at the mouth of the Nishnabotna, somewhat below Council Bluffs, in early November, but did not do well.[77] Zenoni reported at Fort Lisa on February 15 with nothing to show for his efforts.[78] Michael Immel, who had gone directly to the Sioux post to take charge of its operations, returned with the proceeds in early November, but was stopped by the military at Lisa's request. There had been a rumor that Immel planned to withhold part of the cargo, and Manuel, so used to double-dealing by now that he did not even trust one of his oldest and most faithful employees, was not taking any chances that the rumor might be true.[79] Joseph Perkins had gone downstream after the failure at Nishnabotna, and was put in charge of the company's goods at Franklin.[80] In January he headed a small expedition to Fort Lisa with some $3,000 worth of merchandise, including 797¾ gallons of that necessary staple, whisky.[81] Immel, having a good deal of difficulty with his hired hands came

---

[76] Edwin James, *Account*, I, 183.

[77] Letter, Joseph Perkins and John Zenoni to Manuel Lisa and Joshua Pilcher, Nov. 2, 1819, Fur Trade Papers, MHS.

[78] Edwin James, *Account*, I, 191.

[79] Letter, Lt. Col. W. Morgan to Col. Henry Atkinson, Nov. 11, 1819, and Letter, Col. Henry Atkinson to John C. Calhoun, Dec. 5, 1819, War Department Records, National Archives, photostats in author's possession.

[80] Letter, Joseph Perkins to Manuel Lisa and Joshua Pilcher, Jan. 24, 1820, Fur Trade Papers, MHS.

[81] Letter, Joseph Perkins to Joshua Pilcher, Apr. 19, 1820, in *ibid*.

down with another load of pelts in April, indicating that, at the Sioux post, at least, business was brisk.[82]

Moving downstream in the spring of 1820, Lisa was probably well enough satisfied with the beginning of the new company. They did not make enough to pay for the goods being advanced by Stone and Company, but Thomas Hempstead was able, on October 4, 1820, to turn over to Oliver Bostwick $8,074.01 worth of furs and pelts.[83] Thus at least one-third of the first year's goods were paid for before the trading season began.

Lisa returned to St. Louis in an unwell condition, apparently having contracted some illness over the winter, an illness which was to prove fatal before another season could get under way.[84] What the malady was has been impossible to determine, but Lisa must have felt it might have fatal consequences, for shortly after his arrival, he hired Paul Provenchere to put all of his papers in order.[85] Oliver Bostwick appeared in St. Louis that summer and the mortgage arrangement was consumated, but otherwise it was an expensive summer for the company. The Sacs went on the warpath against the whites, and made off with a number of company horses from their Missouri posts.[86] In addition, about 1,800 pounds of beaverpelts were stolen from Thomas Hempstead's house, where they had been stored prior to transferal to Stone and Company.[87] Pilcher, who was actively directing the

[82] Letter, Michael Immel to Joshua Pilcher, Apr. 19, 1820, in *ibid.*

[83] Thomas Hempstead Deposition, Nov. 9, 1824, St. Louis Records, Book I, 447, Office of the Recorder of Deeds, City Hall, St. Louis, Missouri.

[84] Stephen Hempstead Diary, May 14, 1820, notes: "Breakfasted with son Manual [*sic*] who remains unwell."

[85] Bill, Paul Provenchere to executors of Manuel Lisa, May, 1820, Lisa Papers, MHS. The bill was not submitted until after Lisa's death, but was dated when the work was completed. This bill was apparently removed from Lisa's probate file.

[86] Letter, ——— to Thomas Forsyth, June 3, 1820, Thomas Forsyth Papers, MHS. The signature was lost to an autograph hunter.

[87] Michael Immel Deposition, Apr., 1821, St. Louis Court File, Apr. Term, 1821, No. 71.

company during Lisa's illness, had one James Watt arrested for the crime.[88]

Lisa, meanwhile, had somehow gotten involved in a fight with one Antoine Beaudoin, on August 1, in which he "struck with a certain iron bar and his fists the said Beaudoin a great many violent blows and strokes on and about his head face breast back and shoulders and divers other parts of his body, by means of which . . . the said Beaudoin was . . . greatly hurt bruised and wounded, and became sick lame disordered and sore maimed."[89] Even on the point of death, Manuel Lisa was no easy mark.

The scuffle did the victor no good, however, and shortly thereafter Lisa repaired to the sulphur springs a short distance from town in the hopes that those waters, with their reputed healing qualities, would be of some benefit. Such was not the case. Dr. Bernard G. Farrar was in attendance night and day, but could do little for his patient. The sickness, whatever it was, was either too far advanced, or Farrar could not diagnose it, for he tried none of the usual cures, bleeding or emetics, but simply watched and waited.[90] On August 11, Lisa made out his final will and testament, the signature on which, while unmistakably Lisa's, lacked the clarity and vigor which marked his normal hand. In the will, witnessed by Thomas Hempstead and Elijah Beebe, Manuel, after taking care that his debts be paid, expressed his wish for the Missouri Fur Company and, in so doing, betrayed the love he had for the adventurous life of the trader:

> It is my wish that the part I now have in the Missouri Fur Company shall be & continue as long as the articles of Association will permit—in my proper representations—& for that purpose if necessary, my Executors may employ proper persons to act in my place—And as much as I have consented to Execute a Mortgage

[88] Sheriff Order, Aug. 2, 1820, Lucas Papers, MHS.

[89] Antoine Beaudoin vs. Manuel Lisa, St. Louis Circuit Court File, Dec. Term, 1820, No. 6, printed in Peterson, "Warehouse," *loc. cit.*, 74.

[90] Farrar Day Book, 1820, MHS.

on my property in St. Louis to secure a debt to Messrs Stone Bostwick & Co for goods purchased for the said Missouri Fur Company
—if necessary, I hereby authorize and empower my said Executors
to execute such Mortgage according to the terms & for the period
agreed upon between Mr. Bostwick and myself—and lastly I
hereby authorize & empower my Executors to carry into effect
the aforesaid articles of association in as full and ample manner
as I could do—were I living.[91]

Lisa also made provision for his offspring, including Rosalie
and Christopher, his two children by Mitain,[92] and bequeathed
the unmortgaged half of Joaquin's original grant to his brother's
son, and his own godson and namesake, Manuel. The rest of the
personal estate was bequeathed to Mrs. Lisa, and she and her
brother, Charles Hempstead, were named executors, as well as
guardians of the minor children. After affixing his signature,
Manuel's health rapidly declined until his death, "without dis-
tressing struggles," at 6:45 P. M., on August 12, 1820.[93] He was
interred in the Hempstead burial plot the next day, after a
Solemn High Mass in the St. Louis Cathedral, a service attended
by the Presbyterian Hempsteads, not without a good deal of
muttering on the part of the elder Stephen. And so closed the
career of one of the first, and one of the best, traders who ever
ascended the Missouri.

[91] St. Louis Probate Court File, No. 497, Manuel Lisa, Deceased.

[92] Lisa had a last encounter with Mitain shortly before leaving Fort Lisa in the
spring of 1820, when he attempted to take his son Christopher to St. Louis with him.
Mitain refused to let him go, and when Lisa tried to force her to do so, Benjamin
O'Fallon, the Indian agent, intervened, and Mitain was permitted to keep her child.
Edwin James, *Account*, I, 249.

[93] Stephen Hempstead Diary, Sat., Aug. 12, 1820, MHS.

VII

Manuel Lisa
Accomplishments and Legacy

BEREFT of Lisa's dynamic leadership, the remainder of the Missouri Fur Company nevertheless struggled to "carry into effect the . . . articles of association in as full and ample manner as [he] could do—were [he] living," and did a creditable job. Thomas Hempstead took over the firm's financial concerns in St. Louis, while Joshua Pilcher, headquartered at Fort Lisa, became field leader, and later succeeded to Lisa's position as president. Financial problems hit Hempstead almost immediately as fur prices fell off in the late fall of 1820,[1] but Oliver Bostwick was still in town and a favorable agreement was concluded with him for the next year.[2] One-half of the large order of goods was to be paid for in cash, the rest on twelve months' credit, with a provision that 6 per cent interest was to be paid on the remainder if the terms were not met as specified. Not as good as the original agreement, but good enough, for Stone and Company were "honorable men but very scary," an

[1] Letter, Thomas Hempstead to Joshua Pilcher, Sept. 15, 1820, Fur Trade Papers, MHS.

[2] Thomas Hempstead's Deposition, Nov. 9, 1824, St. Louis Circuit Court File, Oct. Term, 1824, No. 35, also printed in Peterson, "Warehouse," *loc. cit.*, 81. Essentially the same statement is contained in St. Louis Records, Book I, 447, Office of the Recorder of Deeds, City Hall, St. Louis, Missouri.

179

opinion which Hempstead was to modify drastically before many more months. Bostwick also agreed to furnish no merchandise to anyone else trading on the Missouri above the mouth of the Grand River.[3]

February, 1821, found Hempstead dispatching about one thousand dollars worth of merchandise upstream to Pilcher, the most conspicuous articles being tobacco, 3,985 pounds, and whisky, 724 gallons, the two indispensables for Indian trade.[4] Business was progressing apace and the new season augured well. Spring brought the necessity of preparing an expedition to take upstream the goods which Bostwick was to have in St. Louis in May or June, which would allow the company time enough to transport the trade articles to the upper posts. June 1 came and went, however, with no sign of either Bostwick or the goods, and Hempstead was forced to look for merchandise in St. Louis, facing the competition of others preparing to embark in the Indian trade. The Bank of Missouri, still operating in defiance of the panic and depression, advanced enough cash to allow Hempstead to get his boats in the water and the men under contract.

Oliver Bostwick arrived in St. Louis on June 23, full of multiple apologies and great promises to see the company through at all costs, as long, of course, as the costs were not his to bear.[5] Taking care of the advances made by the bank, at $2\frac{1}{2}$ per cent, Bostwick proceeded to paint a rosy picture of future prospects, noting that the fur market had risen rapidly, and the cost of trade articles desired by the company had fallen from 50 to, in

[3] Letter, (Thomas Hempstead) to Joshua Pilcher, Oct. 22, 1820, Fur Trade Papers, MHS. The signature is missing, but the handwriting is unmistakably Hempstead's.

[4] Letter, Thomas Hempstead to Joshua Pilcher, Feb. 19, 1821, in *ibid.*

[5] Letter, Thomas Hempstead to Joshua Pilcher, June 27, 1821, Thomas Hempstead Letterbook, June 27, 1821, to February 12, 1823, Coe Collection, MS. No. 345, Yale University Library, New Haven, Connecticut (hereinafter cited as Coe MS); microfilm furnished author by Yale University Library.

some cases, 100 per cent. This was well, for the Astor interests were beginning to stir in St. Louis that spring, and there was the threat that yet another group, Chouteau in nature, was going to send Wilson Price Hunt north with an outfit.[6] The acting partner for Stone and Company was somewhat appalled at the amount he had had to advance to the company thus far. On the original commitment of $25,910.98, secured by Lisa's mortgage, there was still a balance of $16,836.97, and the outfit now en route to St. Louis amounted to $27,815.65. Hempstead, however, was able to turn over to Stone and Company the year's proceeds, totaling $31,875.65, taking care of the original advance and the one-half of the 1821 outfit which had to be paid for in cash upon arrival. This relieved Bostwick considerably, but the tremendous order put in by the company for the next year caused him to ask whether the Lisa mortgage could be extended to cover that. Hempstead referred him to Lisa's executors, who, pressed for funds themselves, refused. Stone and Company later attempted a foreclosure on the terms of the original mortgage, to which the executors had agreed after Lisa's death, but were not entirely successful in collecting.[7]

But while Bostwick was there, talking already about next year's outfit, and dickering over finances, his goods were not, causing Hempstead no little anxiety. Without this year's merchandise, there might not be a next year. Writing to Pilcher, he expressed the hope that the company boat could embark on July 10, providing the goods got there in time (they were always "expected momentarily"), and also noted that Michael Immel and Robert Jones, with their mountain crew of seasoned trappers, were planning to depart St. Louis on July 2. As it was, the mountain party did not get off until July 10, and Bostwick's merchandise did not

---

[6] *Ibid.*

[7] Thomas Hempstead Deposition, Nov. 9, 1824, St. Louis Circuit Court File, Oct. Term, 1824, No. 35.

arrive until July 22, long after it should have been on its way upstream.[8] Immel's contingent was the vehicle by which the Missouri Fur Company returned to the mountains. It returned, in fact, to the very site of the first post on the upper reaches of the Missouri watershed, the mouth of the Bighorn, where Pilcher established Fort Benton. A pity, perhaps, that Lisa was not there to see the fulfillment of his ambition, but in view of the results, it was best.

The Missouri Fur Company, despite Bostwick's procrastination, appeared on the verge of success. The arrival of the goods caused Hempstead to exult: "I have paid every debt that the Company owes in this place with the exception of the few articles that we got this year and Lacroix which I am in hopes to make an arrangement with Mr. Bostwick . . . I think this year will establish the credit and standing of the Missouri Fur Company to the great mortification of some people in this country."[9] Hempstead's joy was to be short-lived, however, for "some people" were determined that the Missouri Fur Company was not going to make it. The company boat, a very substantial, completely watertight craft, was quickly loaded in preparation for the voyage northward, but in the black midnight after final loading was completed, someone cut it loose from the mooring below First Street on the St. Louis water front. At the end of a six-mile chase, with fortune smiling for a change, the boat was caught, undamaged, and brought back to St. Louis. There it was checked carefully, and immediately set sail for Fort Lisa. On the night of August 13, two scant miles above Bellefontaine, the craft sank, soaking all the goods aboard, with a loss which Hempstead estimated at $5,000, but which would prove double that.[10] This was no accident since the boat had been checked at midnight and found bone dry, and two hours later had gone down, sinking so fast that

[8] Letter, Thomas Hempstead to Joshua Pilcher, June 27, 1821, Coe MS.
[9] *Ibid.*, July 22, 1821.
[10] *Ibid.*, Aug. 13, 1821.

the men on board did not have time to save their personal effects.

The blow was a serious one, and Pilcher, not receiving the goods, sent down a long lament, "too late, too late, too late," having been unhappy with arrangements ever since Bostwick had been so tardy that first summer. But there was nothing to do but go on. Hempstead dispatched the company boat to the Kansa post, and noted with increasing apprehension the formation of a new trading organization headed by the Lieutenant Governor of the state, General William Ashley.[11] This was not another experiment, to be tolerated for a few months or perhaps a year before it collapsed, for Andrew Henry, former member of the old Missouri Fur Company, was lending his ability and experience to Ashley's apparently considerable financial backing.

Bostwick sold $6,000 worth of merchandise to Ashley, causing Hempstead, who knew that Ashley was going considerably farther than the Grand, to have a few second thoughts about Stone and Company, and the agent of the Missouri Fur Company turned to Berthold and Chouteau to purchase some necessary knives.[12] The company had also been careful to keep its political fences in good repair, with Hempstead sending gifts of buffalo tongues to such notables in Washington as Henry Clay, John C. Calhoun, William H. Crawford, and President James Monroe.[13] The company boat, loaded with goods for Fort Lisa, Wilson McGunnigle in charge, departed on September 11, after having been held until the last possible moment hoping for a shipment of barley corn and beads which Bostwick had promised would come up from New Orleans that summer. Stone and Company were at least consistent as the goods did not arrive until November 29, and Hempstead was forced to take the corn and beads himself, by pack-horse train, to the posts above.[14] By the time

[11] *Ibid.*, Sept. 2, 1821.

[12] *Ibid.*, Sept. 11, 1821.

[13] Letters of presentation went out to Clay on June 29, 1821, and the rest on October 16, Coe MS.

[14] Letter, Thomas Hempstead to Oliver Bostwick, Jan. 1, 1822, Coe MS.

the operation was completed, the goods had cost more for transportation than their original price. It was well that Bostwick had promised to be in St. Louis by April 15, 1822. Perhaps then the Missouri Fur Company could count on delivery by June.

There was much competition in St. Louis in the spring of 1822, and not all of it according to the rules, as several groups fought to acquire the advantage. Ramsay Crooks, Astor's active agent in the West, attempted to seduce Joshua Pilcher away from the Missouri Fur Company, asking, in a letter written in March, 1822, if the dynamic and forceful leader was free to join another organization, the American Fur Company, for instance, or at least if he would be interested in making some arrangement with that institution. Pilcher answered with a candor worthy of Lisa, although his statement was much more diplomatic than Manuel's would have been. He pointed out that the company was due to expire in July, 1823, and that he could not possibly consider any offers until then. In addition, the partners planned an extension of the agreement at that time. The Missouri Fur Company was doing quite well, despite the fact that they were doing business with Oliver Bostwick, who was always late, multiplying their expenses two or three times. Further:

> . . . there are several young gentlemen who have been ingaged in the service of the Company, and some of them are now interested in it; their fortunes have become identified with my own; they look to me with confidence as a head as a leader; and my confidence in, and attachment for them is unlimited; for in them is united with all the ordinary qualifications for this business; integrity, pride, intelligence spirit and interprise rarely suppressed; and in prosecuting a business of such enormous weight, I should feel much at a loss without the aid of such persons.[15]

Proposition rejected; but Astor had already turned to Berthold and Chouteau.

[15] Letter, Joshua Pilcher to Ramsay Crooks, June 16, 1822, Chouteau Collection, MHS.

Despite the losses suffered the previous autumn, Hempstead was able to report, in the spring of 1823, that the past year had been a success. He turned over to Bostwick, upon the latter's arrival on March 26 (!),[16] furs and skins worth $30,472.30. In October the company turned over another $11,590.25, making the year's total $42,062.55.[17] Stone and Company were prepared to accept another one-year agreement, but the goods for 1822 would be late, as usual. Some of the goods would arrive by April 15, but the important ones, knives, beads, lace, and the rest of the trade articles, would not appear until June 1.[18] This was tragic in view of the competition. William Ashley had purchased everything that floated in and around St. Louis in preparation for his own voyage, and Hempstead was forced as far south as Ste Geneviève to find a boat for company use. Worse for business, although Hempstead did not deem it overly important, Ashley's first boat departed on April 3, and he was planning to send 150 men overland to the Yellowstone to build a post.[19] This would place him on the ground already being covered by Michael Immel and his crew. Hempstead was rather taken aback at the liberality of the contracts Ashley was offering his hunters, although they were the same half-and-half arrangements which Lisa and the Missouri Fur Company had used as early as 1809.

Astor finally made his connection with Berthold and Chouteau that spring, and serious competition was to be expected from that quarter, although the combination was still a tenuous one, with both the American Fur Company and Berthold and Chouteau continuing to make overtures to Hempstead for a partnership. Knowing the strength of his relative position, Hempstead drove too hard a bargain for his suitors, or perhaps they were

16 Letter, Thomas Hempstead to Joshua Pilcher, Apr. 3, 1822, Coe MS.

17 Thomas Hempstead Deposition, Nov. 9, 1824, St. Louis Circuit Court File, Oct. Term, 1824, No. 35.

18 Letter, Thomas Hempstead to Joshua Pilcher, Apr. 3, 1822, Coe MS.

19 *Ibid.*

simply leading him on, hoping to make the Missouri Fur Company dependent on one or the other, and then cutting them off. Hempstead broke off relations with Crooks on August 9,[20] even though he feared that Bostwick would deal only for cash in the coming year, but the negotiations with Berthold and Chouteau went on into 1823.[21] Of more serious consequence, "Mrs. Manuel is compelled to sell her stock as those people have got a judgement against the Estate and have threatened to attach her household furniture."[22] The company did not have $6,000 to purchase it from her, and the loss of such a block of stock to competitors might be fatal. Fortunately no one was in a position to take advantage of the situation. The company boat, *Mary Jane*, departed on May 13, under the command of the inscrutable Frenchman, Lucien Fontenelle, carrying goods purchased in St. Louis, for Bostwick's had not yet arrived, and were now not even expected until June 5.[23] Altogether, it was not a pleasant year, but there had been no massive misfortunes either, and the partners eagerly looked forward to 1823.

However, the evil spirit which had hovered near the Missouri Fur Company from its original inception was about to deal Lisa's legacy a blow from which it would never recover. The weapon used by fate was the same used in the beginning: the Blackfeet. Pilcher well knew the difficulty Manuel had had with these cruel and vindictive savages, and intended to open friendly intercourse with them if at all possible. Led by the faithful Michael Immel and the talented Robert Jones, a party set out in the spring of 1823 from their wintering ground with the Crows near Fort Benton to find the Blackfeet and make arrangements for opening a trade with them. Crisscrossing the Three Forks area, trapping as they went, this small body of men failed to raise a

[20] *Ibid.*, Aug. 9, 1822.
[21] *Ibid.*, Feb. 12, 1823.
[22] *Ibid.*, Apr. 3, 1822.
[23] *Ibid.*, May 14, 1822.

single war whoop, and the unwonted silence caused the men no little trepidation. About the middle of May the group started back to Crow country, totally unsuccessful as far as the diplomatic side of their journey was concerned. On the way out they met a band of Blackfeet, who smoked with the whites in a friendly—almost too friendly—manner, and seemed delighted at Immel's proposal of a fort for their exclusive use and trade to be built below the falls of the Missouri. Both groups made loud protestations of eternal friendship, parted company, and started for their respective camps as quickly as they could travel, the Blackfeet to augment their numbers for an attack, the company men, understanding much more than they let on to the Indians, to get out of that country and safely back to Fort Benton.

Immel and Jones almost made it, but almost was never good enough in the wilderness. The brigade was within ten miles of the Crow camp in which they had wintered when struck from ambush by about four hundred howling Blackfeet. There was no contest. The attack was so sudden, and so unexpected, that Robert Jones did not have time to reflect that he had turned down Thomas Hempstead's offer of the Kansa post in order to go to the mountains before he was struck down by Indian arrows. With him went Michael Immel, who so long had escaped the snares of the wilderness that he had seemed immune, and several others besides. The Blackfeet took, in addition to the men's lives, all the horses and pelts carried by the party and, in the process, destroyed the enterprising spirit which had been the soul of the Missouri Fur Company.[24] Although Pilcher would make several efforts to recoup the company's fortunes, he was never able to overcome the difficulties which beset him. The mountains were now open to a new group of exploiters who would succeed in almost obliterating beaver from the streams of the West.

This resurgence of the Missouri fur trade was led by Manuel

[24] I have generally followed the account in Chittenden, *American Fur Trade*, I, 151–53.

Lisa's old partner Andrew Henry, first man to lead a trapping expedition beyond the Rocky Mountains, and William H. Ashley, businessman and first lieutenant governor of the new state of Missouri. They led the purely American assault on Blackfoot country, and with them came the beginnings of a new brand of frontier character, the mountain man, who was to dominate the West for the next twenty years. Sprung from the same mold which had produced John Colter, George Drouillard, Michael Immel, and the rest of the early devotees of the natural life, these individuals—Jed Smith, Bible in one hand, rifle in the other; Hugh Glass, whose adventures make an American odyssey; Jim Bridger; Bill Sublette; Tom Fitzpatrick; and a host more—would write dramatic pages in the saga of westward expansion. They disdained trading with the lowly tribes of the Missouri, and chose to go directly to the mountains, to deal with Crows and Blackfeet, to trap the rich beaver areas of the northern Rockies. Andrew Henry should have known better.

Henry had been dissatisfied with the operations of the old Missouri Fur Company when he had been a part of it, primarily because of the seeming emphasis on trade rather than on trapping, and probably considered Lisa to be the cause. Manuel, to be sure, never led a brigade of hunters into the forest, was not a trapper, as was Henry, but mainly a trader, and his personal interests were along those lines. However, Lisa had been the one who had originally seen the advantages of trapping. He had sent out the hunters in 1807–1808, and he had sent out Henry himself in 1809–10, recognizing that in capturing the pelts themselves, the company stood to make the greatest profit. Henry never grasped that Manuel's preoccupation with the Missouri tribes kept those Indians friendly, or at least neutral, and that without that friendship or neutrality there was no safe way to get the furs down the Missouri highway to St. Louis. While there had been a good deal of patriotism behind Lisa's activities as subagent during the War of 1812, he was also insuring safe travel for his men and boats. After the discovery of good land routes to the mountains, this necessity was somewhat obviated, but the Rocky Mountain Fur Company and others learned to their sorrow that land travel greatly increased costs and thus cut profits. Henry and Ashley, planning to use the Missouri to transport goods and furs, should have taken precautions to keep the river free for navigation, which meant keeping the amity of the natives who called the banks of the river their home.

Of all the tribes bordering the river, the Arikaras were the most violent and unpredictable, and for good reason. They were not Plains Indians, as were the Sioux, devoted to the chase, accustomed to following the buffalo and subsisting on the products of that animal, nor were they completely sedentary, as were their neighbors to the north, the Mandans. They stood somewhere in transition, living in palisaded villages and growing crops of corn, but also sending out hunting parties to compete with the Sioux, Pawnees, and Gros Ventres for the bounty of the Plains. As competition proved too severe, the Rees developed a main reliance on trade—barter with the Plains Indians of corn for meat, horses, robes, pelts; exchange with the white man of pelts and robes for guns, tools, "strong water," and other goods which rapidly became necessities to the Ree way of life. This trade had developed to the point that the Arikaras protested Lisa's moving his post only twelve miles away in 1812.[25]

For the middlemen Rees, the vicious circle was deep. The more dependent they became on the white man for goods, the more they had to rely on their trade with the nomads of the West. When the Ashley-Henry party went by in 1822, stopping only for the traditional smoke and promise, with Henry even sending out his land party from that point, it took little thought for the Arikaras to understand the significance of this new inva-

[25] See Chapter V in this volume.

sion of the north. The white man was going directly to the source of peltry, cutting off that commodity from the natives, and would deal directly with the mountain and Plains tribes on their own ground. In addition, there were to be no goods left with the Rees, only the promise "next year," thus cutting them off from both ends of their essential trade. Small wonder that they attacked Ashley's boats in 1823.[26]

This incident, coupled with the continued intransigence of the Blackfeet, convinced Henry that there must be easier ways of making a living, and he shortly retired completely from the trade. Ashley, too, quickly discovered what the Chouteaus had always known: the profit in the fur trade was in the supplying of goods to the trading and trapping companies, not in trading or trapping itself. There was little risk involved in that end of the game, and the Chouteaus had early perceived this fact. They sold goods to the Missouri Fur Company in St. Louis, and it was up to the company to transport them safely upriver, trade them off at a profit, and get the proceeds back to St. Louis. Then the Chouteaus, having already made a profit on the goods sold to the company, and interest on the advance made to purchase the goods, would buy the pelts and robes at a discount, usually pre-arranged according to the credit system set up, and sell them at another profit.

If all this was true, why did not Lisa stick to the supply phase of the business as he had begun, supplying men like Robert Mc-Clellan, Jacques Clamorgan, and others? Partly because that was too sedentary. Manuel Lisa was a fantastically active man, constantly on the move, and could usually be found somewhere between New Orleans and Montreal, the Atlantic Coast and the Rocky Mountains. As he said, "I put into my operations great activity; I go a great distance while some are considering whether

[26] A good description of the festivities at the Ree village in 1823 is given in the standard account of Ashley's enterprise, Dale L. Morgan, *Jedediah Smith and the Opening of the West*, 42–77.

they will start today or tomorrow."[27] This was not a man to sit at a desk ordering goods, dispensing them with the push of a pencil, waiting for the returns, and totaling receipts in tedious ledger accounts. There was no ink in his blood.

Then, too, Manuel Lisa had a deep interest in and concern for the Indians he met on the great river. They called him "Father," and with good reason. Lisa fully realized that white settlers would eventually move into the Missouri Valley and push the Indian out or destroy him unless the red man could change his ways. In demanding beaver fur and buffalo robes, Lisa himself was contributing to the destruction of the Indian way of life, the depletion of the animals, particularly the buffalo, upon which the native depended for survival. He compensated for this by helping the Indian adapt to the white man's ways, bringing him domestic cattle, vegetables, pumpkins, beans, turnips, and potatoes; he even brought to him, and taught him to use, the plow. Lisa's blacksmiths labored for the various tribes, making and repairing the tools necessary to the new way of life.[28] Defending them against the activities of unscrupulous whites, Manuel tried to maintain their sovereignty over the lands on which they lived, the lands which had so concerned Big Elk in 1815.[29] Further, Lisa had trapped only the Wind River–Bighorn country, where the Crows had welcomed him, the "Spanish waters" of the Arapahoes, who also had little objection to the activities of traders and trappers, and the Three Forks area, belonging to the Blackfeet. The latter had objected violently to the invasion of their lands, and Lisa had been prevented from ever parleying with them to see whether or not some arrangement could be made.

[27] Letter, Manuel Lisa to William Clark, July 1, 1817, printed in the *Missouri Gazette* (July 5, 1817).

[28] *Ibid.*

[29] Address of Big Elk to William Clark, printed in the *Missouri Gazette* (Aug. 5, 1815).

But the main driving force behind Manuel Lisa was the vision of the Northwest as a giant fur empire, a great source of wealth for himself and his adopted land. Having satisfied his curiosity in 1807–1808, having seen with his own eyes the inestimable value intrinsic in that country, he dedicated his life to exploiting it. Circumstances conspired to thwart his best efforts. This was no small operation he had in mind; the area was vast, the risks enormous. A sizable amount of capital was necessary, and money simply was not available. The War of 1812 interrupted the development of his plans, preventing him from even reaching the area in which he was most interested. But the most damaging thing of all was the attitude of his partners, who did not share the long view, who were unwilling to give up "a bird in the hand" for a whole covey in the bush, forcing Manuel to be content with much less than was available.

Still, the returns from the trade of the river had not been inconsiderable, judging from the steady growth of his estate. In 1805 his tax on one slave, six horses, and two head of cattle amounted to $10.40,[30] while the next year the $10.20 assessment put him on a par with such established citizens as Jacques Clamorgan and Bernard Pratte, though still noticeably below Joseph Robidoux, $24.30, or Auguste Chouteau, wealthiest man in the city, $78.90.[31] By 1816, however, the charge on his assessed valuation had risen to $45.56½, elevating him to the top 10 per cent of those paying taxes,[32] and the following year he appeared among the top very few, paying $157.68¾ on five slaves, one lot, and three houses in St. Louis valued at $18,000.00, and a confirmed landholding of 8,000 arpents on the Mississippi.[33] The year before his death, the tax list showed him maintaining that position with a payment of $121.87½ on six slaves, one lot, and

---

[30] Tax List, City of St. Louis, 1805, Tax Lists Envelope, MHS.
[31] Ibid., 1806.
[32] Ibid., 1816.
[33] Ibid., 1817.

two houses valued at $26,000, placing him among the leading four or five citizens of the community.[34] He used his wealth to provide his family with a good house, fine furnishings, including imported china and glassware, and a fair library of fifty-three volumes, containing everything from Latin grammars to *Don Quixote*.[35]

These figures, and Manuel's relative position on the tax lists, are deceiving, just as they were deceiving to Lisa's friends, enemies, and creditors at the time of his death. Only then, when Mary Lisa and Charles Hempstead attempted to straighten out the trader's accounts, was it discovered how desperately Manuel had sought to fulfill his vision, how confident he had been in the ultimate success of his idea, how willing he had been to stake everything he had in the final attempt of the Missouri Fur Company in 1819. The executors struggled vainly with the estate until 1828,[36] by which time there was absolutely nothing left. As early as 1825, William Clark mentioned in a letter to his son: "the great embarassment [in which] the failure of Manuel's estate to pay for the Board Schooling & Clothes of Keeney & young Manuel placed him—Mr. Manuel's house & everything belonging to the estate was sold for debt last week and purchased by Mr Bostwick in payment for part of the debts due."[37] While Bostwick had been unsuccessful in foreclosing, he still managed to get some sort of settlement from the court, and what the court did not award him he purchased for a song, since no one bid against him at the sale.

Besides the massive mortgage to Bostwick, in which Manuel had given as security his entire St. Louis holdings, there was

---

[34] *Ibid.*, 1819.

[35] St. Louis Probate Court File, No. 497, Manuel Lisa, deceased. The contents of Lisa's library are also printed in John F. McDermott, *Private Libraries in Creole St. Louis*.

[36] *Missouri Gazette* (Nov. 24, 1828).

[37] Letter, William Clark to Meriwether Lewis Clark, Dec. 19, 1825, William Clark Collection, MHS.

still $1,687.50 due to Pierre and Antoine Carraby of New Orleans, for the $3,000.00 mortgage on the 3,000 arpents of the Joaquin Lisa grant made in 1812, when Lisa borrowed money for the reorganized Missouri Fur Company. J. P. Cabanné paid the Carrabys,[38] and was in turn paid by the estate in 1827.[39] Even older than that debt was a portion of the money still owed Geisse, Tayesse, and Snyder for goods purchased by Lisa and Clamorgan in 1806. John Jacob Sommers, of Kaskaskia, had taken over the collection of that sum, and won a favorable ruling from the court in 1826, the interest owing amounting to much more than the principal.[40] In another suit against the estate, John O'Fallon, William Clark, Auguste Chouteau, Bernard Pratte, and Robert Wash were awarded $1,682.71 for alleged incompleted services,[41] Clark's business head apparently outweighing his "embarassment." There were many other minor suits which also helped drain away Lisa's estate. In each of these cases, Manuel's property was sold at public auction to the highest bidder, usually going for ridiculously low figures to Oliver Bostwick, who was attempting to recoup some of what he considered his losses.

Much of the debt could have been erased if the sums owed Lisa had been collectable. At his death Manuel left a long list of people in debt to him, the total reaching several thousand dollars. Unfortunately, the list was replete with the names of former *engagés* to whom Lisa, in his generosity and desire to get ahead with all speed despite costs, had advanced money or merchandise—Jean Baptiste Champlain, $321.00; Forrest Handcock, $99.10—debts that were uncollectable because the

[38] St. Louis Probate Court File, No. 497, Manuel Lisa, Deceased.

[39] St. Louis Records, Book C, 561, Office of the Recorder of Deeds, City Hall, St. Louis, Missouri.

[40] St. Louis Records, Book N, 36, Office of the Recorder of Deeds, City Hall, St. Louis, Missouri. The amount owed on this account was $1,306.25 plus interest. Letter, Sidney Breeze to Executors of Manuel Lisa, n.d., Lisa Papers, MHS.

[41] St. Louis Records, Book M, 354, Office of the Recorder of Deeds, City Hall, St. Louis, Missouri.

people involved were deceased and their estates defunct. Even when some few could be contacted, the majority were generally insolvent, and only a few hundred dollars were ever realized.[42] Lisa's still active share of the Missouri Fur Company did not produce an income to the family because of the expansive policy of the company, and Mrs. Lisa was forced to sell part of that in 1822. After the Blackfeet had finished their inventory of company property in 1823, the stock she retained was not worth very much. Thus Manuel's original tormentors on the upper Missouri helped destroy even his legacy.

At his death there were few to mourn his loss from the trade, fewer still who appreciated what he had accomplished, and none to express their gratitude for the groundwork he had laid. Manuel Lisa had opened the Northwest to the fur trade of the United States. His men had visited all of the important beaver water in the northern Rockies, on both sides of the continental divide, and, in so doing, had served notice to the British and Spanish that America was indeed determined to make the most of her purchase of Louisiana.

But more than that, Lisa had laid down the principles for the successful operation of the fur trade in that area: the combination of permanent posts in the wilderness for trading purposes, with hunting and trapping parties operating out of them. Trade was intended to keep the Indians on friendly terms, and to provide safe access to their lands; trapping was for profit. Those who made names for themselves, if not fortunes, during the revival of the upper Misouri trade in the 1820's failed to heed these principles. And it was left for the American Fur Company, possessed of the capital which Lisa had always lacked, to put his ideas into actual and profitable operation, and ultimately monopolize the fur trade of the Northwest. Thus Kenneth Mc-

---

42 List of Accounts due Manuel Lisa, 1820, Lisa Papers, MHS. This list was apparently removed from the Probate Court File, and just as well. It is well preserved while the Probate Court File is in shreds and scarcely usable any more.

Kenzie of that organization could style himself with the title rightfuly belonging to his predecessor and mentor, Manuel Lisa, "King of the Missouri."

Appendix I
A Typical Fur Hunter's Contract

THE following is a translation from the original French of the contract between Alexis Doza and Pierre Menard, agent for the Missouri Fur Company, in 1809, indicating the nature of the agreements between the hunters and the company as opposed to the ordinary contracts of the *engagés*. While it does not confer the status of free trapper, the possibilities of profit for both the hunter and the company are obvious. This seems to be the typical form of hunter's contract, since there is a similar one in the Chouteau Collection, Missouri Historical Society, between Henley Donnelson and A. P. Chouteau, Jr., for the same voyage.

Articles of Contract, & Agreement made today Between pierre Menard of Kaskaskias Agent of the Missouri Fur Company of the one part; & Alexis Doza also of Kaskaskias territory of the Illinois of the other part, Witness; That the said Alexis Doza voluntarily engages himself in the capacity of Hunter, & fisherman of Beaver, to embark and follow a voyage from St. Louis, to the headwaters of the Missouri, or other places on the waters of the said River, to do, & to assist the said Company or Society; in the transportation of baggage loading; and unloading of the boats & all connected things, relative to the safeguarding of men baggage, merchandise which will be transported from the city of St. Louis to the headwaters of the said Missouri River; & that at his arival at his destination, he is obliged to Hunt, and trap the Beaver of the Missouri the best that he can, to gather together the meat of the furred animals, & peltries, & to remain with the said Company or Society, & to hunt in all the environs that he will find the most suitable on the waters of the missouri for the interest and advantage of the said Society, as also for the said Company, change of place or encampment, he is obliged as above to assist to transport the Baggage, Merchandise & c. . . . in the reloading & unloading; finally he is obliged to do, to obey, to execute with promptness, & diligence all reasonable orders which can be given by those in command of the expedition.

And the said Pierre Menard, to the same name, & for the said Company agrees & is obliged to the said Alexis Doza to furnish him five traps which will be in good condition & repaired at the expense of the said Society besides which he will furnish for (one) year a Horse, ten pounds of powder, twenty pounds of lead, four knives hatchets, ———— awls, kettle,—and if for his risk the said Doza shall find that it shall be for the interest of the said Society to take with him engages of the said Society, he will be given at his choice, in payment by the said Doza one half of their wages for the time that he will keep them, & according to the price he will have given those engages he will take with him; as also if the said Doza wants to go downriver after having stayed two years he will be the master of it, besides the said Alexis Doza is obliged to remit & return to the fort of the said Society before or (on) the fifteenth of June of each year with all the pelts, furs, that he will be able to have made in this time, upon which peltries, & furs he will have the half for his services those which will go downriver in the boats of the Society without having paid any part, nor expense, but they will go down at the risk and peril of the said Alexis Doza— & the other half of the said peltries & furs will belong to the said Society.

This present engagement will remain in full force and virtue for three years unless it should be revoked before by the Society or the said Doza at the expiration of two years, to follow the specific conditions in the said agreement under penalty of five hundred Piastres of damages by those who will break the said conditions, cause their good faith to be doubted, presence of witnesses at Kaskaskias the 8 May 1809

Appendix II
A Standard Indian Treaty

THE standard Indian treaty, of which this is a typical example, was a pretty innocuous affair, which put the burden
of concession primarily upon the natives. The treaty below was
signed with the Oto nation in St. Louis on June 24, 1817.[1]

> *Made and concluded between William Clark and Auguste
> Chouteau, Commissioners on the part, and behalf of the United
> States of America, of the one part; and the undersigned chiefs
> and warriors, of the Ottoes tribe of Indians, on the part and be-
> half of their said tribe, of the other part.*

The parties being desirous of re-establishing peace and friendship between the United States and their said tribe and of being
placed, in all things, and in every respect, upon the same footing
upon which they stood before the late war between the United
States and Great Britain, have agreed to the following articles:

Art. 1. Every injury or act of hostility by one or other of the
contracting parties against the other, shall be mutually forgiven
and forgot.

Art. 2. There shall be perpetual peace and friendship between
all of the citizens of the United States of America and all the
individuals composing the said Ottoes tribe, and all the friendly

[1] Taken from Peters, ed., *Public Statutes of the United States of America*, VII.

relations that existed between them before the war, shall be, and the same are, hereby, renewed.

Art. 3. The undersigned chiefs and warriors, for themselves and their said tribe, do hereby acknowledge themselves to be under the protection of the United States of America, and of no other nation, power, or sovereign, whatsoever.

In witness whereof the said William Clark and Auguste Chouteau, commissioners aforesaid, have hereunto subscribed their names and affixed their seals, this twenty-fourth day of June, in the year of our Lord one thousand eight hundred and seventeen, and of the independence of the United States the forty-first

Signatures
WILLIAM CLARK
AUGUSTE CHOUTEAU
INDIANS
WITNESSES

Appendix III
Articles of Agreement—St. Louis Missouri Fur Company, 1809

ARTICLES of Association and Copartnership made and entered into by and between Benjamin Wilkinson, Pierre Chouteau, senior, Manuel Lisa, Auguste Chouteau, junior, Reuben Lewis, William Clark and Sylvestre Labbadie all of the Town of St. Louis and Territory of Louisiana and Pierre Menard and William Morrison of the town of Kaskaskia in the Territory of Indiana and also Andrew Henry of Louisiana for the purpose of trading and hunting up the river Missouri and to the headwaters thereof or at such other place or places as a majority of the subscribing co-partners may elect, viz:

Article 1st. This Association shall be called and known by the style & firm of the St. Louis Missouri Fur Company; each member of which shall sign & subscribe these articles of association, and shall be bound to furnish for the joint benefit of the company to compose the outfits requisite for such expedition, and generally to pay equal proportions of all and every expense whatsoever, which may be deemed expedient by the aforesaid majority of the company in order to carry out the above mentioned objects of trading and hunting.

Article 2nd. Each member of the association shall be obliged to accompany the expedition in person or to send some person or persons, to be approved of by a majority of the company; and each member of the company failing to do so, shall pay the sum of five hundred dollars per annum for the benefit of and to be divided amongst such of the co-partners as may accompany the expedition.

Article 3rd. Each partner binds and obliges himself to do every thing which may be in his power for the joint benefit of the company during the period of time fixed upon for the existence of these articles of association; to refrain from trading directly or indirectly with all and every party or nations of Indians or the men employed by the company contrary to the true spirit and meaning of these articles of co-partnership or contrary to the joint interest and benefit of the company. And it is expressly agreed and understood that if any member of the company shall during the existence of these articles, be discovered or be known to traffic or trade for his own separate or individual interest or contrary to the true spirit and meaning of these articles of association he shall not only forfeit & pay for the joint benefit of the Company all his portion of the stock and profits but also to be forever thereafter excluded from the Company. Provided however that a majority of all members agree to such forfeiture and expulsion.

Article 4th. No member of this Company shall during the existence of these articles be permitted to traffic or trade with any party or nation of Indians or their towns or villages or usual places of residence for his or their separate and individual profit, nor contrary to the true intent and meaning of these articles, and that a breach of this article shall subject the party offending to the same penalties for the same uses, and also to expulsion as specified in the last preceding article.

Article 5th. And whereas the above named Manuel Lisa, Pierre Menard and William Morrison were lately associated in a trading expedition up the said River Missouri and have now a fort established on the waters of the Yellow Stone River, a branch of the Missoury, at which said fort they have as is alleged by them a quantity of Merchandise and also a number of horses.

Now therefore it is agreed that this Company is to accept from them the said Manuel Lisa, Pierre Menard and William Morrison all the merchandise they may have on hand at the time of the first expedition to be sent up by this Company shall arrive at said fort. Provided however that the same is not then dammaged, and if the same or any part thereof shall be dammaged then the Company shall only be bound to receive such parts and parcels thereof as may be fit for trading or such parts as may not be dammaged, and for the whole or such parts as may be received by a majority of the other members of this company then present this company is to allow and pay them the said Manuel Lisa, Pierre Menard & William Morrison one hundred per centum of the first cost.

Article 6th. The present company is also bound to receive from said Manuel Lisa, Pierre Menard & William Morrison the number of thirty eight horses which it is alleged had been left by them at the said fort when Manuel Lisa took his departure from there or so many of the said Horses as a majority of the other members of this Company then present may approve of, and allow and pay them the sum of thirty dollars for each Horse so approved of and accepted. This Company is also bound to receive from them the said Manuel Lisa, Pierre Menard & William Morrison such other Horses the number and quantity of which is to be approved of in like manner as may have been purchased by their agent for them at the said fort, at the time the aforesaid expedition shall arrive there and which may then be delivered for which this Company is to allow and pay the first cost of the merchandise paid for such Horses and also one hundred per centum of the first cost thereof.

Article 7th. All the Horses purchased by the Agent of the said Manuel Lisa, Pierre Menard & William Morrison since the departure of Manuel Lisa from said fort, for money or

Peltry, and which shall be accepted and approved of as aforesaid are to be received by this Company at first cost to be paid said Manuel Lisa, Pierre Menard & William Morrison.

Article 8th. Every person approved of & accepted as above mentioned to act as agents of any absent member of this Company shall always be subject to the orders of a Majority of the Company then present, and on refusal so to do shall thereupon be discharged and the Partner for whom he acted, shall be bound to pay the same sum of money annually as those who neither attended the expedition in person nor furnish an agent the time to be computed from the time such agent shall be discharged. Which said annual sum shall also be for the exclusive benefit of such members of the Company as may be with the expedition.

Article 9th. When the aforesaid expedition shall arrive at or above the Mandan nation of Indians, each partner accompanying the expedition shall be bound to proceed & reside at such post or place as may be designated for him by a majority of the Company then present and also when there to do and perform as far as may be possible all those duties required of him by such majority of the Company. Each member failing to comply with this article shall be bound to forfeit and pay to the Company one thousand Dollars per annum to be computed from the time of the first breach of this article in each year untill he shall comply with the aforesaid duties required of him by such majority.

Article 10th. The members of this association having contracted with his Excellency governor Lewis to convey the Chief of the Mandan Indians now at St. Louis to his nation: It is hereby agreed that Pierre Chouteau senior shall have the command and complete control of the present expedition: to have the full direction of the march; to have command of such officers as may be appointed under him; to point out their duties and give each officer his command agreeably to rank—so far as the Company is bound by the aforesaid contract with the Executive to observe Military Discipline.

Article 11th. Manuel Lisa and Benjamin Wilkinson are hereby appointed factors to trade with the Indians or men employed by the Company, they shall keep just and fair accounts of all their Company transactions subject to the inspection of the Company or any member of the Company at all times, to use their utmost industry skill and knowledge for the benefit of the Company, to make purchases of peltry and merchandise, to engage men and draw bills of exchange on the agent of the Company hereinafter mentioned residing at St. Louis for such purchases & engagements to the full amount of the funds which said agent may have in his hands belonging to the Company and at that time unappropriated by the Company.

Article 12th. No purchases of Merchandise are to be made without the consent and approbation of a majority of the Company.

Article 13th. The above mentioned factors are to continue as such during their pleasure or that of a Majority of the Company and to be subject to no responsibility except for personal neglect or willful waste of the goods or property they may have in charge or possession.

Article 14th. William Clark is hereby appointed agent of this company to reside at the Town of St. Louis. He is to receive all Peltries, furs, monies or other property sent or delivered to him by the Company or any member thereof; and the same to keep & preserve in the best manner he can for the interest of the Company and said agent shall be paid and allowed all necessary expenditures made by him.

Article 15th. Whenever any Peltries, furs or other property belonging to the company shall be sent down and delivered to said agent, the same shall be (as speedily thereafter as may be) divided equally between all the partners, and their respective proportions paid to them or their agents on demand.

Article 16th. Should the Company or a Majority thereof deem it expedient to purchase a greater quantity of Merchandise, or engage a greater number of men than may at any time be had on hand or engaged, the aforesaid agent is to purchase the said Merchandise and engage the men on the best possible terms, for the interest of the company, always having regard to the Inventories of such Articles as may from time to time be forwarded to him by the aforesaid factors, for all of which said purchases of merchandise or engagement of men each member of the company shall be bound to pay an equal part of the expense.

Article 17th. It is agreed that Pierre Chouteau senior, Manuel Lisa and Pierre Menard are to be the first of the co-partners accompanying the expedition who will be allowed to return to St. Louis. They will however each be bound under the penalty mentioned in the Second Article either personally to return to their respective posts or join the expedition up the river during the Spring succeeding their arrival at Saint Louis; or to send an Agent as is also provided in the Second article; to act in their place—and in ascertaining the amount of forfeitures for a breach of the article the time shall be computed from the arrival of the party at the Town of St. Louis; which said forfeitures shall also be applied and appropriated as is provided in the aforesaid Second Article.

Article 18th. Benjamin Wilkinson and Auguste Chouteau junior are to be the next members of this Company who will be permitted to return to Saint Louis subject to the same provisions as are Contained in the preceeding article and those of Article Second.

Article 19th. No person shall hereafter be admitted to become a member of this Company unless by the unanimous consent of every partner.

Article 20th. The foregoing articles of association and Co-partnership are to have effect and continue in force for and to the full end and expiration of the term of three years and after the date hereof subject to such alterations as a majority of the Company may deem necessary.

In testimony of which we & each of us have hereunto subscribed our names at the Town of St. Louis this seventh day of
March eighteen hundred and nine—interlined in tenth line from
beginning before signed and also Dennis fitzhugh of Louisville
Kentucky

PRE CHOUTEAU
MANUEL LISA
BEN WILKINSON
STRE LABBADIE

Signed in presence of   A. P. CHOUTEAU
MERIWETHER LEWIS   BEN WILKINSON for REUBEN LEWIS
Requirer   WM CLARK
  MANUEL LISA pr PIERRE MENARD
  MANUEL LISA pr WILLIAM MORRISON
  ANDREW HENRY

Article 21st. Previous to the division of the Peltry, fur and
other property mentioned in article 15 all expenditures of whatever nature incurred by the Company previous to said Division
shall first be deducted from the gross amount of Property to be
divided as specified in said Article.

Article 22nd. William Clark and Pierre Chouteau or either of
them in the absence of the other are hereby appointed and fully
authorized by the Company to sign and execute all notes, bills,
obligations, receipts discharges & acquittances for and in behalf
of the Company.

Same signatures

two interlineations approved
Recorded this 20th day of September AD 1809

M. P. LEDUC
Recorder

Appendix IV
Articles of Agreement—Missouri Fur Company, 1812

THE Undersigned do hereby form a company of limited partnership and do associate and agree with each other, to the end of exploring in a commercial way, and hunting in that portion of the country within the claim of the United States, and westwardly of a point, which shall be 500 miles from the United States present factories; and to conduct business within the said boundary, and at the town of St. Louis, under the name and title of the President and Directors of the Missouri Fur company; and they do hereby mutually covenant and agree, that the following shall be the fundamental articles of this their association, and agreement with each other, by which they and all persons who may at any time hereafter transact any business with the said company, shall be bound and concluded.

Article 1st. The capital stock of the company shall not exceed fifty thousand dollars, to be divided into shares of one thousand dollars each, five hundred dollars of which shall be paid on each share when subscribed for, and the residue in installments, not exceeding two hundred and fifty dollars, on each share payable to, and at such times as the President and Directors may require, giving thirty days notice; and in case of non payment of the said residue, or any part thereof at the time or times required, the share or shares subscribed for, and upon which such default of payment arises; shall be forfeited to the company, together with all and every sum or sums of money previously paid thereon.

Article 2nd. Twenty three thousand dollars of the said capital stock shall be subscribed for by individuals, and the funds of the former St. Louis Missouri Fur Company, which is now up the Missouri, calculated at twenty nine thousand nine hundred and eighty five dollars, in goods wares and merchandize, and debts due by hunters who are now out as will appear by a reference to the settlement of accounts of that company in the possession of Gen. William Clark of St. Louis, shall constitute twenty seven thousand dollars of the said fund, and taken into the common stock of the association. Subject to the future direction of the president and directors aforesaid, and the undersigned individual members of the former St. Louis Missouri Fur Company shall be entitled to three shares each in the association, for the goods, wares, merchandise & c. which they have up the Missouri aforesaid.

Article 3rd. That for the purpose of constituting the said stock, subscriptions for the sum of twenty three thousand dollars, in shares of one thousand dollars each, shall be opened in the town of St. Louis, under the directions of Gen. Wm. Clark, Manuel Lisa, and Salist Labade, or any two of them, commissioners, hereby appointed to receive the said subscriptions, and the money due thereon, and to give acquaintance therefor; three directors shall be chosen annually on the first Monday of December hereafter, and receive for their compensation one hundred dollars each; when more than half the capital stock is subscribed for, the stockholders may proceed to elect three directors, to serve until the next annual election.

Article 4th. The stockholders in all elections may vote either in person or by proxy, authorized by letter of attorney, and should any vacancy happen among the directors, by death, resignation, or otherwise during the year for which they are elected, the remaining directors, shall elect a director to fill such vacancy until the next election thereafter; the commissioners shall deliver the subscription for shares in their hands, and the money received thereon, to the directors when called for by them.

Article 5th. The board of directors for the time being, shall have power to sell, exchange, barter, purchase, engage, hire hands, clerks, establish trading houses, stores, and generally do all and every thing, which in their opinion they may think best for the interest and advantage of said association, not inconstant with law, and subject to the restrictions and limitations herein contained, as to them or a majority of them shall deem expedient, to render full accounts and make a report of the situation of the said association, including a statement of the amount which they may think requisite for the next years outfit, to the members or stockholders at their meeting which shall be on the first Monday of Dec. annually, at which time a majority of all members of the company being present, they shall direct the necessary outfits to be made and are empowered to order a dividend to be made by the directors out of such funds, as may not be necessary to carry on the association, and two thirds of the whole of those entitled to vote may change or alter the whole or any part of these articles of association.

Article 6th. One of the directors at the time of election, shall be elected by the members of the company, president of the board of directors, whose duty it shall be, in addition to other duties, to keep or cause to be kept under him the accounts, books, papers &c. of the company for which he is to be allowed for clerk hire stationary and storage, six hundred dollars per annum, one other member of the said board of directors, so to be appointed shall be obliged to ascend the Missouri to the highest post on the Missouri below the falls at such time and with such supplies as the board may direct, he is to settle the accounts of the company in that quarter bring or send down the proceeds, and as soon as possible after his return to St. Louis, he is to make his report and deliver the accounts settled by him to the board, to be entered on the books of the association for which additional services, he is to be allowed one thousand dollars per annum.

Article 7th. Not less than two directors shall form a board for the transaction of business, of which the president shall be one, except in the case of sickness or necessary absence, in which his place may be supplied by another director, who shall be named by the president.

Article 8th. The number of votes to which each stockholder shall be entitled shall be according to the number of shares he shall hold; in the proportion following, that is to say for each share of one thousand dollars, shall until it amounts to three thousand dollars be entitled to one vote, each stockholder possessing shares to the amount of five thousand dollars shall be entitled to four votes, each stockholder possessing shares to the amount of eight thousand dollars shall be entitled to five votes and no more. All shares that are disposed of previous to the first day of April next ensuing, shall be entitled to the full years dividend with the present stockholders.

Article 9th. The shares of capital stock shall be transferable on the books of the company, according to such rules as may be conformable to law established in that respect, by the board of directors.

Article 10th. No transfer of stock in the company shall be considered as binding upon the company, unless made in a book or books kept for that purpose by the company, and it is further expressly agreed and declared, that any stockholder who shall transfer in the manner aforesaid all his stock or shares whatever shall thenceforth cease to be a member of this company, and every person or persons whatever who shall accept a transfer of any stock or shares in this company, shall thenceforth become and be a member of this company, according to the articles of association.

Article 11th. All bonds, notes, and every other contract and engagement on behalf of the company shall be signed by the president and one of the members of the board of directors;

except in contracts for or by the partner or agent, authorized by the board of directors and the funds of the company shall in no case be held responsible for any contract or engagement whatever, unless the same should be signed as aforesaid, and the books, papers, correspondence, and funds of the company, shall at all times be subject to the inspection of the directors aforesaid.

Article 12th. Dividends of the profits of the company, or so much of the said profits as shall be deemed expedient and proper, shall be declared and paid yearly, to be computed from the date in conformity with the fifth article and subject to the conditions contained in the eighth article of association; the dividends shall in no case exceed the amount of the nett profits actually acquired by the company so that the capital stock thereof shall never be impaired.

Article 13th. It is hereby expressly and explicitly declared to be the object of the persons who associate under the firm of the Missouri Fur Company, that the property or joint stock of said company, exclusively of the dividends to be made in the manner herein mentioned, shall alone be responsible for the debts and engagements of the company, and that no persons who shall or may deal with the said company, or to whom they shall or may become in any wise indebted shall on no pretense whatever, have recourse against the separate property of any present or future member of the company, or against their persons, but all persons accepting any bonds, bills, notes, or other contract of the company, signed by the president for the time being, or dealing with it in any manner whatsoever, thereby give credit respectively to the joint stock or property of said company, and thereby disavow having recourse or any pretense to the person, or separate property of any present or future members of this company, except as above mentioned, and all suits brought against the company (if any shall be) shall be brought against the president and directors for the time being, and in case of their death or removal from office pending any such suit against them; measures shall be taken at the expense of the company, for substituting their successor in office as defendants, so that persons having demands upon the company may not be prejudiced or delayed by that event, or if the person sueing should go on against the persons first named as defendants, notwithstanding his or their death or removal from office, the company shall take no advantage by writ of error or otherwise, of such proceedings on that account, and all recoveries had in the manner aforesaid, shall be conclusive upon the company as far as to render the company's joint stock or property liable thereby, and no further; and the company shall immediately pay the amount of such recovery out of their joint stock, but not otherwise; and in case of any suit at law, the directors or one of them shall sign his appearance, or file bail therefor, it being expressly understood and declared, that all persons dealing with the said company agreeable to these terms are bound thereby.

Article 14th. The directors shall keep fair and regular entries on a book provided for that purpose, of their proceedings, and on any question when one of the directors shall require it, the yeas and nays, of the directors votes shall be inserted on their minutes, and those minutes be at all times on demand produced to the stockholders, when at a general meeting the same shall be required.

Article 15th. No members of the association shall either directly or indirectly sell, exchange, barter, any goods wares or merchandize of any kind whatever, or purchase, hunt or contract debts of any kind in a mercantile way contrary to the interest of the company, within the limits westwardly of the United States Factories aforesaid, but for the sole use and profit of the said company, under the penalty of ten thousand dollars, to be paid by him to the directors for the use of the said company, and to be recovered on his share or capital in stock as other debts.

Article 16th. These articles of agreement shall be published for three weeks in the Louisiana Gazette, & for the further information of all persons who may transact business with, or in any manner give credit to this company, every bond, bill or note, or other instrument of contract, by the effect or terms of which the company may be charged or held liable for the payment of money, shall especially declare in such manner as the board of directors may prescribe, that payment shall be made, out of the joint funds of the company according to the present articles of this association, and not otherwise, as it is expressly declared that no engagement can legally be made in the name of said company, unless it contains a limitation or restriction to the effect above recited, and the company hereby expressly disavows all responsibility for any debt or engagement which may be made in their name, not containing a limitation or restriction to the effect aforesaid.

Article 17th. In case of the death of any of the contracting parties entitled to a share or shares in the Company, such share or shares is to continue until the expiration of these articles of association, and whatever sum or sums of money which would have been paid yearly to the deceased, shall then be delivered to his legal representative, who shall be entitled to a vote or votes agreeable to the amount of stocks aforesaid.

Article 18th. Each director before they enter on the duties of their office shall if required, give a bond with two securities to the satisfaction of the stockholders assembled, in such sums as by them may by their bye laws order & direct, not exceeding double the amount of the compensation allowed them, with a condition for the faithful performance of their duties.

Article 19th. If any one or more members of this association shall be thought necessary by the directors to continue in the upper Missouri or bounds aforesaid to superintend the interest of the company, their compensation shall be fixed by the board of directors out of the funds of the company.

Article 20th. This association shall continue until the first monday of December eighteen hundred and eighteen, but the proprietors of two thirds of the capital stock of the company, may by their concurring votes at a general meeting to be called for that express purpose dissolve, the same at any prior period, provided that notice of such meeting and of its objects, shall be published in Louisiana, previous to the time appointed for such meeting.

Article 21st. Immediately on the dissolution of the association, effectual measures shall be taken by the existing directors for closing all the concerns of the company, and for dividing the capital and profits which may remain among the stockholders in proportion to their respective interest.

IN WITNESS whereof we have hereunto set our names, this twenty fourth day of January, eighteen hundred and twelve

Bibliography

THE pole toward which all students of the Lisa era—indeed, scholars of the entire fur-trade period—necessarily must be attracted is the archives of the Missouri Historical Society, located in the Jefferson Memorial Building, St. Louis, Missouri. This organization, founded shortly after the Civil War by a group of dedicated people to collect and preserve materials pertaining to the history of St. Louis, the Louisiana Territory, and Missouri, has, over the years, built up a priceless collection of primary sources and rare secondary accounts. Under the long-term direction of Charles van Ravenswaay, now of Sturbridge, Massachusetts, and, presently, George R. Brooks, the Society has added, and continues to add, significant materials to its accumulation of treasures. Mrs. Frances H. Stadler, archivist, and her predecessors have labored mightily to sort and catalogue most of the documents, making them readily available for scholarly use. In the section below labeled "Manuscript Materials," all manuscripts will be from the Missouri Historical Society unless otherwise noted.

I. Manuscript Materials

Bates Papers. [This grouping, concerned mainly with Frederick Bates, at one time a territorial official, is especially valuable for information concerning land claims and titles, as Frederick Bates was a land commissioner.]

Billon, Frederic, Collection. [One of the earliest of St. Louis historians, Billon's notes are valuable in that he saw materials no longer in existence. Contained herein are several plats of St. Louis in the early days, showing the position of the lots and houses, and indicating ownership at various times.]

Chouteau Collection. [This compendium of materials pertaining to the Chouteau family fills several file drawers, but is put together chronologically for easy access. It is the most complete of the early collections, shedding light on all activities in early St. Louis, and particularly on the fur trade. While there are some unaccountable gaps in places, there are also, perhaps as a compensation, many letters and documents which do not properly belong to the Chouteaus but were gems of knowledge with regard to Lisa.]

Chouteau, Pierre, Ledger Account, 1802–17. [As frustrating as it is valuable, this ledger provides some knowledge regarding the Missouri Fur Company, but it also contains many referrals to other ledgers which are, unfortunately, nonexistent.]

Chouteau, Pierre, Letterbook. [A vital source for much of the activity of that gentleman.]

Clark, George Rogers, MSS. Draper Collection, Wisconsin State Historical Society, Madison, Wisconsin. [This collection throws only sidelights on the Missouri fur trade and deals mostly with Clark's land claim.]

Clark, William, Collection. [A large repository of records of that famous member of the Lewis and Clark expedition, it is of especial interest because it contains so many photographic reproductions of materials in the National Archives, thus consolidating in one place the scattered references to Lisa and his work with the Indians in the War of 1812. Curiously, there is nothing concerning Clark's connection with the Missouri Fur Company.]

Clark, William, MSS. Kansas State Historical Society, Topeka, Kansas. [Most valuable for the two Missouri Fur Company Ledger Books—1812–14; and April, 1812–June, 1813, and 1817, the latter entirely in Lisa's handwriting. The more than thirty volumes in the collection are now on microfilm to protect the originals from repeated handling. Like the Clark Collection in St.

Louis, these papers contain no direct reference to Clark's position as president of the Missouri Fur Company.]

Crooks, Ramsay, Letterbook, 1816–20. [These letters written by the moving force of the American Fur Company chronicle the rise to eminence of that company in St. Louis and on the Missouri at that early date.]

Dyer, Henry Chouteau, Collection. [As yet only a vast pile of un-catalogued materials, some of it pertaining to the period under scrutiny, this collection may prove of some value to early St. Louis history when it is put in order.]

Early Litigations Envelope. [A gathering of many court cases in St. Louis dating back to the Spanish era, it contains the documents of a number of probate cases.]

Farrar, Bernard, Daybooks. [There are several of these daybooks of one of St. Louis' early medical men who treated many of her most prominent citizens.]

Fitzhugh, Dennis, Papers. Filson Club, Louisville, Kentucky. [This is the business record of that prominent Louisville family which had many connections in St. Louis.]

Forsyth, Thomas, Papers. [Although pertaining mostly to activities east of the Mississippi, this small group of documents does have some relevance to Lisa and the War of 1812.]

Fur Trade Papers. [A single envelope containing references to many aspects of the fur trade throughout its existence, this is a treasure trove of isolated gems of knowledge.]

Graham, Richard, Papers. [A small collection, this, which pertains particularly to the Illinois country.]

Gratiot, Charles, Collection. [While containing references to all manner of things in early St. Louis, the two letterbooks—March 6, 1798, to January 6, 1816; and September 9, 1812, to June 20, 1819—are of greatest value. The former comprises a series of letters to John Jacob Astor stretching over a long period of years, while the latter contains what little is known of the activities of Cabanné and Company.]

Hempstead, Stephen, Diary. [A thoroughly human document

which covers Hempstead's life in St. Louis, it also helps to place Lisa's whereabouts during the last year of his life.]

Hempstead, Thomas, Letterbook, January 27, 1821, to February 12, 1823. Coe Collection, MS No. 345, Yale University Library, New Haven, Connecticut. [Not only does this book provide a chronicle of the activities of the Missouri Fur Company after Lisa's death, but it is also valuable for the sidelights thrown on the various groups in competition with Pilcher, Hempstead, *et al.*]

Hertzog, Joseph, Letters from, 1811–15. [This Philadelphia merchant kept in close touch with his St. Louis partner, Christian Wilt, and his letters provide a running commentary on the fluctuations of the Philadelphia market over that period.]

Hunt, John Wesley, Papers. Filson Club, Louisville, Kentucky. [These records contain the Hunt genealogy and some reference to the activities of young Theodore, although most of them are concerned with his more famous brother, Wilson P. Hunt.]

Hunt, Theodore, Papers. [A small grouping of papers, they show something of the relationship between Lisa and Hunt, even though leaving much to the imagination.]

Indians Papers. [This single envelope, curiously titled, holds many scattered references to Lisa and other important men in and about St. Louis during the era of the fur trade.]

Indian Trade and Fur Companies Papers. [Like the one mentioned above, this envelope is a hodgepodge of documents, valuable for much of the period.]

Jefferson, Thomas, Collection. [These documents comprise the fourth largest collection of Jeffersoniana in America, and graphically demonstrate that great gentleman's lively interest in the West.]

Journal of the Proceedings of the Legislature of the Territory of Louisiana Commencing June 3, 1806. MSS, Mercantile Library, St. Louis, Missouri. [This journal notes the actions taken by that body, some of which have to do with Lisa and the fur trade.]

Kaskaskia Papers. [A compendium of materials pertaining to the Illinois town, this proved a wonderful find because it contained several letters written by Pierre Menard while on the 1809 voyage. These letters supplement the only other source for that voyage, Thomas James, *Three Years among the Indians and Mexicans,* and, in addition, help fill out the story of Lisa's 1807 trip.]

Lewis, Meriwether, Collection. [Contained herein are the letters of Reuben Lewis, a fine addition to knowledge of the Lisa era.]

Lisa, Manuel, Papers. [This small set of three envelopes contains practically all of the papers pertaining to the fur trader, although much of the total documentation consists of court-case announcements. They are of particular value during his first years in St. Louis, providing the documents outlining his various encounters with Spanish officialdom. One can only wish for a Manuel Lisa letterbook.]

Lucas Papers. [This is a compilation of papers pertaining to the prominent Lucas family, especially those of J. C. B. Lucas, an important early judge in the Louisiana, and later Missouri, Territory.]

Menard Family Papers. Illinois State Historical Society, Springfield, Illinois. [An assortment of documents pertaining to Pierre Menard and his family, this accumulation indicates the closeness of the relationship between William Morrison and Menard.]

Menard, Pierre, Collection. Illinois State Historical Society, Springfield, Illinois. [The massive Menard Collection contains one volume of importance to this study: Book 4, 1785–1818. In it are not only letters of Menard himself but letters to Menard and Mrs. Menard from other members of the Missouri Fur Company.]

Missouri Minute Book of the Supreme Court. [This manuscript, beautifully preserved in the new plastic-laminating process, covers, in three volumes, the years, 1805 to 1821, providing a chronological survey of some of Lisa's court actions over the period.]

Morrison, William, Records. Illinois Historical Survey, Lincoln Hall, University of Illinois, Urbana, Illinois. [These four rolls of microfilm consolidate all the known records of Morrison and his business ventures. They were gathered from such various places as the Chester, Illinois, Courthouse and the Chicago Historical Society by John L. Tevebaugh in the course of researching for his dissertation, "Merchant on the Western Frontier."]

New Madrid Archives. [A collection of early references and documents concerning the history of New Madrid collected by the WPA writers' project, it illustrates the early history of the Louisiana Territory.]

O'Fallon Papers. [Most of these papers have to do with James O'Fallon's later career, although there are scattered references to the period under consideration.]

St. Louis Archives. [Like the New Madrid Archives above, this collection contains references no longer available in the original.]

St. Louis Circuit Court Files. Civil Courts Building, St. Louis, Missouri. [Here is a relatively untapped lode of historical material, court cases involving mortgages, divorces, land claims, etc. Difficult to find, they sometimes provide wonderful rewards for persistence in research.]

St. Louis History Envelope. [This is a conglomeration of references and documents relating to the whole history of the city.]

St. Louis Probate Court File. [Lisa's probate envelope is contained herein, but time has taken its toll, and the file is practically useless.]

St. Louis Records. Office of the Recorder of Deeds, City Hall, St. Louis, Missouri. [Several of these early deed-books contain references to Lisa and to practically all citizens of importance in early St. Louis.]

Santa Fe Papers. [The Southwest trade references possessed by the Society are in this single envelope.]

Tax Lists Envelope. [Many of the early tax lists for residents of St. Louis are preserved here.]

Vigo Collection. Indiana Historical Society, Indianapolis, Indiana. [The records of this prominent trader show the close relationship between Vincennes and St. Louis during the early period.]

War Department Records. National Archives, Washington, D.C. [Scattered through these files are references to the early fur trade, but fortunately the Missouri Historical Society has most of them on file in photostatic copy.]

Wilt, Christian, Letterbook, 1812–15. [Wilt, an important St. Louis merchant, provides a fine record of the ups and downs of business in the Mound City during the War of 1812.]

II. Government Documents

American State Papers. 38 vols. Washington, D.C., Gales & Seaton, 1834.

Carter, Clarence E., comp. and ed. *The Territorial Papers of the United States.* 25 vols. Washington, Government Printing Office, 1934–60.

Laws of the Territory of Louisiana Passed by the Governor and Judges Assembled in Legislature, in the Month of October, 1810. St. Louis, Public Printer, 1810.

Morse, Jedediah. *Report to the Secretary of War of the United States on Indian Affairs.* New Haven, S. Converse, 1822.

Peters, Richard, ed. *The Public Statutes at Large of the United States of America.* Vol. VII. Boston, Little, Brown & Co., 1861.

United States Congress, Senate. *Sen. Doc. No. 56,* 18 Cong. 1 sess. Serial 91, Vol. III.

———, ———. *Sen. Doc. No. 67,* 20 Cong., 2 sess. Serial 181, Vol. I.

III. Newspapers

Arkansas Gazette, Little Rock, Arkansas. [Typed excerpts are contained in the Dale L. Morgan Collection, Henry E. Huntington Library, San Marino, California.]

Missouri Gazette, St. Louis, Missouri.

Niles' Weekly Register, Baltimore, Maryland.

St. Louis Enquirer, St. Louis, Missouri.

Western Intelligencer, Kaskaskia, Illinois.

IV. Primary Sources

Ashe, Thomas. *Travels in America, 1806.* London, W. Sawyer & Co., 1808.

Beck, Lewis C. *A Gazetteer of the States of Illinois and Missouri; Containing a General View of Each State—A General View of Their Counties—and a Particular Description of Their Towns,*

Villages, Rivers, Etc., Etc. Albany, New York, C. R. & G. Webster, 1823.

Bolton, Herbert E. "New Light on Manuel Lisa and the Spanish Fur Trade," *Southwest Historical Quarterly*, Vol. XVII (July, 1913).

Brackenridge, Henry M. *A Journal of a Voyage up the River Missouri, Performed in Eighteen Hundred and Eleven*. Baltimore, Coale & Maxwell, Pomery & Toy, 1816. [This is a second printing of a portion of the work cited immediately below.]

——. *Views of Louisiana, Together with a Journal of a Voyage up the Missouri River, in 1811*. Pittsburgh, Cramer, Spear, and Eichbaum, 1814. [A second edition was published in Baltimore by Schaeffer and Maund in 1817.]

Bradbury, John. *Travels in the Interior of America in the Years 1809, 1810, and 1811; Including a Description of Upper Louisiana, Together with the States of Ohio, Kentucky, Indiana, and Tennessee, with the Illinois and Western Territory, and Containing Remarks and Observations Useful to Persons Emigrating to Those Countries*. Liverpool, Sherwood, Neely & Jones, 1817.

Bradley, James H. "Journal," *Montana Historical Society Contributions*, Vol. II (1896).

Clyman, James. *James Clyman, American Frontiersman, 1792–1881*. Ed. by Charles L. Camp. San Francisco, California Historical Society, 1928.

Coues, Elliott. "Letters of William Clark and Nathaniel Pryor," *Annals of Iowa*, Vol. I (April, 1893).

Cutler, Jervase. *A Topographical Description of the State of Ohio, Indiana Territory, and Louisiana*. Boston, Charles Williams, 1812.

Darby, John F. *Personal Recollections*. St. Louis, G. I. Jones & Company, 1880.

Flint, Timothy. *Recollections of the Last Ten Years*. Boston, Cummings, Hilliard, & Company, 1826.

Henry, Alexander, and David Thompson. *New Light on the Early History of the Greater Northwest; The Manuscript Journals of Alexander Henry of the Northwest Company and of David*

Thompson, Official Geographer and Explorer of the Same Company. Ed. by Elliott Coues. 3 vols. New York, F. P. Harper, 1897.

Holmes, Captain Reuben. "The Five Scalps," *Missouri Historical Society Glimpses of the Past,* Vol. V (1938). [This is a reprint of an article appearing in the St. Louis *Beacon* (n.d., 1828), and redone in the St. Louis *Reveille* (July 17 and 24, 1848).]

Hunter, John Dunn. *Memoirs of a Captivity among the Indians of North America.* London, Longmans, Hurst, Rees, Orme, & Brown, 1823.

Irving, Washington. *Astoria, or Anecdotes of an Enterprise beyond the Rocky Mountains.* Philadelphia, Carey, Lea, & Blanchard, 1836.

James, Edwin. *Account of an Expedition from Pittsburgh to the Rocky Mountains, Performed in the Years 1819 and '20.* 2 vols. Philadelphia, H. C. Carey & I. Lea, 1822–23.

James, Thomas. *Three Years among the Indians and Mexicans.* Waterloo, Illinois, War Eagle Press, 1846. [There is another edition, with annotations by Walter B. Douglas, published in St. Louis by the Missouri Historical Society in 1916].

Jusseaume, René. "Letter to President Jefferson by René Jusseaume," *Missouri Historical Society Collections,* Vol. IV (1913).

Kurz, Rudolph F. *Journal of Rudolph Friederich Kurz.* Trans. by Myrtis Jarrell; ed. by J. N. B. Hewitt. Washington, D.C., Government Printing Office, 1937.

Larocque, Antoine. "Journal of Larocque: From the Assiniboine to the Yellowstone, 1805," ed. by Lawrence J. Burpee, *Publications of Canadian Archives,* No. 3, Ottawa, Government Printing Service, 1910.

Lewis, Meriwether. *Original Journals of the Lewis and Clark Expedition, 1804–1806.* Ed. by R. G. Thwaites. 8 vols. New York, Dodd, Mead & Co., 1904–1905.

Luttig, John C. *Journal of a Fur Trading Expedition on the Upper Missouri, 1812–1813.* Ed. by Stella M. Drumm. St. Louis, Missouri Historical Society, 1920.

Maximilian, Prince of Wied-Neuwied. *Travels in the Interior of America.* Trans. by H. Evans Lloyd. London, Ackerman & Co., 1843.

Nasatir, A. P., ed. *Before Lewis and Clark; Documents Illustrating the History of Missouri, 1785–1804.* 2 vols. St. Louis, Historical Documents Foundation, 1952.

Paxton, John A. *The St. Louis Directory and Register.* St. Louis, Author, 1821.

Pike, Major Zebulon M. *An Account of Expeditions to the Sources of the Mississippi and through the Western Parts of Louisiana, to the Sources of the Arkansaw, Kans, La Platte, and Pierre Jaune, Rivers; Performed by the Order of the Government of the United States during the Years 1805, 1806, and 1807. And a Tour through the Interior Parts of New Spain, When Conducted through These Provinces, by Order of the Captain-General.* Philadelphia, C. & A. Conrad & Co., 1810.

———. *The Expedition of Zebulon Montgomery Pike, to the Headwaters of the Arkansaw, Kans, La Platte, and Pierre Jaune, Rivers; Performed by the Order of the Government of the United States during the Years 1805, 1806, 1807.* Ed. by Elliott Coues. 3 vols. New York, F. P. Harper, 1895.

———. "Papers of Zebulon M. Pike, 1806–1807," ed. by Herbert E. Bolton, *American Historical Review,* Vol. XIII (July, 1908).

———. *Zebulon Pike's Arkansas Journal.* Ed. by S. H. Hart and Archer B. Hulbert. Denver, Denver Public Library, 1932.

Rollins, Philip A. *The Discovery of the Oregon Trail; Robert Stuart's Narrative.* New York, C. Scribner's Sons, 1935.

Stoddard, Capt. Amos. "Transfer of Upper Louisiana: Papers of Captain Amos Stoddard," *Missouri Historical Society Glimpses of the Past,* Vol. II (1935).

Tabeau, Pierre-Antoine. *Tabeau's Narrative of Loisel's Expedition to the Upper Missouri.* Ed. by Annie Heloise Abel; trans. by Rose Abel Wright. Norman, University of Oklahoma Press, 1939.

Thompson, David. *David Thompson's Narrative of His Exploration in Western America, 1784–1812.* Ed. by J. B. Tyrrell. Toronto, Champlain Society, 1916.

Wislizenus, F. A. *A Journey to the Rocky Mountains in the Year 1839.* Trans. by F. A. Wislizenus. St. Louis, Missouri Historical Society, 1912.

V. Secondary Sources

A. BOOKS AND THESES

Baldwin, Leland D. *The Keelboat Age on Western Waters*. Pittsburgh, University of Pittsburgh Press, 1941.

Berry, Don. *A Majority of Scoundrels*. New York, Harper, 1961.

Billington, Ray A. *Westward Expansion*. 2d ed. New York, Macmillan, 1960.

Billon, Frederic L. *Annals of St. Louis in Its Early Days under the French and Spanish Dominations*. St. Louis, Author, 1886.

――――. *Annals of St. Louis in Its Territorial Days from 1804 to 1821*. St. Louis, Author, 1888.

Branch, E. Douglas. *Westward, The Romance of the American Frontier*. New York, Appleton, 1930.

Cable, John Ray. *The Bank of the State of Missouri*. New York, Columbia University Press, 1923.

Chittenden, Hiram M. *The American Fur Trade of the Far West*. 2 vols. Palo Alto, Stanford University Press, 1954.

Clark, Thomas D. *Frontier America; The Story of the Westward Movement*. New York, Scribners, 1959.

Cleland, Robert Glass. *This Reckless Breed of Men; The Trappers and Fur Traders of the Southwest*. New York, Alfred Knopf, 1950.

Coman, Katherine. *Economic Beginnings of the Far West*. 2 vols. New York, Macmillan, 1912.

Conard, Howard L., ed. *Encyclopedia of the History of Missouri*. 6 vols. New York, Scribners, 1901.

Connelley, William E. *History of Kansas, State and People*. 5 vols. Chicago, American Historical Society, 1928.

Coyner, David H. *The Lost Trappers; A Collection of Interesting Scenes and Events in the Rocky Mountains*. Cincinnati, J. A. & U. P. James, 1847.

Culmer, Frederic A. *A New History of Missouri*. Mexico, Missouri, McIntyre, 1938.

Dale, Harrison C., ed. *The Ashley-Smith Explorations and the Discovery of a Central Route to the Pacific, 1822–1829*. Cleveland, Arthur C. Clark, 1918.

Dellenbaugh, Frederick S. *Breaking the Wilderness*. New York, Putnam, 1905.

DeVoto, Bernard. *Across the Wide Missouri*. Cambridge, Houghton-Mifflin, 1947.

Dick, Everett. *Vanguards of the Frontier*. New York, D. Appleton Century, 1941.

Duffus, R. L. *The Santa Fe Trail*. New York, Longmans, Green & Co., 1930.

Dye, Eva E. *The Conquest; The True Story of Lewis and Clark*. Chicago, Doubleday, 1902.

Edwards, Richard, and M. Hopewell. *Edwards's Great West*. St. Louis, Edwards' Monthly, 1860.

Ewers, John C. *The Blackfeet: Raiders on the Northwestern Plains*. Norman, University of Oklahoma Press, 1958.

Gardiner, Dorothy. *West of the River*. New York, Crowell, 1941.

Garraghan, Rev. Gilbert J. *Chapters in Frontier History; Research Studies in the Making of the West*. Milwaukee, Bruse, 1934.

Ghent, W. J. *The Early Far West*. New York, Longmans, 1931.

Gilbert, E. W. *The Exploration of Western America, 1800–1850; An Historical Geography*. Cambridge, England, Cambridge University Press, 1933.

Goetzmann, William H. *Army Exploration in the American West, 1803–1863*. New Haven, Yale University Press, 1959.

Goodman, Cardinal Leonidas. *The Trans-Mississippi West, 1803–1853*. New York, Appleton, 1922.

Greenbie, Sydney. *Furs to Furrows: An Epic of Rugged Individualism*. Caldwell, Caxton, 1939.

Hafen, LeRoy R., and C. C. Rister. *Western America*. New York, Prentice-Hall, 1941.

Harris, Burton. *John Colter: His Years in the Rockies*. New York, Scribners, 1952.

Hebard, Grace R. *The Pathbreakers from River to Ocean*. 6th ed. Glendale, Arthur H. Clark, 1933.

Holcomb, R. I. *History of Vernon County, Missouri*. St. Louis, Brown & Co., 1887.

Hollon, W. Eugene. *The Lost Pathfinder: Zebulon Montgomery Pike*. Norman, University of Oklahoma Press, 1949.

Houck, Louis. *A History of Missouri from the Earliest Explorations and Settlements until the Admission of the State into the Union*. 3 vols. Chicago, R. R. Donnelley, 1908.

Hyde, George E. *Pawnee Indians*. Denver, Brown Book, 1951.

Jennings, Sister Marietta. *A Pioneer Merchant of St. Louis, 1810–1820: The Business Career of Christian Wilt*. New York, Columbia University Press, 1939.

Kelly, Charles. *Old Greenwood*. Salt Lake City, Western Printing Co., 1936.

Kyski, Walter J. "The Missouri Fur Company." Typescript, M.A. Thesis, St. Louis University, 1942.

Leonard, Zenas. *Adventures of Zenas Leonard, Fur Trader*. Ed. by John C. Ewers. Norman, University of Oklahoma Press, 1959.

––––––. *Leonard's Narrative: Adventures of Zenas Leonard Fur Trader and Trapper, 1831–1836*. Ed. by Walter F. Wagner. Cleveland, Arthur H. Clark, 1904.

Lewis, Oscar. *The Effects of White Contact upon Blackfoot Culture with Special Reference to the Rôle of the Fur Trade*. New York, Columbia University Press, 1942.

McDermott, John F. *Private Libraries in Creole St. Louis*. Baltimore, Johns Hopkins University Press, 1938.

McFarling, Lloyd, ed. *Exploring the Northern Plains, 1804–1876*. Caldwell, Caxton, 1955.

McNally, Sister Mary Hubert, O. P. "Manuel Lisa: A Pioneer St. Louisan." Typescript, M.A. Thesis, St. Louis University, 1945.

Marshall, Thomas M. *The Life and Papers of Frederick Bates*. 2 vols. St. Louis, Missouri Historical Society, 1936.

Monaghan, James. *The Overland Trail*. Indianapolis, Bobbs-Merrill, 1947.

Morgan, Dale L. *Jedediah Smith and the Opening of the West*. Indianapolis, Bobbs-Merrill, 1953.

Music, James B. *St. Louis as a Fortified Town*. St. Louis, R. F. Miller, 1941.

Neill, Rev. Edward D. *The History of Minnesota: From the Earliest French Explorations to the Present Time.* 4th ed. Minneapolis, Minnesota Historical Company, 1882.

Nelson, Bruce. *Land of the Dakotahs.* Minneapolis, University of Minnesota, 1946.

Peake, Ora B. *A History of the United States Indian Factory System, 1795–1822.* Denver, Sage Books, 1954.

Peck, John Mason. *Memoir of John Mason Peck, D.D., Edited from His Journals and Correspondence.* Ed. by Rufus Babcock. Philadelphia, American Baptist Publishing Society, 1864.

Phillips, Paul C. *The Fur Trade.* 2 vols. Norman, University of Oklahoma Press, 1961.

Porter, Kenneth W. *John Jacob Astor, Business Man.* 2 vols. Cambridge, Mass., Harvard University Press, 1931.

Riegel, Roy E. *America Moves West.* 3rd ed. New York, Holt, Rinehart & Winston, 1956.

Rothensteiner, Rev. John. *History of the Archdiocese of St. Louis.* 2 vols. St. Louis, Catholic Historical Society of St. Louis, 1928.

Russell, Carl P. *Guns on the Early Frontiers.* Berkeley, University of California Press, 1957.

Scharf, J. Thomas. *History of St. Louis City and County, from the Earliest Periods to the Present Day.* 2 vols. Philadelphia, Louis H. Evarts & Co., 1883.

Seifert, Shirley. *Those Who Go against the Current.* Philadelphia, J. B. Lippincott Company, 1943.

Shepard, Elihu H. *The Early History of St. Louis and Its First Exploration by White Men in 1673 to 1843.* St. Louis, Southwestern Book and Publishing Co., 1870.

Shoemaker, Floyd C. *Missouri and Missourians.* 5 vols. Chicago, Lewis, 1943.

Smith, Ambrose C. *Memorials to the Life and Character of Mary Manuel Lisa.* Philadelphia, Lippincott, 1870.

Spencer, Thomas E. *The Story of Old St. Louis.* St. Louis, St. Louis Pageant Committee, 1914.

Steiner, Bernard C. *The Life and Correspondence of James Mc-*

Henry, Secretary of War under Washington and Adams. Cleveland, Arthur H. Clark, 1907.

Stevens, Walter B. *Centennial History of Missouri.* 4 vols. St. Louis, S. J. Clarke, 1921.

———. *Missouri: The Center State, 1821–1915.* 4 vols. Chicago, S. J. Clarke, 1914.

———. *St. Louis: The Fourth City, 1764–1909.* 3 vols. St. Louis, S. J. Clark, 1909.

Sunder, John E. *Bill Sublette: Mountain Man.* Norman, University of Oklahoma Press, 1959.

Tevebaugh, John L. "Merchant on the Western Frontier: William Morrison of Kaskaskia, 1790–1837." Typescript, Ph.D. Thesis, University of Illinois, 1962.

Tohill, Louis A. "Robert Dickson, British Fur Trader on the Upper Mississippi: A Story of Trade, War, and Diplomacy." Typescript, Ph.D. Thesis, University of Minnesota, 1926.

Vandiveer, Clarence A. *The Fur Trade and Early Western Exploration.* Cleveland, Arthur H. Clark, 1929.

Vestal, Stanley. *The Missouri.* New York, Farrar & Rinehart, 1945.

Vinton, Stallo. *John Colter, Discoverer of Yellowstone Park.* New York, E. Eberstadt, 1926.

Violette, Eugene M. *A History of Missouri.* Boston, D. C. Heath, 1918.

Wheeler, Olin D. *The Trail of Lewis and Clark, 1804–1904.* 2 vols. New York, G. P. Putnam's Sons, 1904.

Williams, Walter, and Floyd Shoemaker. *Missouri, Mother of the West.* 5 vols. Chicago, American Historical Society, 1930.

B. ARTICLES

Adams, Franklin G. "Reminiscences of Frederick Chouteau," *Kansas State Historical Society Collections,* Vol. VIII (1903–1904).

Atherton, Lewis M. "The Pioneer Merchant in Mid-America," *University of Missouri Studies,* Vol. XIV (April, 1939).

Bassford, Homer. "Manuel Lisa, St. Louis Pioneer," St. Louis *Star-Times* (April 28, 1936).

Briggs, Harold E. "Ranching and Stock Raising in the Territory of Dakota," *South Dakota Historical Collections,* Vol. XIV (1928).

Chappell, Philip E. "A History of the Missouri River," *Kansas State Historical Society Transactions,* Vol. IX (1905–1906).

Cox, Isaac J. "Opening the Santa Fe Trail," *Missouri Historical Review,* Vol. XXV (October, 1930).

DeWolf, Edwin A. "The Story of a Great but Forgotten St. Louisan," St. Louis *Globe-Democrat* (May 29, 1904; June 1, 1904).

Douglas, Walter B. "Manuel Lisa," *Missouri Historical Society Collections,* Vol. III, (1911).

Forsyth, Thomas. "Journal of a Voyage from St. Louis to the Falls of St. Anthony, in 1819," Lyman C. Draper, ed., *Wisconsin Historical Collections,* Vol. VI (1869–72).

French, Kathryn M. "Manuel Lisa," *South Dakota Historical Collections,* Vol. IV (1908).

Frost, Donald M. "Notes on General Ashley, the Overland Trail, and the South Pass," *Proceedings of the American Antiquarian Society,* Vol. LIV (October, 1944).

Fynn, Arthur J. "Furs and Forts," *Colorado Magazine,* Vol. VIII (November, 1931); Vol. IX (March, 1932).

Gianini, Charles A. "Manuel Lisa," *New Mexico Historical Review,* Vol. II (October, 1927).

Graustein, Jeannette B. "Manuel Lisa and Thomas Nuttall," *Missouri Historical Society Bulletin,* Vol. XII (April, 1956).

Gregg, Kate L. "The History of Fort Osage," *Missouri Historical Review,* Vol. XXXIV (July, 1940).

Hamlin, Hannibal, ed. "The St. Louis Missouri Fur Company; The Story of Mona [*sic*] Lisa, Missouri River Trail Blazer Who Built the First Fort on Its Upper Reaches," *Pony Express,* Vol. XII (July, 1945).

Hill, J. J. "An Unknown Expedition to Santa Fe in 1807," *Mississippi Valley Historical Review,* Vol. VI (March, 1920).

Jones, Brackenridge. "One Hundred Years of Banking in Missouri," *Missouri Historical Review,* Vol. XV (January, 1921).

Klein, Ada P., ed. "The Missouri Reader: The Fur Trade," *Mis-*

souri Historical Review, Vol. XXXIII (October, 1948); Vol. XXXIV (January and April, 1949).

Lippincott, Isaac J. "A Century and a Half of Fur Trade at St. Louis," *Washington University Studies,* Vol. III, Pt. 2 (April, 1916).

McDermott, John F. "Cadet Chouteau: An Identification," *Missouri Historical Review,* Vol. XXXI (April, 1937).

Mattes, Merril J. "Behind the Legend of Colter's Hell: The Early Exploration of Yellowstone Park," *Mississippi Valley Historical Review,* Vol. XXXVI (September, 1949).

Mattison, Ray H. "Report on Historical Aspects of the Oahe Reservoir Area, Missouri River, South and North Dakota," *South Dakota Historical Society Collections,* Vol. XXVII (1954).

Nasatir, A. P. "Jacques Clamorgan: Colonial Promoter of the Northern Border of New Spain," *New Mexico Historical Review,* Vol. XVII (April, 1942).

Parker, Donald D. "Early Exploration and Fur Trading in South Dakota," *South Dakota Historical Collections and Report,* Vol. XXV (1950).

Peterson, Charles E. "French Houses of the Illinois Country," Historical Houses of Missouri, Missouri Historical Society Scrapbook IV.

———. "Manuel Lisa's Warehouse," *Missouri Historical Society Bulletin,* Vol. IV (January, 1948).

Phillips, Paul C. "William Henry Vanderburgh: Fur Trader," *Mississippi Valley Historical Review,* Vol. XXX (December, 1943).

Richman, Irving B. "Manuel Lisa," *Dictionary of American Biography,* XI.

Robeson, George F. "Manuel Lisa," *Palimpsest,* Vol. VI (January, 1925). [Reprinted in *Palimpsest,* Vol. XXXIX (February, 1958).]

Robinson, Doane. "A History of the Dakota or Sioux Indians from Their Earliest Traditions and First Contact with White Men to the Final Settlement of the Last of Them upon Reservations and the Consequent Abandonment of the Old Tribal Life," *South Dakota Historical Collections*, Vol. II (1904).

———. "A Sioux Indian View of the Last War with England," *South Dakota Historical Collections*, Vol. V (1910).

———. "South Dakota and the War of 1812," *South Dakota Historical Collections*, Vol. XII (1924).

Ross, Frank E. "The Early Fur Trade of the Great Northwest," *Oregon Historical Quarterly*, Vol. XXXIX (December, 1938).

Traux, Allen L. "Manuel Lisa and His North Dakota Trading Post," *North Dakota Historical Quarterly*, Vol. II (July, 1928).

Voelker, Frederick E. "The Mountain Men and Their Part in the Opening of the West," *Missouri Historical Society Bulletin*, Vol. III (July, 1947).

Watkins, Albert. "The Evolution of Nebraska," *Mississippi Valley Historical Association Proceedings*, Vol. III (1909–10).

White, J. B. "The Missouri Merchant 100 Years Ago," *Missouri Historical Review*, Vol. XIII (July, 1918).

Index

American Fur Company: 95, 168, 184–85, 195; in Great Lakes area, 63, 161; moves onto Mississippi, 165; Lisa asks for aid, 171–72

Americans: 10, 23, 57–58, 63, 65, 162–63; description of, 28; take over Louisiana, 31; on 1809 expedition, 75–92; Indian hostility to, 112, 116, 122, 138, 141; assault on Blackfoot country, 188

Antoine, Baptiste, alias Machecou: 134

Antonio, Pedro: 162

Arapaho Indians: 34, 115, 134–35, 191; Champlain sent to, 131; at war with Americans, 141

Archambeau, Louis: 140

Arikara Indians: 80–84, 111, 128, 135–36, 140, 163; confront Lisa, 48–49; attack Pryor, 51–53; outfit left with, 90; meet Astorians, 113; difficulties with, 129f.; hostility to Gros Ventres, 133; description of, 189f.; attack Ashley, 190

Arikara villages: 48, 75, 83, 129; battle at 50–52; Astorians at 113f.; post at, 124; at war with Americans, 141

Arkansas River: 16; Osages on, 26; Pike to explore, 36

Articles of Agreement, St. Louis Missouri Fur Company: 68, 93, provisions of, 70f.; modified, 108

Ashley, William: vii, 70, 183–84, 188–90

Assiniboine Indians: 50

Astor, John Jacob: 96, 161, 168, 181; makes overtures to St. Louis, 63; plan for Astoria, 104; offered share of Missouri Fur Company, 117

Astorians: viii, 112, 150

Atlantic Coast: 190

Au Jacques River: *see* James River

Aunt Manuel: *see* Lisa, Mary Hempstead Keeney

Austin, Moses: 143

Ayres, ———: 94

Baird, James: 123, 135

Bank of Missouri: 143, 180

Bank of St. Louis: 143

Barges: 76

Bates, Frederick: 52–53

Beads: 57, 120, 183

Beaudoin, Antoine: 177

Beaudoin, Louison: 35

Beauvais, Jean Baptiste: 85

Beaver: 28, 46, 54–57, 59, 66, 81, 85, 98, 134, 153, 166, 175; as money, 7; value of in mountains, 60, 89; failure of Indians on Missouri to hunt, 90; on Henry's Fork, 116; brought to St. Louis by Lisa, 140; musk, 142

Beebe, Elijah: 177

Bellefontaine, Mo.: 126, 182

Benoît, Francis Marie: 27, 30; partnership with Lisa, 23; shares Osage trade, 25; factor at Mandan village, 111

Berthold, Bartholomew: 170

Berthold and Chouteau: 168, 170–71, 183–86

Bigbellies: see Gros Ventre Indians

Big Elk: 157, 159, 191; accompanies Lisa to St. Louis, 156; address to Clark, 158

Big Horn Mountains: 54

Bighorn River: 54, 88, 182, 191

Bijou, Louis: 127, 133, 140–41; in charge of Sioux post, 129; death reported, 135; writes to Lisa, 139

Bissonette, Antoine: 3–5, 45

Blackbird (Omaha chief): 111

Blackbird Hill: 111

Blackfeet Indians: 34, 58n., 64, 66, 89, 103, 114, 133, 186, 188, 190–91, 195; hostility to whites, 56–58, 95–97; drive out traders, 85; kill Potts and capture Colter, 86f.; attack trappers, 94, 115; kill Immel and Jones, 187

Blankets: 57, 120

Boons Lick: 151

Boston, Mass.: 173

Bostwick, Oliver, 178–79, 181–82, 184, 186; does business with Lisa and Missouri Fur Company, 173f.; in St. Louis, 173, 176, 180, 185; Lisa's mortgage agreement with, 173–74; sells goods to Ashley, 183; buys up Lisa estate, 193–94

Bouché, Jean Baptiste: 41, 54, 139; holds up expedition, 47–48; Lisa blames for loss, 55; refuses to bring in meat, 58; tries to foment mutiny, 59; sues Lisa, Morrison, and Menard, 102

Bourgeois: 80

Bourne, Mrs., School for Young Ladies: 106

Bouvet, Jean Baptiste: 170

Brackenridge, Henry Marie: 70n., 112;

on expedition of 1811, 109; discourages discontent, 111; mediates dispute between Lisa and Hunt, 113; returns to St. Louis, 114

Bradbury, John: 88n.; warns Dorion, 108; mediates dispute between Lisa and Hunt, 113; returns to St. Louis, 114

Brandt, Étienne: 58–59

Brandy: 147

Brazeou, Joseph: 170

Breeze, Sidney: 194n.

Bridger, James: vii, 188

British: 29, 33, 64, 101–102, 122, 126, 141, 152, 153n., 155, 158, 160, 172, 195; take over Illinois, 15; traders, 32, 53, 95; relations with Blackfeet, 57–58; on Missouri, 84–85, 109; influence Sioux, 107; intrigues of, viii, 129; influence with Gros Ventres, 130; in Northwest, 133; wampum of, 135; activities near St. Louis, 138

Brown, William: 94

Browne, Joseph: 37

Brownsville, Pa.: 143

Buffalo: 15, 45, 54, 86, 153, 189; supplies necessities for Blackfeet, 57; tongues, 183; basis of Indian life, 191

Buffalo robes: 90, 189, 191; use of, 57; value of, 141, 144

Cabanné, Jean Pierre: 18–19, 164, 169, 170–71; description of, 168; pays Lisa's debt, 194

Cabanné and Company: 164, 166–67, 169n., 172; composition of, 168f.; demise, 171

Caddoan Indians: 48

Calhoun, John Caldwell: 183

Calloway, James: 138

Cantonment Missouri: 36–37

Carondelet, François Luis Hector: 16n.

Carr, William: 5

Carraby, Pierre and Antoine: 123, 150, 194

Carson, Moses B.: 170, 172

Casa-Calvo, Marques de: 19

Cedar Island: 34, 124; post with Sioux,

83; post at burns, 97; Lisa proposes post at, 112; post rebuilt, 116

Champlain, Jean Baptiste: 95, 128, 194; with Crows, 85; suggested for advancement, 93; return to Fort Mandan, 115; Lisa's letter to, 131–32; death of, 134–35

Charbonneau, Baptiste: 111–12; hired as interpreter, 109; return from Gros Ventres, 140

Chariton River: 156

Charless, Joseph: 5n., 74, 166

Charlo: 127

Chatigny, Tynan: 12

Chauvin, Jacques: 19

Cheek, James: leads mutiny, 83; confrontation with Lisa, 92; death of, 94

Chevalier, Cadet: 134

Chew, Polly Charles: *see* Lisa, Polly Charles Chew

Chew, Rachel: 10

Chew, Samuel: 10

Cheyenne Indians: 140–41

Chicago, Ill.: 101

Chihuahua, Mex.: 39

Chittenden, Hiram Martin: 58n.

Chouteau, Auguste: 3, 15, 18–19, 29–31, 34, 63, 67, 147, 190, 192; assists at murder trial, 4; description of, 6–8; proposes post at Osage village, 16; granted Osage trade, 16; prestige of, 22; opposition to Lisa, 24–25, 27; demands payment of note, 26; bank commissioner, 143; position in St. Louis, 148–49; appointed subagent, 152; at Prairie du Chien, 157; sues Lisa's estate, 194; signs treaty with Otos, 200–201

Chouteau, A. P., Jr.: 72, 117, 137, 142, 197, 207; partner in St. Louis Missouri Fur Company, 69, 202, 208; reports loss of Cedar Island, 97; at stockholders meeting, 103

Chouteau, Cadet: *see* Chouteau, Pierre

Chouteau, Pierre: 18–19, 29, 34, 37, 67, 70n., 78, 89, 92, 94, 98, 101, 103, 117, 119, 142, 181, 190; position in St. Louis, 6–8, 15; brings in hostile

Osages, 16; splits Osages, 26; in formation of St. Louis Missouri Fur Company, 68f., 202, 208; description of, 69; agent of company, 72; note to St. Louis Missouri Fur Company, 73n.; commands militia, 75&n., 205; supplies merchandise, 76; lectures Arikaras, 84; to return to St. Louis, 90, 207; return to St. Louis, 99; collects fee for return of Shahaka, 100; director of Missouri Fur Company, 137; supplier to Missouri Fur Company, 147–48; witnesses Lisa's wedding, 167

Chouteau, Pierre, Jr.: 79, 117; accompanies Pryor, 51; commended by William Clark, 53

Cincinnati, O.: 11

Claibourne, William: 31

Clamorgan, Jacques: 19, 34, 39–40, 168, 190, 192; forms Company of Discoverers and Explorers of the Missouri, 17; description of, 18; partnership with Lisa, 35

Clamorgan, Loisel, and Company: 34

Clark, William: 6, 8, 28, 40, 45–46, 51–54, 93n., 95, 104, 117, 122, 124, 137, 142, 145–46, 151, 156, 168, 193, 210; Lewis' correspondence with, 30–31; prepares maps for government, 60; partner in St. Louis Missouri Fur Company, 69–70, 202, 208; Indian agent, 69; agent of St. Louis Missouri Fur Company, 71, 206; Lisa's correspondence with, 77–78, 80; in Washington, 101–102; at stockholders' meeting, 103; contribution in 1811, 108; president of Missouri Fur Company, 118; puts up note, 122, 148; gives contract to Lisa and Egliz, 143; appoints subagents, 152; at Prairie du Chien, 157; meets Indians in St. Louis, 158–60; signs treaties, 163; grants license to Farnham and Lapeche, 165; witnesses Lisa's marriage, 167; sues Lisa's estate, 194; signs treaty with Otos, 200–201

Clay, Henry: 183
Clermont (Osage chief): 26
Coal: 54
Coles' Fort: 151
Colter, John: vii, 30, 58–60, 188; returns to mountains with Lisa, 46–47; sets out to notify Indians, 55; joins Crow to fight Blackfeet, 56; race for life, 86f.; veracity noted, 88n.; sells equipment to James, 89; guides Henry and party to Three Forks, 93; leaves mountains, 94
Colter's Hell: 55
Columbia River: 64, 95–96, 104, 114, 150
Company of Discoverers and Explorers of the Missouri: 17–18, 34
Congress of the United States: 155
Connecticut: 167
Cordelle: 44
Corn: 80–82, 183, 189
Côte Sans Dessein: 76–77
Council Bluffs: 99, 152; winter quarters of Crooks and McClellan, 54, 80; posts at, 81, 162, 174–75
Coureurs du bois: 15
Crawford, William H.: 183
Creoles: 76, 162
Crooks, Ramsay: 99, 109, 113, 186; partnership with McClellan, 53; meets Lisa at Fort Osage, 80; escapes from Sioux, 100; partner in Pacific Fur Company, 104; leads American Fur Company in West, 161, 165; Lisa's letter to, 171; attempts to hire Pilcher, 184
Crow Indians: 34, 58, 60, 63, 87, 140, 186–88; located by Colter, 55; Colter joins in battle, 56; taught to trap beaver, 57; Rose trader with, 61; Rose joins tribe, 62; trade with, 66, 85, 132; steal horses, 116; rob trappers, 134; at war with Americans, 141
Cuba: 9

Dabuche, ———: see Dubuque, Julien
Danis, Jean Baptiste: 134

Davis, Charles: 96
Deerskin: 7, 15
Delassus, Charles Dehault: 12, 21, 30–32; recommends trade licenses, 19; activities as governor, 24–28, 30–32
Delaware Indians: 75
Denison, Captain: 78
Deserters: from 1809 expedition, 77–80; law regarding, 105
Des Moines River: 19, 154
Detroit, Mich.: 74, 76, 100–101, 104
Dickson, Robert: 153n., 162; stirs up Indians, 138; activities with Santee, 153
Dixon, Joseph: 46
Donnelson, Henley: 197
Dorion, Baptiste: 158–59
Dorion, Pierre: warrant issued against, 107; Lisa tries to hire, 113
Dougherty, John: 83, 94
Doza, Alexis: 89&n., 197f.
Drips, Andrew: 172
Drouillard, George: 29, 47, 56, 58–59, 69, 102, 188; murder trial of, 3–5; represents Menard and Morrison, 40; explores from Fort Raymond, 60; in Lisa's debt, 62n.; full partner in Lisa, Morrison, Menard, and Drouillard, 66; death of, 96
Dubois, Touissant: 39, 74, 101; citizen of Vincennes, 11; travels to Detroit with Lisa, 100
Dubrouil, Augustin: 5n.
Dubuque, Julien: 30
Duchoquette, Baptiste, dit Larme: 37

Easton, Rufus: 5
Egliz, Hyacinte: 35, 143
Embargo Act: 76; curtails trade, 97; effectiveness, 101
Engagés: 4, 20, 37, 48, 58, 61; contracts with, 41; bound to trappers, 46n.; mountain prices charged to, 80; in debt to Lisa, 194; lawsuits against, 102; with Sanguinet, 131; sent to meet Sanguinet, 139; thrown out of Fort Manuel, 139; notes due from, 145

Falls of the Missouri: 94–95, 118, 187, 211
Far East: 104
Farnham, Russell: 165
Farrar, Dr. Bernard G.: 177
Fitzhugh, Dennis: 66
Fitzhugh, Samuel: 144
Fitzpatrick, Thomas: 188
Flathead Indians: 85, 95–96
Flint, Timothy: 159
Flour: 81
Fontenelle, Lucien: 186
Fort Benton: 182, 186–87
Fort Hunt: 153–56
Fort Lisa: 174–75, 178n., 179, 182–83
Fort Mandan (Lewis and Clark's): 46
Fort Mandan (Lisa's): 75n., 92, 100, 114&n., 124; prices charged at, 107&n.; Sioux hostility around, 112; Champlain returns to, 115
Fort Manuel: 136; completed, 134; hostility of natives at, 138–39; evacuated, 140
Fort Osage: 82, 110, 127, 143; established, 69; expedition stops at, 78–80
Fort Raymond: 58n., 62, 73, 76, 79, 88, 90, 100, 174; built, 54; winter life at, 55, 58; closed, 85; party leaves, 92
Fort Washington (Cincinnati): 10n., 11
Fortin, Casé: 85
Fox Indians: 152, 160
France: 27, 31
Franklin, Mo.: 175
Freeharty, ———: 94
Free trapper: 46&n.
French: 7–8, 57, 76, 82; society, 15; transfer Louisiana, 31
Furs: 57

Gallatin River: 66, 93
Gasconade River: 77
Gatzeze, Juan: 18
Geisse, Tayesse, and Snyder: 35, 40, 194
Genêt, Citizen Edmund: 15
Giddings, Salmon: 167
Gillespie, G., and Company: 40
Glass, Hugh: 188

Grand River: 78, 180, 183
Gratiot, Charles: 30, 137; counsels merger with Astor, 63; reorganizes company, 117
Great Britain: 115, 122, 136, 148, 157
Great Lakes: 63, 161
Green River: 134, 191; trappers on, 67, 85; beaver on, 95
Greenwood, Caleb: 127
Grizzly bears: 47, 58
Gros Ventre Indians: 58n., 114, 124, 133, 189; post with, 84, 90; plunder Yellowstone cache, 97; hostility of, 130–31, 140; at war with Americans, 141
Gulf Coast: 9
Gulf of California: 34, 95
Gun powder: 49, 52, 59, 109
Guns: 29, 52, 57–58, 189; company sells, 119, 142

Handcock, Forrest: 46, 194
Harrison, William Henry: 10n., 11
Hempstead, Charles: 193; witnesses wedding, 167; named Lisa's executor, 178
Hempstead, Edward: 3, 5
Hempstead, Stephen: 167
Hempstead, Thomas: 177, 186–87; partner in Missouri Fur Company, 172; goes East, 173; turns furs over to Bostwick, 176; difficulties with Bostwick, 180f.; optimism of, 182; sends gifts, 183; competition with Ashley, 185
Henry, Andrew: 69n., 73, 93n., 100, 108–109, 112, 114, 117, 137, 146; description of, 70, 91; leads expedition to Fort Raymond, 90; goes to Three Forks, 93; crosses divide, 96; letter of, 96–97; left without support, 103; arrives at Mandan villages, 115; joins with Ashley, 183; opinion of Missouri Fur Company, 188; retires from trade, 190; partner in St. Louis Missouri Fur Company, 202, 208
Henry's Fork of the Snake River: 116
Hertzog, Joseph: 115

Hoback, John: 45n., 114
Horses: 73, 176, 189, 192; stolen by Gros Ventres, 130; St. Louis Missouri Fur Company purchases, 204
Hubert, Antoine: 15
Hudson's Bay Blankets: 57
Hudson's Bay Company: 104
Hull, ———: 94
Hunkpapa creek: site of Fort Manuel, 130&n.
Hunt, Theodore: 168, 170; joins with Lisa, 150; overseer of bridge, 151
Hunt, Wilson Price: viii, 109, 150, 181; partner in Pacific Fur Company, 104; prepares for Astorian venture, 105f.; leaves St. Louis, 107; race with Lisa, 110f.; makes purchase from Lisa, 114
Hunt and Bright: 150
Hunter, John Dunne: 160&n.

Ildefonso, Treaty of: 27
Illinois: 15, 39, 138, 147
Immel, Michael: 127, 185, 188; in charge of Omaha post, 141; in Cabanné and Company, 170f.; trades with Sioux, 175; departs for mountains, 181–82; expedition to Blackfeet, 186f.; death of, 187
Indiana: 10–11, 138
Indians: viii, 11, 15, 18, 47–48, 50, 53, 59, 61, 64, 67, 76, 80, 90, 99, 103, 109, 121, 139, 162, 172, 203, 206; attack Chew family, 10; Wayne's campaign against, 32; Colter sent to find, 55–56; Lisa's treatment of, 67; visit James, 91; in St. Louis, 107; hostility of, 111, 131, 138, 151; British influence over, 122; around Fort Manuel, 134; Lisa's understanding of, 146; kill John Dunne Hunter, 160; demand Mrs. Lisa trade with them, 174; Lisa's concern for, 191; see also under specific tribes
Indian trade, goods used in: 120f.
Iowa Indians: 152, 159; defeated by Omahas and Poncas, 154; crops destroyed, 156

Jackson, Andrew: 151
Jackson's Hole: 55
James, Thomas: 75n., 84, 93n., 107n., 160n., 174; chronicles voyage, 81; feelings toward Lisa, 82; purchases equipment from Colter, 89; winter camp of, 91; goes to Fort Raymond, 92; at Three Forks, 94f.; claim against Missouri Fur Company, 145
James River: 83, 153
Jefferson, Thomas: 29, 31, 50–51
Jefferson River: 66, 86f., 93, 96
Jessaume, René: 51
Jones, Robert: 181; expedition to Blackfeet, 186; death of, 187

Kansa Indians: 19, 37, 45, 152, 160n., 187
Kansas River: 45
Kaskaskia, Ill.: 39, 76, 194
Keelboat: 10, 40, 44–45, 76, 108f., 112
Keeney, Christopher: 193
Keeney, Mary Hempstead: see Lisa, Mary Hempstead Keeney
Kennerly, George: 170
Kentucky: 10, 28, 144

Labbadie, Sylvestre: 37, 92, 117, 137, 142, 210; description of, 69; in charge of Fort Mandan, 93; letter to Menard, 93; at stockholders meeting, 103; director of Missouri Fur Company, 118; puts up note, 122, 148; reasons for joining Missouri Fur Company, 147; partner of St. Louis Missouri Fur Company, 202, 208
Lacroix, Michel: 168, 171, 182
Lafargue, Jean: 134
La Lande, Baptiste: 40
Landreville's: 3
Lange, Pierre: 139
Langlois, Adrien: 74, 76, 81, 90
Langlois, Alex: 15
Lapeche, Pierre: 165
Larme, Baptiste Duchoquette dit: see Duchoquette, Baptiste
Larocque, Antoine: 57
Latoulipe, Baptiste: 127

Latour, Charles: 139
Laurison, Daniel: 127
Law for the Benefit of Insolvent
  Debtors: 59
Le Bourgne: chief of Gros Ventres, 130;
  dethroned, 140
LeCompt, François: 45
LeDuc, M. P.: 77, 103, 117, 208
Lemos, Manuel Gayoso de: 17n.
Lewis Meriwether: 205; with William
  Clark, 6, 8, 40, 45–46, 51, 53; pre-
  pares for expedition, 28–31; kills two
  Piegans, 56, 58n.; as governor, 65,
  69, 75, 100; signs contract for return
  of Shahaka, 74–75; death of, 99
Lewis, Reuben: 103, 117, 134, 139–42,
  146; partner in St. Louis Missouri
  Fur Company, 69, 202, 208; com-
  mands boat, 79, 81; writes brother,
  94–96; at Fort Raymond, 100; meets
  expedition at Mandan village, 114;
  hired as clerk, 124; leads trapping
  party, 133; report from Little Horn,
  136
Lewis and Clark Expedition: viii, 3, 33,
  50, 56, 109, 126, 157
Lexington, Ky: 150
Liguest, Pierre Laclede: 7
Liquor: 25, 159; as trade item, 121,
  175, 180, 189; price of at Fort
  Mandan, 107; supplied by Chouteau,
  147
Lisa, Benoît, and Company: 24, 26–27,
  32–33
Lisa, Christobal de: 9
Lisa, Christopher: 178&n.
Lisa, Joaquin: 123, 178, 194; birth of,
  9; granted land, 13; deeds land to
  Manuel Lisa, 29
Lisa, M., and Company: see Lisa and
  Hunt
Lisa, Manuel: vii-ix, 17, 34, 53, 76,
  89, 97, 99, 104, 107n., 119, 124–25,
  182, 184, 188; involved in Drouillard
  murder trial, 3–6; expedition of
  1809, 4–7, 40f.; description of, 8;
  birth, 9; in Vincennes, 10–11; early
  years in St. Louis, 12f., 18; petitions

government, 19f.; partnership with
  Benoît, Sarpy, and Sanguinet, 23;
  obtains Osage trade, 23–24; supplies
  Lewis and Clark, 29f.; suits against
  Robert McClellan, 32–33; partnership with Clamorgan, 35f.; troubles
  with Pike and Wilkinson, 36f.; partnership with Morrison and Menard,
  39; meets Colter on Missouri, 46;
  trouble with Arikaras, 48; trouble
  with Mandans, 49–50; trouble with
  Assiniboines, 50; acused by Pryor,
  52–53; builds Fort Raymond, 54;
  notifies Indians of arrival, 55;
  threatens Brandt, 59; pays $3.00 per
  pelt for beaver, 60; fight with Rose,
  61f.; relations with Rose, 63; return
  from mountains, 63; vision of Northwest, 63; searches for capital, 66f.;
  forms St. Louis Missouri Fur Company, 68f.; factor of St. Louis Missouri Fur Company, 72; inventories
  goods, 74; granted trading license,
  76; writes to Clark, 77f.; sends
  statement of debtors, 79; description
  of by James, 82; meets Vasquez, 85;
  confrontation with James Cheek, 92;
  returns to St. Louis, 99; suspected of
  inciting Sioux, 100; in Detroit, 101;
  administrator of Drouillard's estate,
  102; dispute with Morrison, 106;
  contribution to voyage of 1811, 108;
  takes goods on account, 109; race
  with Astorians, 110f.; speaks to
  Arikaras, 113; agreement with Astorians, 114; attempts Santa Fe contact, 115; director of Missouri Fur
  Company, 118; as a trader, 120f.;
  puts up note, 123; joins 1812 expedition, 126; builds post with Sioux,
  128–29; goes to Gros Ventres, 130;
  attempts to open Santa Fe trade,
  131f.; maintains peaceful Indian relations, 133; learns of Champlain's
  death, 135; replaced as director, 136–
  37; discharges *engagés*, 139; evac-
  uates Fort Manuel, 140; participates
  in termination of company, 141–42;

involved with Bank of St. Louis, 143; contract with William Clark, 143; Chouteau's opposition to, 148–49; gains new support, 150; bridge commissioner, 151; appointed sub-agent, viii, 152; marriage to Mitain, 153; sets Missouri tribes on warpath, 154f.; takes Indian delegation to St. Louis, 156f.; at Prairie du Chien, 157; takes Indians upriver, 159; writes public letter, 161; on death of Pedro Antonio, 162f.; brings down Mitain's child, 163; marriage to Mary Keeney, 167; joins Cabanné and Company, 168f.; breaks up Cabanné and Company, 170; requests supplies from Crooks, 171; forms new Missouri Fur Company, 172f.; goes to Fort Lisa, 174; has Immel stopped by Army, 175; illness, 176&n.; fight with Beaudoin, 177; will, 177–78; death of, 178; activity of, 190; position in St. Louis, 192–93; as partner in St. Louis Missouri Fur Company, 202f.; as partner in Missouri Fur Company, 209f.

Lisa, Manuel, Jr.: 193
Lisa, Manuel (Joaquin's son): 178
Lisa, Maria Ignacia Rodriquez: 9–10
Lisa, Mary: 168
Lisa, Mary Hempstead Keeney: 186, 193; marriage to Lisa, 167; goes upriver to Fort Lisa, 174–75; named executor, 178; sells portion of stock, 195
Lisa, Morrison, and Menard: 40, 63, 73n., 102, 118; partnership formed, 4, 39; division of funds, 65; settlement with St. Louis Missouri Fur Company, 73, 203–205
Lisa, Morrison, Menard, and Drouillard: 66–67
Lisa, Polly Charles Chew: 30, 35, 150, 163; marriage to Lisa, 10&n.; signs petition, 65; death of, 166
Lisa, Rosalie: 163, 178
Lisa and Hunt: 151, 161, 169–70;

partnership terminated, 164; value of, 168
Little Dish: 157
Little Horn River: 131, 133n., 139; Lewis sets up post on, 133; report from, 136
Little Osage Indians: 37
Loisel, Regis: 34, 83
London, Eng.: 8, 55, 107, 169
Lorimier, Louis: 136; leads trappers, 132; leaves Bijou's post, 140
Louisiana: ix, 9, 17, 23, 216
Louisiana Gazette: see Missouri Gazette
Louisiana Territory: 29, 36, 195, 202; ceded from Spain to France, 27; ceded to the United States, 31
Louisville, Ky.: 52, 66, 70, 76, 124, 144, 169, 208
Lucas, Anne: 166n.
Lucas, J. C. B.: 4
Luttig, John C.: 126, 130, 133n., 136, 140

Maccoun, J. & D.: 150
Machecou, Baptiste Antoine (alias): *see* Antoine, Baptiste
McClellan, Robert: 59n., 80, 109, 171, 190; difficulties with Lisa, 32–33; partnership with Ramsay Crooks, 53; escapes from Sioux, 99–100; partner in Pacific Fur Company, 104; threats of, 112–13
McDaniel, James: 89, 91
McDonough, Michael: 123
McGunnigle, Wilson: 183
McKenzie, Kenneth: 195–96
Mackey's Saline: *see* Boons Lick
Mackinac boat: 80
McKnight, Robert: 123, 135
McKnight expedition: 127–28
Madison, Dolly: 157
Madison River: 66, 93, 95
Mahas: *see* Omaha Indians
Mandan Indians: 52, 99, 140, 163, 189, 205; meeting with Lisa, 49–50; greet Shahaka, 84; outfit left with, 90
Mandan villages: 18, 49, 51, 71, 79, 108; return Shahaka to, 84; Vasquez

waits at, 85; F. M. Benoît factor at, 111; Lewis waits at, 114; post at, 114n., 124
Marie, Baptiste: 60
Mary Jane (boat): 186
Mayette, Jan Baptiste: 126
Menard, Madam: 100
Menard, Pierre: 72–73, 73n., 76, 117, 137, 142, 207; partnership with Lisa and Morrison, 4, 39–40; in debt to Lisa, 62n.; partnership in St. Louis Missouri Fur Company, 69, 202, 208; inventories goods, 74; writes from Osage River, 77; writes from Fort Osage, 81; leads boats to Fort Raymond, 90, 92; at Three Forks, 93f.; leaves mountains, 96; return to St. Louis, 97; at stockholders' meeting, 103; contributions to 1811 voyage, 108; goes into politics, 147; writes contract with Alexis Doza, 197f.
Michaels, Myers: 40
Michigan: 53
Michilimackinac: 33, 40, 53, 104, 169
Militia: 75&n., 78, 83
Miller, William: 89, 91
Miró, Esteban Rodriguez: 21
Mississippi River: 10–11, 15, 27–28, 33, 36, 41, 63, 116, 138, 152, 155f., 161, 165, 192
Missouri: 10, 188
Missouri Fur Company (1812–14): 121, 135, 150, 164, 167, 188, 190; created, 117; description of, 118f., 209f.; credit problem of, 122f.; attempt to enter Santa Fe trade, 131–32; end of, 141–42, 145–46; Lisa's role in, 146
Missouri Fur Company (1819): 179, 195; formation of, 172f.; in Lisa's will, 177–78; Lisa's faith in, 193; activities after 1820, 182–86
Missouri Gazette: 74, 97, 102, 106, 116–17, 138, 141–42, 145, 151, 161, 164, 165–66, 214
Missouri Indians: 163
Missouri Loup Indians: 19
Missouri River: 7–8, 25, 34, 36, 39, 54,

56, 60, 63, 67, 70, 74, 97, 100, 103–104, 108, 118–19, 124–25, 135, 146, 149, 151–52, 161, 166, 172, 178, 182, 188–89, 195, 202–204, 210–11; Lisa arrives from 3–4, 6; Lisa applies for land on, 12–13; Spanish on, 17–18; Lewis and Clark to ascend, 28–29; British traders on, 32, 116; description of, 41, 44–45, 76–77; trip up in 1807, 48f.; trip up in 1809, 76f.; trip up in 1811, 109f.; Lisa's experience with, 121; trip up in 1812, 126f.; Lisa ascends, 164; Cabanné and Company on 169f.
Missouri Territory: 13
Missouri Valley: 191
Mitain: 162–63, 178&n.; marriage to Lisa, 153; sent into forest, 175
Monongahela River: 143
Monroe, James: 183
Montreal, Can.: 8, 60, 76, 101, 104, 138, 190
Morrison, William: 73, 108, 147; partnership with Lisa and Menard, 4, 39–40; partner in St. Louis Missouri Fur Company, 69, 202, 208; purchases beaver, 97n.; receives credit, 98; disputes with Lisa, 106, 165; credit to Missouri Fur Company, 123; joins Missouri Fur Company, 145
Mountain men: 61, 188
Mountain prices: 80
Mulattoes: 80

Nadowa River: 105, 107
Napoleon I: 27
Natchez, Miss.: 28
New Madrid, Mo.: 10, 13
New Mexico: 35
New Orleans, Battle of: 157
New Orleans, La.: 8–11, 13, 19–20, 23–24, 26–29, 31, 60, 123, 183, 191
New York, N. Y.: 60, 104
New York Company: *see* American Fur Company
Nishnabotna River: 175
North Dakota: 18
Northwest: 7, 34, 63, 70, 166, 192, 195;

British activities in, 53, 133; furs in, 56; Lisa's vision of, 146, 149, 151
North West Company: 57, 84, 104
Northwest Territory: 10
Nuttall, Thomas: 108

O'Fallon, Benjamin: 178n.
O'Fallon, James: joins Missouri Fur Company, 124; in Cabanné and Company, 168–70
O'Fallon, John: 194
Ohio: 10
Ohio River: 15, 28, 33, 144, 156, 157
Omaha Indians: viii, 19, 32, 153, 159; post with, 81; defeat Iowas, 154; held in check by Lisa, 162
Omaha village: 111, 156, 159, 175; post at, 141, 151
Ortiz, José: 25
Osage Indians: 19, 31, 33–34, 61, 160&n.; trade with, 7–8, 15–17, 24; village, 16, 37–38, 78; Lisa obtains trade of, 22, 24–28; Pike's arrival with, 37; Chouteau subagent for, 152
Osage River: 5, 45, 76–78, 110
Oto Indians: 19, 154; Astorians winter with, 105; sign treaty, 163, 200–201

Pacific Fur Company: 104, 113
Pacific Ocean: 8, 17, 29, 69
Panis: see Pawnee Indians
Papin, Alex: 128–29, 170
Partizan (Teton Sioux chief): 157
Pattinson, Richard: 101
Pawnee Indians: 19, 20n., 48, 163, 166, 189
Pennsylvania: 10
Perkins, Joseph: 172, 175
Philadelphia, Pa.: 35, 101, 115
Pierre's Hole: 55
Pike, Zebulon M.: 36–40, 38n., 107
Pilcher, Joshua: 172, 180–81, 186–87; trades with Omaha, 175; directs company, 176; field leader, 179; laments lateness of goods, 182
Pirogue: 78&n., 127
Plains: 34, 189
Plains Indians: 57, 189

Platte River: 34, 46–47, 75, 77, 81, 83, 111, 115, 128
Ponca Indians: viii, 18; attack Iowas, 154; sign treaty, 163
Pork: 81–82
Portage des Sioux: 119, 138
"Possibles": 47&n.
Potts, John: 30, 45; saves Lisa, 61; death of, 86
Prairie du Chien: 157, 163, 165
Pratte, Bernard: 192, 194; partner in Cabanné and Company, 167–68; contribution to Cabanné and Company, 170
Pratte, Joseph: 19, 170
Presbyterians: 167
Price, Ridson: 168
Provenchere, Paul: 176
Pryor, Nathaniel: 75; defeated by Arikaras, 51–53; James's comment upon, 82
Psoralea esculente: 88

Red Head's Town: 114; see also St. Louis
Red River of the South: 48
Rees: see Arikara Indians
Regnier, F., & Company: 76
Renville, Joseph: 153n.
Republican Osage Indians: 35
Republican Sioux Indians: 19
Reznor, Jacob: 45n., 114
Richard, ———: 171
Río Grande River: 95
River of the Spaniards: see Green River
Robidoux, Joseph: 11–12, 19, 192
Robinson, Edward: 30, 45&n., 114
Rocky Mountain Fur Company: 189
Rocky Mountains: viii, 6, 8, 17, 29, 41, 46, 63, 74, 164, 166, 188, 190, 195
Rodriguez, Maria Ignacia: see Lisa, Maria Ignacia Rodriguez
Rose, Edward: vii, 113, 158; adventures at Fort Raymond, 61f.; goes to live with Crows, 62; paid to guide Lorimier, 140
Rucker, ———: 94

Sacajawea: accompanies expedition of 1811, 109; death of, 139

Sac Indians: 152, 160, 176

St. Augustine, Fla.: 9

St. Charles, Mo.: 5, 41, 52, 108–10

St. Joseph, Mo.: 105

St. Louis, Mo.: viii, 3, 8, 10n., 12, 16, 18–20, 23, 32–33, 35–36, 39–40, 47, 54, 59, 61–63, 66–67, 69, 71–72, 89–90, 93, 96–97, 99–101, 108, 114–15, 122, 127, 131, 135–36, 140, 147–50, 152, 154, 157, 162, 164, 167–71, 173, 176, 178–82, 184–86, 188, 190, 192, 202, 205f.; founded, 7; description of, 13f., 65, 106–107; society of, 15; Indians brought to, 17, 158–60; prison, 25–26; change in ownership, 27–29; Pryor's activities in, 51–53; incorporation into a city, 65; expedition leaves, 75–77, 126; Astorians in, 104f.; worried by Indians, 138, 151; visited by Timothy Flint, 159; Cathedral, 178

St. Louis Missouri Fur Company: 31, 58, 74, 84, 99–100, 102, 104, 107n., 115, 118, 210; formed, 68f.; purchases goods from Lisa, Morrison, and Menard, 73; meets Crooks and McClellan, 80; activities in Northwest, 90, 95; opposition to Astorians, 102, 104–105, 107; meeting of, 107; demise, 117

Ste Genevieve, Mo.: 11, 13, 185

Salcedo, Manuel Juan de: 26–27

Salt: 82

Sanguinet, Charles: 132, 135; petitions for trade with Omahas and Poncas, 19; partnership with Lisa, 23, 25, 27; leads trappers, 85; sent to Arapahoes, 131; report from Arapahoes, 134; arrives at Fort Manuel, 139

Santa Fe, N. M.: viii, 28, 34, 40, 60, 67, 115, 124, 135; Lisa attempts to open trade with, 35, 38, 131–32; Morrison's connection with, 39–40; McKnight attempts to trade with, 127–28

Santee Indians: 152–54

Sarpy, Gregory: 18–19, 23, 25, 27

Sarpy, Juan Bautista: 23

Saskatchewan River: 57

Shahaka: 82, 98, 100, 102, 205; Pryor attempts to return, 50–52; contract to return, 74–75; complains of Indian life, 114

Shawnee Indians: 75

Sherman, John: 77

Shoshone River: 55

Sioux Indians: viii, 34, 83, 100, 109, 113, 135, 141, 152, 154, 160, 175, 189; location of, 47–48; Lisa leaves outfit with, 50, 90, 116, 124, 128; actuated by British intrigue, 107; stop Lisa's boat, 112; called to council, 153; council with Lisa, 155; attack Iowas, 156; smallpox kills chiefs, 159; kill Pedro Antonio, 162; sign treaty, 163; *see also* Teton Sioux Indians, Santee Indians, Yankton Sioux Indians, etc.

Sioux of the Lakes: 157

Sioux of the River St. Peters: 157

Smallpox: 159

Smith, Adam: 8

Smith, Jedediah: vii, 188

Snake Indians: 60, 93, 95f.

Sommers, John Jacob: 194

Southwest: 36

Spaniards: viii, 31f., 36, 38, 40, 60, 64, 134, 195; government of, 12, 16, 21–23; in upper Missouri area, 60; Lisa attempts contact with, 128, 131–32; of Mexico, 115

Spanish Boy: 166

Spanish Waters: *see* Green River

Stoddard, Amos: 31

Stone, Bostwick and Company: 176, 179; connection with Missouri Fur Company, 172f.; Lisa's mortgage to, 178; late with goods, 181; sell goods to Ashley, 183

Sublette, William: 188

Swivels: 49–50, 61, 108

Taillon, Joseph: 12

Tamaha (Teton Sioux chief): 153

Tecumseh: 116
Tennessee: 29
Territorial Legislature at Missouri: and law concerning boatmen, 105; and Bank of St. Louis, 143; and Bank of Missouri, 143
Tetaus: *see* Teton Sioux Indians
Teton Mountains: 55
Teton Sioux Indians: 38, 153n., 155, 157; meet St. Louis Missouri Fur Company, 83; threaten Santee Indians, 153
Texas: 143, 160n.
Thomas, Dr.: 75n.
Three Forks of the Missouri: 58, 89–90, 92, 135, 186, 191; in Blackfoot country, 56–57; trappers go to, 66, 94; British posts at, 84; site of Colter's race, 86f.; post at, 93f.; Henry leaves, 115; abandoned as a trapping possibility, 133
Tibeau, Baptiste: 60
Tobacco: 109, 180
Tomahawks: 120, 162
Trudeau, Zenon: 11–13

Union Hall, St. Louis: 161
United States: viii, 8–9, 38, 50, 146, 153n., 154–55, 159, 195, 209; purchases Louisiana, 27–29; Shahaka visits, 50; threat of war with Britain, 115, 148; Indian hostility to, 140, 153; declaration of war with Britain, 136; treaties made with Indians, 157; Yellowstone expedition of, 172

Vallé, Francis: 96
Vasquez, Baroney: 36–37
Vasquez, Benito: 19; Lisa's second-in-command, 59; in Lisa's debt, 62n.; in charge of Fort Raymond, 66; meets Lisa at Mandan village, 85

Vigo, Francisco: 11, 39
Vincennes, Ind.: 10–11, 13, 33, 39, 74, 100–101
Virginia: 28, 46

Wabash River: 10, 33
Wampum: 116, 135
Wash, Robert: 194
Washington, D.C.: 52–53, 100–101, 107, 154, 160, 173, 183
Watt, James: 177
Wayne, Anthony: 10n., 32
West Indies: 18
Whisky: *see* liquor
Wier, William: 94
Wilkinson, Benjamin: 70n., 79, 103, 117, 202, 207; description of, 69; factor of St. Louis Missouri Fur Company, 72, 206; partner in St. Louis Missouri Fur Company, 208
Wilkinson, James: 36–39
Wilkinson, Walter: 103, 117
Williams, Ezekiel: 135
Wilt, Christian: 115; supplies Missouri Fur Company, 123; competes with Lisa, 144
Wind River: 132, 191
Wind River Mountains: 54–55
Wiser, Peter: 30, 45, 96
Wolves: 58
Wood River: 28–29
Woods, Andrew: 172

Yankton Sioux Indians: 155, 157
Yellowstone Expedition: 172
Yellowstone Park: 55
Yellowstone River: 34, 54, 56, 88, 91, 97, 131, 133n., 185, 203
York (William Clark's servant): 127
Yosti's: 3

Zenoni, John B.: 172, 175